Reimagining Philanthropy in the Global South

While there have always been high levels of philanthropic giving in the Global South, the urgency and unexpectedness of COVID-19 transformed the parameters within which philanthropy operates. *Reimagining Philanthropy in the Global South* examines how newer models of philanthropy are tackling development challenges, including poverty, inequality, and access to health care and education, and questions how organisations are coping with structural changes in donor-driven philanthropy; how changes in traditional grant-making are impacting the imperatives of recipient organisations; and how indigenous philanthropy is making a difference. The chapters provide frank assessments of the priorities, challenges, and opportunities of emerging market philanthropy, and the lessons learned from the pandemic. The authors highlight the deeper issues at play, as well as offering ideas and positive examples of how diverse stakeholders are coming together to solve social challenges in creative and practical ways. This title is also available as Open Access on Cambridge Core.

CLARE WOODCRAFT is the former Executive Director of the Centre for Strategic Philanthropy at the University of Cambridge. She was CEO of Emirates Foundation and Deputy Director at Shell Foundation and is a board member of Fondation Chanel and WINGS. She writes about catalytic philanthropy, sustainable development, and the power imbalances therein.

KAMAL MUNIR is Pro-Vice-Chancellor and Professor of Strategy and Policy at the University of Cambridge and the Academic Director of the Centre for Strategic Philanthropy. His research focuses include organisational inequality and strategy in the face of disruption. He has won several teaching awards and given policy advice to the World Bank, the Asian Development Bank, and the State Bank of Pakistan.

NITYA MOHAN KHEMKA is Director of Global Alliances at PATH, a global health think tank, and a visiting fellow at the Judge Business School at the University of Cambridge, where she researches topics spanning gender inequality, poverty, and human development. She lectures on sustainable development and gender.

Reimagining Philanthropy in the Global South

From Analysis to Action in a Post-COVID World

Edited by

CLARE WOODCRAFT
University of Cambridge

KAMAL MUNIR
University of Cambridge

NITYA MOHAN KHEMKA
University of Cambridge

CAMBRIDGE
UNIVERSITY PRESS

Shaftesbury Road, Cambridge CB2 8EA, United Kingdom

One Liberty Plaza, 20th Floor, New York, NY 10006, USA

477 Williamstown Road, Port Melbourne, VIC 3207, Australia

314–321, 3rd Floor, Plot 3, Splendor Forum, Jasola District Centre,
New Delhi – 110025, India

103 Penang Road, #05–06/07, Visioncrest Commercial, Singapore 238467

Cambridge University Press is part of Cambridge University Press & Assessment,
a department of the University of Cambridge.

We share the University's mission to contribute to society through the pursuit of
education, learning and research at the highest international levels of excellence.

www.cambridge.org
Information on this title: www.cambridge.org/9781009400541

DOI: 10.1017/9781009400565

First published 2024

A catalogue record for this publication is available from the British Library

A Cataloging-in-Publication data record for this book is available from the
Library of Congress

ISBN 978-1-009-40054-1 Hardback

This book is dedicated to philanthropy practitioners in the Global South who are pioneering new models of social investment.

Contents

Figures

Tables

Contributors

Silvia Bastante de Unverhau, Co-Impact
Katy Bullard, Independent
Prakash Fernandes, CIPLA Foundation
Rumana Hamied, CIPLA Foundation
Maysa Jalbout, Independent
Olivia Leland, Co-Impact
Natasha M. Matic, King Khalid Foundation
Takalani Netshitenzhe, Vodacom
Sahra Noor, Grit Partners
Deval Sanghvi, DASRA
Naina Subberwal Batra, AVPN
J. Satrijo Tanudjojo, Tanoto Foundation
Kathleen Wai Lin Chew, YTL Foundation

Foreword

Over the past few years, a range of adverse external factors has converged, transforming the basic notion of philanthropy from a 'nice to have' to a 'must-have'. This makes it important to improve the impact of philanthropy while simultaneously expanding the size of philanthropic investment and its scope.

The paradigm shift in philanthropy that is required to maximise its potential is unlikely to occur without a fundamental and durable change in the underlying mobilisation and deployment mechanisms: moving away from inequitable power dynamics fraught with tensions and blame games to much more cooperative, enabling, and trust-based set-ups. Such a change would open up opportunities for systemic transformation and the full empowerment of both recipients and donors.

The need for such a change is obvious at a macro level. The world has become unusually uncertain and susceptible to frequent and violent socio-economic, political, and geopolitical shocks. From the COVID pandemic and the escalating cost of living crisis to China–United States tensions and Russia's invasion of Ukraine, the basic drivers of welfare enhancement have been weakened. This urgency is exacerbated by worsening inequality, not just in terms of income and wealth, but also in terms of opportunity. The vulnerable segments of our global society are particularly hard hit.

The need is also obvious at a micro, community level. The frictions inherent in the power imbalance between donors and recipients is hindering the effectiveness of philanthropic capital and stymieing the sense of joint accomplishment that is so essential for sustaining cooperative and growing relationships. Collaboration is too often undermined by mutual suspicion, misunderstandings, and incentive misalignments. The desire of donors to give and the needs of recipients become harder to match.

However, amidst these concerning developments, two silver linings emerge.

Firstly, there is a growing recognition among more privileged segments of society of the importance of supporting the less privileged. This recognition is driven not only by moral considerations but also by self-interest. There is an understanding that one cannot thrive as an isolated entity in a challenged neighbourhood.

Secondly, this recognition has been accompanied by a broader acknowledgement of the need to enhance the effectiveness of philanthropy through collaborative and incentive-aligned dynamics that include both donors and recipients. Beyond mere financial considerations, donor generosity and flexibility must be met with stewardship and accountability from recipients. Both parties must work together with aligned and shared goals that can foster multi-actor partnerships. This approach leads to a more sustainable and comprehensive process of creating long-term, sustainable system change.

This book plays an important role in advancing this agenda. By focussing on three challenges – building networks, effective partnerships, and institutional resilience – it aims to stimulate discussions and actions centred around strategic and catalytic philanthropy. It comprises insightful essays written by practitioners that address risks and opportunities in an action-oriented manner. From the experiences of individual foundations to those of philanthropic networks, it offers engaging discussions not only on pursuing promising practices and approaches but also on avoiding potential pitfalls and diversions.

All three themes emphasise the importance of not only minimising the risk of falling but also swiftly recovering from the falls in our increasingly unpredictable world. This highlights the significance of a robust social-sector foundation, particularly in health and education, and underscores the need for collective responsibility rather than individual action.

Regrettably, there is little indication that our world will become more accommodating in the coming years. Also, there is little to suggest that, without external support, the most vulnerable segments of society will be able to reduce the multiple debilitating risks they face.

There are neither quick nor readily available solutions to the climate crisis or to the economic pressures stemming from inadequate growth, burdensome indebtedness, onerous inflation, and excessive inequality. We must make a concerted effort to act where there are windows for feasible and desirable improvements.

The insights provided in this book contribute significantly to this endeavour. They offer actionable guidance on how to enhance private philanthropy in a mutually beneficial and sustainable manner.

Mohamed A. El-Erian
President of Queen's College
University of Cambridge

Introduction

Clare Woodcraft, Kamal Munir, and Nitya Mohan Khemka

THE PARADIGM SHIFT

In 2020, as COVID-19 shut down operations in multiple industries, long-standing calls for a 'paradigm shift' in the philanthropic sector gained momentum with a slew of reports highlighting inefficiencies and the need for change. From claims that philanthropic capital was insufficiently flexible and overly bureaucratic, to criticism of its often myopic approach and lack of 'risk-taking', practitioners seized the opportunity of crisis to champion long-awaited structural transformation. The pandemic amplified the growing feeling that philanthropy was not empowering its recipients enough, with too many micro decisions about the allocation of funding taken remotely rather than by the communities in need. At a macro level, concerns were raised about the absence of co-funding and collaboration in the sector and the missed opportunities that this represented for a capital market estimated at several trillion US dollars.

In our respective work, including the report written in 2020 for the Centre for Strategic Philanthropy (CSP) at the Judge Business School on the impact of COVID on philanthropy,[1] we set out to better understand these issues. Why wasn't philanthropy able to effectively do more, more quickly, and more collaboratively? Why was this well-intentioned source of social investment with the potential to change lives positively and permanently not systematically delivering value at scale? We explored the extent to which the pandemic

---

[1] Munir, K., and Woodcraft, C. 2020. *Philanthropy and COVID 19: Is the North–South Balance of Power Finally Shifting?* Centre for Strategic Philanthropy, www.jbs.cam.ac.uk/wp-content/uploads/2020/12/csp-report-covid-2020-executive-summary.pdf.

had reinforced the need for change, accelerated it, or both, and sourced empirical evidence around how practitioners had overcome operational challenges.

As evidenced throughout this book, we observed that the pandemic highlighted the imbalanced power relationship between the Global North and South and that

> this is particularly true in the case of the North–South
> relationship in philanthropy which has long been characterized
> by an unequal power dynamic. Global South philanthropy is
> as old as that of the Global North with often long traditions of
> community support and local giving. However, the resource-poor
> nature of many Global South SPOs [social purpose organisations]
> has meant that many are reliant on Global North foundations
> for funding. This in turn has meant that these foundations have
> tended to set the parameters around which various programmes
> and interventions are identified for funding and the way in which
> resources are allocated to them.[2]

These imbalances are further compounded by the source of the capital which, as the Organisation for Economic Co-operation and Development (OECD) points out, tends to be highly concentrated.[3] Of the 143 foundations included in their 2018 global survey, the Bill & Melinda Gates Foundation (BMGF) is by far the most significant philanthropic donor, having provided almost a half of total giving for international development (49 per cent). In addition, 81 per cent of the total philanthropic giving during 2013–2015 was provided by only twenty foundations. Moreover, philanthropic flows, at 5 per cent, are still modest in volume compared to official development assistance (ODA).

Our findings resonated not just with practitioners in the Global South but also with a growing movement that sprung up in preceding

---

[2] Ibid.

[3] OECD. 2018. *Private Philanthropy for Development*, www.oecd.org/dac/private-philanthropy-for-development-9789264085190-en.htm.

years. Recognition of this phenomenon of imbalanced power structures coalesced into a new aligned community calling for solidarity and system change. What began as a simple hashtag (#ShiftThePower) has now evolved into a dedicated website, a grassroots-driven movement, and a broad-based practitioner community calling for radical change.

The pandemic empowered practitioner organisations to insist on less funding conditionality, and catalysed funders to openly acknowledge the need to listen better, act faster, and adapt quickly to new ways of doing business. The gravity of the situation meant that 'business as usual' was no longer an option and a new level of understanding, responsiveness, and flexibility in philanthropy was critical to prove philanthropy's worth for practitioners on the front line in desperate need of help. We found multiple examples of impressive new practices that cut across geographic boundaries, sectors, and issues, to demonstrate that philanthropists can do things differently and, more importantly, should.

CORE SECTOR CHALLENGES

Our research found that there are core areas where the change that the pandemic catalysed was sufficiently positive and progressive that it should be encouraged and institutionalised. Three opportunities to radically improve impact stood out.

Mobilising Networks

First, we call for more funding for networks and a general commitment to fund infrastructure. We note that funding Global South professional philanthropic networks plays a significant role in supporting the development and institutionalisation of philanthropy in these markets. They help under-resourced SPOs collectively bargain for better conditions where they might fear repercussions were they to do so alone. By articulating the collective demands of the sector to local governments, global grant-makers, and the broader development community, philanthropic networks in the Global South can elevate the voice of SPOs, create stronger collective advocacy platforms to lobby for improving practices, connect Global South SPOs to their peers for knowledge exchange, and help build richer and more accurate analysis of the needs and potential of the sector. Professional networks allow for faster scale-up of knowledge-sharing, technology transfer, and the creation of operational partnerships. Only with a collective voice can Global South SPOs make the case for system change.

Since the publication of our 2020 research report, we have seen professional networks in the sector gain exponential momentum and demonstrate their value. Two venture philanthropy networks focused on the Global South – the Africa Venture Philanthropy Alliance (AVPA) and the Asian Venture Philanthropy Network (AVPN) – launched an initiative that unites Global South practitioners for peer learning, in collaboration with the Oxford Said Business School. The Africa-Asia Impact Fellowship nurtures asset owners and capital managers to become effective impact investing practitioners and explicitly leverages its respective networks to build capacity and knowledge to increase social investment into these regions. Similarly, on the back of AVPN's annual conference in July 2022, in partnership with The Rockefeller Foundation, the seeds were sown for the creation of the Global South Impact Community (GSIC), which subsequently contributed a statement to the 2022 G20 summit in Jakarta,[4] calling for a shift in the architecture of global development finance to empower Global South voices and enable philanthropic investment.

Partnerships with Governments

Secondly, we call for increased Global South government/ grant-maker partnerships, arguing that as emergency market philanthropy grows (largely due to the multi-trillion-dollar intergenerational wealth transfer expected in coming decades), there

---

[4] GSIC G20 Statement: www.rockefellerfoundation.org/news/the-global-south-impact-community-presents-public-statement-to-g20-leaders-at-the-t20-summit-indonesia/.

is an opportunity for Global South philanthropists to work more closely with governments. Such partnerships increased during the pandemic and served to respectively highlight the mutual benefits that they offer. Governments get much needed additional capital and social innovation. Global South SPOs and grant-makers have an opportunity to align with national development policy and scale up their initiatives faster. Perhaps most importantly, Global South philanthropists and governments can build harmonious – rather than contentious – working relationships to create a new narrative around system change.

In 2021, our partners at the OECD Centre on Philanthropy produced the second edition of their Philanthropy for Development report,[5] which demonstrated that progress is accelerating in this space as more philanthropists commit to pooling their capital with that of development funds and government-underwritten efforts. The report noted that the percentage contribution of philanthropy to global development funding is increasing, and according to the OECD's Secretary-General Mathias Cormann, it is 'playing a pivotal role in providing targeted resources, leveraging private capital, and testing innovative approaches in support of many communities in the Global South'. As Cormann acknowledges, this newfound commitment to partnering with governments brings previous unseen levels of innovation and agility as philanthropy – essentially 'risk' capital – is married with governmental capacity to scale. The report further notes that more can be done to promote this form of collaboration, including encouraging greater transparency in the sector through formal reporting and enabling regulation that removes constraints on cross-border philanthropy, including differential tax exemption for activities carried out domestically versus abroad, or denial of tax exemptions for activities whose beneficiaries are foreign public benefit organisations.

---

[5] OECD. 2021. Philanthropy in Development, www.oecd.org/dev/private-philanthropy-for-development-second-edition-cdf37f1e-en.htm.

Indeed, since COVID-19, partnership with government no longer feels like an alien practice and more like a logical step to ensure real system change. Even some of the most 'third-sector averse' regimes that fear the threat of civil society insurgency are now embracing the possibility of deploying philanthropic capital for more scalable and sustainable outcomes (shrinking public-sector spending no doubt also plays a role). In the Kingdom of Saudi Arabia, the government is actively trying to build capacity in the sector and encourage its investment in critical areas such as health care, education, housing, research, and social programmes. This support was epitomised by the 2021 announcement that the country would create an entire city dedicated to the not-for-profit sector. While such lofty ambitions may not translate quickly into systemic outcomes, they do evoke a burgeoning enabling environment in stark contrast to earlier years where SPOs might face abject hostility from the ruling regime. It also suggests new opportunities for building trust where historically a third-sector partnership might have been perceived as a threat.

Building Resilience

Finally, the importance of core philanthropic funding for building resilience cannot be overstated. Grantees all over the Global South want the simpler, faster due diligence and application processes that COVID-19 engendered to continue. These reduced time and transaction costs and quickly freed up funding for unexpected purposes where previously it might have been rigorously restricted.

Since the initial publication of the CSP's report, the drive for more core funding and unrestricted philanthropic capital has gained further momentum. As NPC reported in July 2022,[6] funders must 'give more and give flexibly if they're to achieve any impact' during the cost-of-living crisis, which it said was 'as big a crisis as COVID,

---

[6] www.civilsociety.co.uk/news/funders-told-to-offer-urgent-covid-type-support-to-charities-amid-cost-of-living-crisis.html.

possibly bigger'. One of the core outcomes of the AVPN's annual conference in July 2022 was the conclusion from hundreds of practitioners attending that

> there is the need for social investors to take greater risks with their capital and give investees the freedom to decide how they use their funding. Unrestricted funding is also essential in providing investees with the flexible support they need to build resilience and remain sustainable. Further, for funding to be catalytic, investors need to be open to risks, learning from mistakes and making long-term commitments.[7]

GENESIS OF THIS BOOK

Upon publishing our overview of the grassroots-level shifts that were underway in the sector, we quickly realised the need for further insight into actual cases of SPOs in the Global South engaging in these dynamics. That is when we – Clare Woodcraft, Kamal Munir, and Nitya Khemka – came together as an editorial team to identify exemplars and request them to contribute to a volume that would bring their experiences to a wider audience. This volume is thus an effort to showcase the possibility of a different way of using philanthropic capital to create system change. It is an opportunity to amplify the voices of leaders in the Global South who have already developed their own parameters around best practice and have already tested new thinking and new ideas about how we can do things better. It is also a call to action for a more united community of global change-makers who believe that philanthropy can have a disproportionately powerful role in changing and improving socio-economic realities of the developing world but only if it undergoes a radical transformation.

In this edition, you will find contributions from thirteen Global South philanthropic experts on three themes that we have derived from

---

[7] www.sei.org/wp-content/uploads/2018/12/avpn-global-conference-2022---post-event-report-compressed.pdf.

our original research findings, which we felt merited additional exploration. These are areas that we deem critical to the improvement and institutionalisation of best practice in philanthropy. They comprise building multi-sector partnerships, fortifying networks, and creating institutional resilience. Each of our authors has produced their chapter by drawing on their actual work and experience. They have shared their views with us candidly so that other practitioners can not only benefit from the potential replicability of their work but also appreciate the myriad challenges they face in delivering system change.

WHAT TO EXPECT

This compendium presents a view of how 'newer' models of private philanthropy in the Global South are grappling with the most pressing development challenges. The curated essays provide a frank assessment of the challenges and opportunities of emerging market philanthropy and lessons learned from how the pandemic has affected giving. It highlights how philanthropy in the Global South can become more independent of its reliance on large Northern foundations. Several topical themes are examined: What steps can be taken to share data and best practices among local philanthropic organisations? What new strategies should the philanthropic sector adopt to increase its impact? How can the philanthropic sector work more closely with the state? What initiatives are already underway that need to be strengthened in this respect? How has COVID highlighted new possibilities for a more robust, impactful, and democratic philanthropic sector in emerging markets? Through our contributing authors, we explore further some of the COVID-induced sector changes and the responses to them of recipient organisations in emerging markets within the framework of our three themes:

Building Networks: Infrastructure, Capacity, and Knowledge

This theme brings together authors who have developed networks to improve 'philanthropic infrastructure', be it databases, knowledge-sharing platforms, professional associations, or events and outreach.

Their work allows us to appreciate how emerging market professional philanthropic networks can potentially play a huge role in supporting the development and institutionalisation of Global South philanthropy. This section (Chapters 1 and 2) gives real world examples of how professional association can drive greater impact through knowledge-sharing, co-funding, peer learning, and practical operational collaboration.

In Chapter 1, 'From Transactional to Transformational: Leveraging Networks to Catalyse Bold Philanthropic Action in Asia', Naina Subberwal Batra examines the power of networks with the creation and growth of the AVPN. Batra explores how connecting like-minded Global South peers and building bridges to collaboration is a core function of ecosystem builders such as AVPN. Since it was established in 2011, AVPN has grown into Asia's largest social investment network and has incubated several successful partnerships. However, the journey has not always been smooth sailing – building networks is challenging given the heterogeneity of their communities and the need to build compromise and clear collective 'value add'. Batra explains how the network strove to create a robust value proposition and against the odds built an entity that is inclusive, responsive, and resilient.

In Chapter 2, 'A Model for Promoting Systems-Change Philanthropy by Leveraging Networks', Olivia Leland and Silvia Bastante de Unverhau provide a nuanced understanding of philanthropic networks to promote collaboration and impact. By highlighting the experiences of Co-Impact, a global collaborative that advances inclusive systems change through grant-making and influencing philanthropy, the chapter flags a novel approach to higher-impact philanthropy through pooled funds. By analysing the constraints in philanthropic practice that the Co-Impact model is designed to address, the chapter discusses how to advance 'trust-based philanthropy' that both learns from and inspires others as well as provides a practical approach to addressing inherent power dynamics in philanthropy.

Forging Multi-Stakeholder Partnerships: Global South Governments, Global South Philanthropists, and Civil Society

Authors who have been involved in the development of multi-stakeholder partnerships congregate around this theme. As emergency market philanthropy grows, there is an opportunity for Global South philanthropists to build strong partnership with fellow Global South actors and particularly with Global South governments. These have increased on the back of the pandemic and served to respectively highlight the mutual benefits that they offer. Our authors provide their perspectives on the value of such partnerships. This section (Chapters 3, 4, 5, and 6) highlights the mutually beneficial value of such partnerships.

Chapter 3, 'Building Effective Philanthropy through Strategic Partnerships: A Case Study of the Tanoto Foundation', by Dr Satrijo Tanudjojo, focuses on efforts by the Indonesia-based Tanoto Foundation to engage in knowledge exchange via the creation of collaborative networks and global communities of practice. The chapter highlights how the Foundation effectively partnered with local and national organisations to create collaborative regional platforms that respond to endemic threats, supporting a more sustainable social system and a resilient community through education. In doing so, this chapter examines how the institutionalising of cross-sectorial partnerships and implementation of scalable human capital development programmes can allow philanthropic organisations to expand their value proposition and improve their inherent know-how, ultimately impacting the lived daily realities of communities they serve.

In Chapter 4, 'Forging Multi-Stakeholder Partnerships: Global South Governments, the Private Sector, Philanthropists, and Civil Society', Dr Natasha Matic explores philanthropic partnership best practices in the post COVID-19 world through lessons learned from Saudi Arabia-based King Khalid Foundation's philanthropic partnerships journey. The chapter argues that historically, the philanthropic sector in the Global South has been siloed, with few foundations working together and even fewer engaged in multi-sectoral collaborations. The scale and urgency of the pandemic transformed the way philanthropists work, creating the case for more active collaboration between governments, the private sector, philanthropic capital, and the ultimate stakeholders they serve. The chapter identifies several critical elements of a successful partnership and provides insights and practical tools that will help initiate, develop, and sustain high-impact partnerships over time between governments, the private sector, and philanthropists.

In Chapter 5, 'The Whole Is Greater than the Sum: Forging and Sustaining Multi-Stakeholder Philanthropic Partnerships in Africa beyond the Pandemic', Sahra Noor discusses the vital multi-sector partnerships between the African Union (AU), local governments, and the private sector that arose from the pandemic and helped curb the massive spread of infections due to COVID-19. The chapter highlights the uniqueness and significance of these partnerships at the local and continental levels and some of the values underpinning them. Several salient themes are discussed, including the importance and impact of the AU's strategic leadership and multi-sectoral partnerships in advancing the continent's health and economic agenda, the challenges inherent in sustaining and scaling these alliances in Africa, as well as forging the way forward post-pandemic.

Chapter 6, 'Gender-Based Violence in South Africa and Multi-Stakeholder Partnerships: The Vodacom Foundation Experience', by Takalani Netshitenzhe, examines the extent of gender-based violence in South Africa and the role of multi-stakeholder partnerships to tackle this fundamental violation of human rights. Using the work of the Vodacom Foundation, the chapter outlines how the Foundation's contribution to the fight against gender-based violence has evolved into an ecosystem that supports prevention, response, and survivor empowerment through strong, sustainable partnerships with civil society organisations (CSOs) and the roll out of information communication technologies (ICTs). Most critically, the chapter underscores key transformative impacts of this evolution in the relationships between the Foundation and CSOs into mutually beneficial and supportive partnerships. The case study serves to demonstrate that big business can do more than just generating revenues and can also work in tandem with governments and the civil society to address societal ills.

Creating Resilience: Philanthropic Financing for Sustainable Development

Finally, we bring together authors whose work showcases how new ways of thinking and innovation in Global South philanthropy can offset some of the historical fragility of emerging market third sectors and ensure sufficient resilience to survive future crises. Here in Chapter 7, 8, 9, and 10, authors share both COVID-19 and non-pandemic experiences of how they build institutional capacity in the third sector and ensure sustainable finance for their initiatives.

Chapter 7, 'Philanthropy in Emerging Economies: A Call to Invest in Resilience', by Maysa Jalbout and Katy Bullard, outlines current philanthropic trends in emerging economies, exploring the extent to which philanthropists are investing in resilience. Three dimensions are considered: what philanthropists invest in, how they invest, and with whom they invest. The chapter presents a detailed understanding of emerging economy philanthropy – both pre-COVID-19 and in the wake of the pandemic – and articulates frameworks and considerations for understanding resilience in philanthropy. Drawing on case studies of philanthropic organisations in Brazil, India, and Saudi Arabia, the chapter advocates for investing in resilience, discussing both challenges and opportunities for doing so.

In Chapter 8, 'How Strategic Philanthropy Can Shake Up the Ecosystem and Build Resilience: A Case Study on Increasing Access to Palliative Care in India', Rumana Hamied and Prakash Fernandes highlight the crucial role that indigenous philanthropy plays in the Global South despite systematic philanthropy from the Global North. Using palliative care in India, the chapter outlines the two-decade journey of the Cipla Foundation to support palliative care and bridge the gaping unmet need for end-of-life care. The chapter presents a systematic discussion of how the Foundation has mobilised a multi-stakeholder ecosystem including civil society, public health experts, government and private-sector professionals, the health-care community, patients, and the media. It presents valuable learnings of how indigenous philanthropy can unveil less visible but potent local needs and underscores that even when funding remains domestic, institutional learning and knowledge can be disseminated globally.

Chapter 9, 'Building Resilience for the Malaysian Education Ecosystem during the Pandemic and Beyond', by Kathleen Wai Lin Chew, describes the challenges faced by the Malaysian education system to address remote learning during lockdown and school closure in Malaysia because of the pandemic. The chapter discusses the role the YTL Foundation played in bringing together a raft of technological solutions, alongside key partnerships with the government and the community, to ensure continuity in learning, particularly for low-income students across the country. The uniqueness of this case study underscores the importance of partnerships that enable the scaling of locally identified solutions. The chapter also explores the elements necessary for building resilience into the Malaysian education ecosystem in a future where hybrid education will be the norm.

In Chapter 10, 'Creating Resilience and Rebuilding India through Philanthropy', Deval Sanghvi outlines the approach that Dasra took in their 'Back the Frontline' initiative to combine COVID-19 rapid response efforts with building long-term resilience in helping India's most vulnerable communities. Drawing on insights from Dasra's twenty-two years of experience, this chapter provides a nuanced understanding of the urgent need to shift giving practices towards an equity-focused approach, committed to supporting locally led scalable solutions that have measurable outcomes of justice, diversity, and inclusion. The chapter proposes providing rapid response funding for local frontline organisations, while simultaneously unlocking more thoughtful philanthropy, strengthening institutional backbone through capacity-building support, and promoting learning and knowledge exchange between key stakeholders to accelerate development.

CONCLUSION

In this book, we have attempted to curate the lived experiences of leading Global South practitioners in philanthropy. We hope to evolve this work into a community of institutional peer learning onto which we can build and to which others can contribute. We acknowledge the enormous power and potential of philanthropic capital but equally recognise its often spectacular failure to create sustainable change. We believe passionately that the constellation of crises the world currently faces coupled with the rapidly growing pool of philanthropic capital demands a more focused, researched attempt to build standards, share best practice, acknowledge failures, and ensure positive system change. We see this book as just the beginning of the overall work and welcome input – positive or critical – from others who believe in its importance to the future of the philanthropic sector in how it supports the United Nations' Sustainable Development Goals (SDGs).

This is meant to be a 'thinking and doing' book for readers seeking to understand how philanthropy in emerging markets is forging a common agenda. The featured chapters highlight the deeper issues at play but also offer up ideas and positive examples of how diverse stakeholders can solve big social challenges in creative and practical ways. We have created an inclusive publication that speaks to all readers, practitioners, scholars, policy influencers, and non-governmental organisations (NGOs), and can also serve as a foundational text to those seeking a deeper understanding of the shifts in emerging market philanthropy and how best to maximise impact.

This publication makes a crucial contribution towards understanding the current state of Global South philanthropy in the aftermath of COVID-19 and identifies future opportunities and challenges.

Currently there is a dearth of research and literature on Global South philanthropy, and specifically our chosen focus of the Middle East, Southeast Asia, and Africa. This is a significant market gap given that philanthropy in these markets – where institutional voids prevail and often create significant barriers to impact – is often very different from that in the Global North. Specifically, many emerging market governments are struggling to navigate the development of relevant regulatory framework, tax incentives don't always play a role, and philanthropic giving may be blocked by state actors rather than encouraged.

The time is ripe for a radical rethink of Global South philanthropy, not only in how to best get resources to where they are most needed but also to support national governmental plans driving sustainable development. We aspired to create work that helps underwrite the ongoing and important debate about how delivering on the SDGs might be accelerated if philanthropic capital were systematically pooled to this effect. We hope that practitioners and grantmakers alike will take inspiration from this work and collectively help us move forward effectively on our mission towards improving the impact of philanthropy in the Global South.

Further, this book contributes to the ever-growing appetite for collaboration that is uniting the voices of Global South philanthropic practitioners. We hope it represents an opportunity to create a centralised force and repository for evidence-based practices from the developing world that defy those historically entrenched through structures born out of the Global North. We thank all our contributors for being part of this project and for taking the time to share their experiences, energy, drive, and passion with fellow practitioners. We thank them also for capturing these experiences in technical detail and in a way that enables replication in other parts of the world. We hope this collection of chapters will prove a catalyst for similar exchanges whereby game-changing case studies can bring about new hope for innovation and system change using private capital for public good.

ACKNOWLEDGMENT

We are beholden to several associates, colleagues, and partners for encouraging us to put together this volume, and to the many detailed comments we have received along the way. Grateful thanks must also go to our contributors who dealt with our feedback and correspondence with promptness, diligence, and patience. We are also appreciative of Valerie Appleby and Carrie Parkinson at Cambridge University Press for being so patient with us during the various iterations of the book. Special thanks must go to Di Kennedy and Charles Goldsmith of the Judge Business School their assistance. Particular gratitude goes to Dr Shonali Banerjee, also of Judge Business School, for her painstaking editorial guidance and support. We are also very grateful to Faiza Ahmed and Tania Nadia Kossberg for their critical help in the final stages. Finally, we remain grateful to The Defeat-NCD Partnership for providing additional support to ensure the timely publication of this volume.

I   From Transactional to Transformational

Leveraging Networks to Catalyse Bold Philanthropic Action in Asia

Naina Subberwal Batra

INTRODUCTION

The COVID-19 pandemic has been a clarion call to philanthropists to collaborate.[1] It has proven that large-scale systemic challenges such as pandemic response and relief cannot be addressed sustainably through unilateral effort. According to Bridgespan, the highest number of philanthropic collaboratives established in a single year was in 2020, right as the pandemic was unleashing its full wrath. If all of these organisations acted alone, the burden on frontline support organisations to coordinate well-intentioned efforts would have been insurmountable, let alone the level of duplication, waste, and inequity in reach. We have to build on this openness to collaboration to extend its value to address other wicked problems.[2]

Ecosystem builders are the lynchpin in this process, giving philanthropists and resource providers a neutral platform to identify the right partners, connect with peers and unlikely allies, share learnings openly and honestly, and build trust. Those new to philanthropy can also leverage the network to leapfrog the knowledge accumulation process and identify partners with the required expertise on the ground. Although time and resources seem more stretched than ever,

---

[1] The author wishes to acknowledge the contributions of Denderah Rickmers, Nadya Pryana, Sangeetha Watson, and Siddharth Chatterjee in the development of this chapter.

[2] www.bridgespan.org/getmedia/5590afe6-fe08-452e-9afd-bedfbc586cf6/releasing-the-potential-of-philanthropic-collaborations-2021.pdf.aspx.

there is an influx in actors, innovations, and risk-taking behaviour in the ecosystem that must be capitalised on.

Ecosystem builders often act behind the scenes. More than providing a safe space for conversations and convenings, ecosystem builders are constantly connecting the dots and choreographing opportunities for the likeminded to converge. Often they are at the heart of introductions to unusual allies, as was the case with Kellogg's, the Breakfast Revolution, and Sesame Workshop India. In 2018, each of these organisations were addressing India's malnutrition problems in isolation: Kellogg's was implementing holistic nutrition programmes in rural childcare centres and Sesame Workshop India was looking to address malnutrition through broadcasted content. At the Asian Venture Philanthropy Network's (AVPN's) Global Conference in 2018, these organisations were brought together to speak on the same panel and this led to a series of conversations that culminated in the creation of Bright Start, a network of implementation partners, funders, and content and advocacy leaders who share the goal of ending morning hunger.

While AVPN's annual conference is its most well-known convening, yearly team members organise close to 100 opportunities for members across the region to meet and engage on various topics, and countless informal ones. It is through the constant process of making connections, opening doors, and facilitating introductions that AVPN has helped build a robust social investment community in Asia, as its sister networks have done in other regions. Without such effort, the scale of collaboration that is necessary in this post-COVID world would be far from achievable.

Leveraging ecosystem builders as partners is a win-win opportunity for philanthropists. It opens doors not only to a ready network of partners, but also curated engagement to ease the hurdles of collaboration. The deep local roots of ecosystem builders ensure grounded insights and access to impact organisations with proven solutions. It means being part of a long-term, robust solution, not a transient one.

In order for philanthropists to be bold, ecosystem builders need to be bolder. But the contribution of ecosystem builders often goes unrecognised. The function of an ecosystem builder is far-reaching, from making quick connections and sharing information, to supporting fund deployment, both during and outside of times of urgency. However, they are often seen merely as platforms for affiliation. The inherent benefit of an intermediary of this form to support and grow a community of action for change often goes unnoticed. This is partly because the contributed value of a network is difficult to separate from its attributive value. Indeed, it takes more than a local presence to be a meaningful partner at the market-specific level. One also needs to have strong expertise in the local market and context. At a regional level, being a valued and valuable ecosystem builder means guiding the activities of organisations working on various issues coherently and cohesively. It requires a deep and nuanced understanding of every member's expertise and interests so as to pinpoint areas of synergy. However, while this effort is appreciated it is often difficult for philanthropists to justify supporting it with financial resources in the same way as they do with impact organisations. The impact of ecosystem builders is seen over a long period of time, and progress towards this cannot always be tangibly demonstrated. The conflict is in the perceived opportunity cost of funding an ecosystem builder which will yield systemic impact over time versus an impact organisation that can address beneficiary needs tangibly today.

Voices from Asia Pacific: AVPN's Journey in Building the Social Investment Ecosystem in the Region

This chapter provides insights from AVPN's journey and teachable moments in its path to becoming an effective ecosystem builder of social investment in the Asia Pacific.

By examining how AVPN's approach and guiding principles have evolved over its ten-year journey, this chapter will demonstrate the network's growth from providing a safe space for members to being an ecosystem builder pushing the frontiers of social impact.

It will address how various elements of AVPN's work have been adapted, refined, and revamped in this process.

As philanthropists in the Global South continue to leverage networks in delivering social impact, this chapter will give an understanding of how the backbone of the ecosystem was strengthened. Lessons learned in this chapter will help philanthropists identify opportunities to amplify the capacity of networks and ecosystem builders to do more, and in doing so, setting *themselves up* to do so much more. By doing so, philanthropists, too, can play an active role in building the social impact ecosystem in the region.

COVID-19 sharpened the need for systematic ecosystem builders. Whereas before philanthropists would be laser focused on direct giving to implementing organisations, the complex logistical challenges brought forth by the pandemic made them realise the amplified value of intermediary organisations with influence and reach across the ecosystem. In a time of uncertainty and urgency, a network like AVPN could help translate their intent into measurable, impactful outcomes. In AVPN's case, the groundwork and *'thought work'* had already been done over ten years; the network had built trust and credibility. All of this came together in new and powerful ways in the face of COVID-19.

KEY CHALLENGES IN BUILDING AN EFFECTIVE ECOSYSTEM BUILDER

This section discusses the challenges that confront a network looking to become an effective ecosystem builder, reflecting on the experience of AVPN as the largest social investment network in Asia.

Principally, there were two kinds of challenges AVPN faced. First was the *challenge of identifying and articulating the true value of the network.* How can members' efforts go beyond tracking impact to creating a safe space for members to connect, resulting in them exploring innovative approaches, structures, and partnerships? How does our work account for and get recognised for the complex value it creates? Finally, how do we scale operationally and get funded adequately for our contribution and goals?

Second was the *challenge of being globally, regionally, and locally relevant* to diverse members, regional markets, and the network's own changing goals and capabilities. How does a network accommodate the needs of its diverse members across the region while connecting to global trends? How should it maintain neutrality within the regional diversity of the markets it supports? How does a network adapt to the changing shape of the industry vis-à-vis its own capabilities and goals? This section addresses each challenge in turn.

Identifying and Articulating the True Value of the Network

The importance of ecosystem builders is often under-recognised. The function of a network is far-reaching, from making quick connections and sharing information, to supporting funding deployment, both during and outside of crises. Nevertheless, network organisations are often seen merely as platforms for affiliation, promotion, or endorsement, operating entirely on a transactional basis. In the early days of AVPN, its engagement activities were driven by members. Its role was to provide a safe space and neutral platform for convening relevant stakeholders and participants. The members led the conversation, speaking from their experience and asking others to join them or guide them in the process. AVPN soon became aware that its value far exceeded a role as a mere meeting ground for its members. But how could members articulate this value clearly?

Accounting for a network's role in outcomes is not easy. The contributed and attributive value of a network is often tricky to delineate. It is one thing for the network to recognise its own capacity, but for true credibility it must also have an evidence-based track record that is visible to its members. Essentially, a network must find ways to demonstrate that it is not just 'nice to have' for members, but an integral part of their success. Most AVPN members join the network with pre-established giving practices, so the network must show how it is able to amplify the impact of those activities through collaboration, as well as creating new opportunities for giving.

The nebulous quality of a network's true value also comes with operational hurdles. Because of the under-recognised value of networks, organisations like AVPN struggle to receive consistent and committed unrestricted funding which are integral to ensure, streamline, or grow their operations. In AVPN's case, less than 4 per cent of its funds annually are unrestricted, with membership fees covering less than 30 per cent of the annual budget. While the AVPN team has grown from four to more than seventy-five in just ten years, the organisation faced considerable challenges in funding this growth. How can networks communicate value to funders and clients to raise the funds needed to accomplish their goals?

Adaptation

Change is uncomfortable but inevitable, and there is no end to it. AVPN challenged itself to keep innovating as a way to grow the ecosystem and support members in achieving and expanding their impact goals. While most of these strategies have proven to be successful, a few haven't quite panned out as expected. For example, in its early days, AVPN attempted to mainstream the concept of *venture philanthropy*,[3] at that time a new way of doing philanthropy in the region, and started its proposition as the Asian Venture Philanthropy Network. As years went by however, AVPN recognised that there were several occasions where the team spent more time and resources ironing out theoretical and conceptual elements of the concept rather than focusing on catalysing the action itself. It was essential for AVPN to embrace the change and adapt to its new role.

A network must master a way to be an accommodative partner while remaining a neutral platform. As AVPN enlarged its focus

---

[3] Defined as an approach whereby an investor for impact supports a social purpose organisation (SPO) to help it maximise its social impact.

from venture philanthropy to see social investment as a continuum that encompasses everything from philanthropy and venture philanthropy to impact investing, corporate social responsibility (CSR), and sustainable investment, it faced a second challenge. How can a network stay a neutral platform while serving diverse members with widely ranging goals?

It takes more than local presence to be a meaningful partner at the market-specific level. One also needs to have strong expertise in the local market and context. AVPN was established in Singapore in 2011 by an American looking to replicate an idea and network that flourished in Europe. Since its initial premise was not based on a formal needs analysis of the Asian philanthropic ecosystem, figuring out how AVPN could best add value to the ecosystem came after its foundation. As AVPN started to build its presence on the ground, it faced the challenge of accommodating regional differences. It wasn't easy to speak a common language with members across the board given differences in terminology and language in different markets. And AVPN services, which initially stemmed from ideas in Singapore, were met with mixed responses in different countries in the region.

Any network that attempts to create value in its ecosystem is likely to experience challenges similar to AVPN's. However, AVPN's experience shows that these challenges can be overcome. AVPN's response to the challenges it faced can be characterised first in its *strategy*, and second in *implementation*. This chapter details the strategies that AVPN chose and how they were implemented.

AVPN addressed the challenges faced by embracing change and iterating constantly to re-envision its role in Asia's impact space. As a network spanning a broad geographical base, a wide spectrum of social investment approaches, and a diversity of stakeholders, AVPN had the unique opportunity to take a bird's-eye view of the space, its opportunities, and its challenges. Unrestrained by conventional boundaries, AVPN was able to imagine new ways of working, building on exciting ideas often emerging at the fringes and supporting members to take considered risks. This can be attributed to the ethos of constant self-investigation, with an acute conscientiousness of evolving contexts, and has been key to each stage of AVPN's growth.

It took AVPN three years from inception to clarify its position in the ecosystem and product offerings. It was not a straightforward journey to identifying, refining, and articulating AVPN's value proposition: a platform for practitioners to share knowledge and build capacity, centred on the Asian context, and to offer practical solutions, and allow a space for sharing challenges, best practices, and collective learning. This clarity emerged from AVPN's deliberate and reflexive responsiveness to its members' needs; built on AVPN's adaptability rather than a pre-defined model that members needed to try to fit into.

AVPN continues to refine its value proposition. AVPN has embraced its role as a bold ecosystem builder, pushing the frontiers of what a social investment network can do. It does so by trying new approaches, introducing new programmes, and facilitating collaboration, especially pioneering ideas that are uncommon in Asia but needed in the face of current challenges. AVPN is also open to letting go of ideas that do not work. As it refined its core, widened offerings, and let go of its initial proposition, it changed its name from the Asian Venture Philanthropy Network to simply AVPN.

In adapting to market needs, AVPN empowers local market teams to function with autonomy. AVPN has expanded regional presence by leveraging local teams in over thirteen markets. These local representatives bring with them market-specific expertise and influence, ensuring that the right people, resources, and solutions are mobilised to respond to opportunities and problems that have surfaced. AVPN market representatives are engaged in conceptualising and operationalising activities, ensuring local market relevance and regional alignment. This extended autonomy is not without the full support from core functions housed in the headquarters, demonstrating AVPN's commitment to 'empower the edges'.

AVPN's strategy, rooted in a consistent openness to innovate, iterate, and explore new ways of engagement has contributed to the clarification and concretisation of its values, even in an ever-changing ecosystem. The network has been able to withstand market shifts and be nimble in its response to the evolving needs of its membership across the continuum as well as the distinct local contexts across the region. The adaptive, forward-thinking, and experimental nature enshrined in AVPN's process has been richly rewarded. This is evident not just in AVPN's exponential growth, but also in the way it was able to pivot quickly during COVID-19, creating novel opportunities and providing a blueprint for a social investment ecosystem builder in the post-COVID world.

The Three Pillars: Connect, Learn, Act

The philanthropic ecosystem relies on iteration to reassess models of working and structuring. AVPN members are eager to revisit solutions, improve efficiency, increase transparency, and assess impact. In this climate, AVPN wanted to offer consistency in the process of how the organisation functions as a network. It mapped its work under three pillars: *connect*, *learn*, *act*, all of which are pathways to *lead*, or network leadership. The pillars are a reflection of the core characteristic of AVPN's activities: convening. AVPN is in the business of connecting people, providing members with opportunities to meet and learn from each other with the goal of eventually taking collaborative action in moving capital towards impact. The framework has helped AVPN systematically articulate its value proposition and impact, while being able to innovate and adapt on the specific product offerings under each pillar allows AVPN to adapt to its dynamic ecosystem.

AVPN continuously grows, adds, and refines products and offerings within the Connect, Learn, Act pillars. The objective is to build and influence the ecosystem by piloting ideas in collaboration with members and sharing these tested solutions with the broader community. Below are the activities AVPN has undertaken under each pillar of the organisation (Figure 1.1).

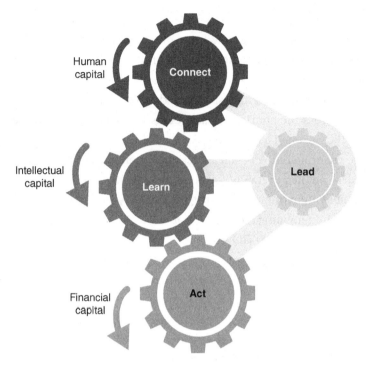

FIGURE 1.1 The three AVPN Pillars: Connect, Learn, Act

'Connect': Support Member Action and Identify Ideas that Move Capital

'Connect' happens at several levels in different forms: hosting large conferences, providing personal introductions, and more. The idea is to connect unlikely allies within the network to foster collaboration for greater impact.

- **Conferences**: AVPN's cornerstone is its power to convene. The network now runs forty events per year. In the wake of the pandemic, AVPN has tried and tested countless ways for members to engage and connect virtually with each other. Its Virtual Conference in 2020, right at the start of the pandemic, attracted almost 7,500 attendees. Yet there is no adequate substitute for in-person meetings, especially at scale. Networking is not the same when it is not face to face, and scheduled zoom meetings and webinars do not allow for chance encounters with new people, topics, or ideas.

With this in mind, AVPN made a bold move to host the Global Conference 2022 as one of the first in-person conferences since the start of the COVID-19 pandemic. AVPN's initiative was rewarded with the participation of over 1,100 delegates in 119 sessions across the 3.5 days. Over the duration of the conference, these members made over 8,100 connections on the conference app, sharing ideas, finding allies, and learning together. The network is more committed than ever to providing a safe and collaborative space to discuss effective ways of moving capital towards impact, fostering connections in the industry, and creating opportunities for learning.

- **Platforms and communities of practice**: As a network, AVPN is intentionally cause-agnostic. However, with a deep understanding of what individual members are working towards, AVPN saw that members were organically converging around issues like gender, climate, youth opportunities, and health. Sector-specific platforms, by creating a space for targeted conversations, knowledge-sharing, and ideation, presented the potential for members who were either already knee-deep in these issues or who were working in areas that intersect with these issues to learn from and collaborate with one another. AVPN's platforms build communities of like-minded individuals and strengthen the network's own capacity around specific causes. At the time of writing, AVPN has hosted platforms for gender equality, climate action, and youth opportunities, with emerging platforms in health and sustainable livelihoods. These platforms are currently still in their early stages, and they will evolve as the needs of the ecosystem change.

'Learn': Surface Actionable Insights for Asian Leaders through Pilots and Research

Across the 'Learn'-related work, AVPN engages members through collaborative content development and delivery. Through the co-creation process, members are on a journey with AVPN and can influence their ecosystem.

- **Knowledge Centre**: Early on, AVPN noticed that many of its members were on a learning journey in clarifying their impact theses. Members could learn from each other through connections made in the network, but there had to be a structured approach to providing knowledge-building opportunities and developing mastery and confidence in scaling social impact. This consideration drove the decision to launch a dedicated Knowledge Centre in 2014.

The Knowledge Centre has also shifted over time. For example, among its initial portfolio were research projects which served the agenda of specific funders. Yet, as AVPN continues to embody its role as an ecosystem builder, the Knowledge Centre has been subsumed into the organisation's research and insights pillar to ensure connectivity across the organisation and the ecosystem as a whole.

- **AVPN Academy**: The limited number of Asian best-practice case examples was a formidable challenge for members. It was important for them to learn from others who had experiences in similar contexts and cultures. Many of them had participated in often prestigious academic programmes in the United States and Europe, but still felt unable to implement their learnings on their return. The AVPN Academy was established to address these issues. The platform allows for practitioners to learn from each other, through self-paced video modules as well as live interactive sessions on various topics. These include a learning circle series where peers can exchange ideas, solutions, and insights in a safe space under the Chatham House Rule.

  AVPN Academy also has fellowship programmes that are four to six-month-long structured learning opportunities for selected cohorts. Examples of AVPN fellowship tracks include an Impact Investing Fellowship to support asset owners and wealth managers in building impact-focused portfolios, a Policy Leadership Lab to help policymakers engage with key industry leaders in refining their proposals, and a programme for emerging philanthropists to build a community of practice based on a shared understanding of social investment approaches and responsible leadership.

Act: Scale Repeatable Solutions that Work

Driving action and moving the needle are the ultimate outcomes AVPN strives towards. AVPN's objective is to identify best practice and clarify benchmarks in the ecosystem, enabling its members to set higher standards.

While AVPN is at its core a network for funders and resource providers, we are cognisant that impact is demonstrated when there is a change in outcomes for the end beneficiary. Consequently, a central pillar of AVPN's 'Act' work is capital mobilisation, where the team works with capital providers and impact organisations to bridge the gap between demand for and supply of human, intellectual, and financial capital. Recognising the diverse needs of our network, the network hosts case studies of impact organisations, coordinates curated engagements between stakeholders for potential collaboration, and offers capacity-building programmes.

- **Deal Share Platform**: The AVPN Deal Share Platform hosts a list of investment-seeking impact organisations that are endorsed by other members and enables funders and resource providers to connect with those impact organisations and co-invest in them.[4] The idea has empowered many impact organisations and social investors to create impact on the ground and, like all of AVPN's projects, is constantly updated and refined.

  One aspect that is being refined is building a common language around the types of organisations listed on the Deal Share Platform. It is often the case that funders and impact organisations employ different terminology, this is true even before we take into consideration inter-market discrepancies. For example, 'foundations' in most markets refers to funders or resource providers, but in some markets could be used to refer to impact organisations and non-profits. The AVPN Deal Share Platform understands these differences and aims to introduce some degree of uniformity in the way these terms are used so that impact organisations are in the best position to access the resources they need, eliminating the barriers to entry that funders might otherwise face in navigating the complexities of the social investment ecosystem.
- **Philanthropic funds**: In the wake of COVID-19, AVPN recognised the desire among members to collaborate and contribute to the pandemic recovery efforts. However, with the wide breadth of urgent needs, funders began to look to AVPN to not only identify credible impact organisations they could support but also to deploy the capital. AVPN responded to this need from both the funders and the impact organisations by launching a

---

[4] Deal Share increases the visibility of quality impact organisations that have previously partnered with and been endorsed by funding AVPN members, but also enables members to further collaborate and co-invest in those organisations in a more targeted manner.

philanthropic pooled fund in May 2021. This was the first of its kind in Southeast Asia and sought to support COVID-19 resilience and long-term primary healthcare solutions. This was a defining moment for AVPN, where its convening, learning, and strategising roles culminated in all-out execution.

Since then AVPN has launched six other philanthropic funds, both single donor and pooled, and now offers an end-to-end process of project management, pipeline sourcing, grant deployment, monitoring and evaluation, and capacity-building, thus expanding its work even beyond grant funding. In all of its philanthropic funding work, AVPN aims not to merely channel funds from funders to impact organisations, but to advance radical investment based on trust-based giving to allow impact organisations the unrestricted funding they need to best advance their goals.

- **Adaptability and iteration remain at the core of AVPN's identity.** While AVPN's offerings have become more clearly articulated with time, the organisation continues to embody dynamism and experimentation – as members' needs and the ecosystem they operate in evolve, so does AVPN.

This commitment has allowed AVPN to capture the breadth of possibility within the impact space. The network introduced the concept of 'Continuum of Capital' in 2018, building on the understanding that financial, human, and intellectual capital is situated across a non-prescriptive spectrum from impact-first to finance-first. AVPN aims to demonstrate to funders that all the work that they do can be impactful, whether they receive a financial return or not. AVPN sees that it is essential for organisations of all kinds to participate in learning and champion social investment causes together in order to create lasting systems change. By providing opportunities for both targeted learning and also for cross-stakeholder engagement AVPN has been able to address a wide range of organisational needs.

Lessons Learned in Becoming an Effective Ecosystem Builder in Asia Pacific

In its journey, AVPN has learned from experience. Here is a summary of some key lessons learned, which can hopefully guide other intermediaries and field builders, as well as support philanthropists in identifying ways through which they can help build the ecosystem more collaboratively.

Being more than just a network takes persistence, creativity, and nimbleness. Change is constant and inevitable, and organisations need to regularly think and rethink their approach, managing the balance between being bold and confident about their offerings, whilst at the same time critically questioning their core proposition. *Is this the best approach to achieve our goals? Are there better ways to do this?* Being an ecosystem builder means pushing the frontier, and pioneering ideas without having all the answers. The social investment field is an evolving field space so practitioners must constantly be open to experimentation, and consequently, have the humility to learn and move on from projects that fail. This is true especially for ecosystem builders who operate amongst many unknowns. It is crucial for ecosystem builders to find unique ways to create value. For AVPN, it was about going beyond the standard approach of organising events and connecting actors in the field in that way. Whilst conversation is undeniably an essential starting point for learning and building intent, networks must see that these conversations eventually lead to collaboration and action, which is where impact truly lies.

Networks must be able clearly to conceptualise, identify, and articulate the additionality of their work. Whilst the relationship between a network and its parts is symbiotic, it is important to distinguish, and therefore strike a balance, between acting on one's own behalf and that of members in one's network. This will enable potential partners to perceive and consequently buy into the value of networks and intermediaries. This is undoubtedly a complex balancing act: on the one hand a network serves to elevate its members, on the other hand it must not only recognise but also communicate its own accomplishments in order to be appreciated as a credible leader and field builder. AVPN has learned to build trust by being transparent about its intent and committing to its leadership role as a field builder.

Similarly, networks need to concentrate on getting things done while integrating learnings in real time and making space for new members in the community. It can be difficult to align activities around learning for new members while coordinating action for others. It is a continuous and conscious choice to foster diversity while trying to build a cohesive network and organisation. This boils down to offering products and services that are specific enough to lead to action, while being inclusive enough to be accessible to most members.

Without public-sector buy-in, social change and progress at scale are often not possible and never sustainable. Many of AVPN's members – philanthropists and social investors – manage and deploy significant amounts of capital. However, to attain the full potential of these resources, public-sector support is essential, whether financial or non-financial, including access to data and regulatory accommodations. Dialogue with policymakers continues to focus on how to steer those resources towards, first, those who can most effectively employ them and secondly, those that need them most. AVPN is in a fairly unique position to work closely with the government and affiliated agencies, as it serves the interests of the entire ecosystem. The network recognises that governments and policymakers play pivotal and central roles in championing and encouraging multi-sector collaboration. As a network and neutral platform based out of Singapore, AVPN looks to achieve common ground and clarity on how the public, private, and social sectors can complement each other and avoid duplicating efforts. An exciting result of these efforts was AVPN's appointment as the impact partner for the Ministry of Tourism and Creative Economy of the Republic of Indonesia (Kemenparekraf) as part of the G20 in October 2022.

As AVPN continuously develops to effectively and collaboratively build an ecosystem in social investing, the results are evident. The following discusses this in more detail.

AVPN has grown immensely. In 10 years, AVPN has grown from having just 4 staff to 75, with over 600 members in Asia who are actively building the social investment ecosystem in the region. In this time, AVPN's offerings have mirrored its growth, with several new initiatives introduced, including thematic platforms, the AVPN Academy, and most recently, Philanthropic Funds. At the time of writing this chapter, AVPN leads collaborations of funders in six other philanthropic funds, amounting to a total fund size of over $30 million. Additionally, the number of deals hosted by the Deal Share Platform has increased more than 200 per cent from 2016 to 2021, with 1,130 nominations and connections made between funders and impact organisations in 2021 alone.

AVPN strengthens the impact-seeking capital field in Asia. The network continues to build an adaptive infrastructure based on convening and collaborating, with the aim of being the backbone that connects unusual allies, inspires collaboration, and enables personalised matchmaking. AVPN works with the full spectrum of actors in the ecosystem, offering products and services to communities: the members, fellows, online learners of the Academy, and impact organisations. It drives a field-level agenda through impact communities, spearheading thought leadership in flexible, nimble, and cause-agnostic ways. It further aggregates resources and acts as a conduit to fund underinvested causes and deserving, but under-resourced, organisations through their capital mobilisation efforts. AVPN also keeps building the knowledge base of its network across a range of formats that focus on both the depth and breadth of knowledge and expertise.

In the earlier sections, it was noted that one of the deep challenges networks face is in identifying and articulating the actual value they create. So perhaps the best way to grasp AVPN's true contribution is to consider what Asia's social investment space would be if it did not exist. Certainly, social investment would not have disappeared if an ecosystem builder like AVPN did not exist. But it seems equally clear that the social investors would not collaborate, innovate, and take risks in the same way without AVPN. This hints at the true value of ecosystem builders, one which can only be appreciated in hindsight: ecosystem builders do not just enable its members to achieve their existing goals, they make it possible for the ecosystem to succeed in ways that were not even conceivable before.

What AVPN Members Say

Ultimately, AVPN's role is to help the ecosystem generate greater impact, and a key way it accomplishes this is by equipping members to become moral leaders that drive change in the ecosystem. Thus, a key part of AVPN's mission is to help its members understand the depth and potential of their own impact, and one way to evaluate success in this endeavour is to hear from the members. Here are some reflections:

> 'I think the Asia Gender Network is a great platform to really drive change. Each of us is working in our ecosystem to bring change, and through this platform, we can create a ripple effect where change can happen much *faster* than working at issues individually.' Neerja Birla, Founder and Chairperson, Aditya Birla Education Trust
>
> 'Personally, I think it's a really interesting way to engage. It's really great just to step back and hear from others about what they're doing and *benchmark* yourself informally against where you're up to. If we take this fund as an example, we can take some lessons from that and apply it to other philanthropy.' Susan Clear, Regional Director Asia, Macquarie Group Foundation
>
> 'The more you work in philanthropy, the more you *value the lens that other funders have* when they look at the same situation, the same grantee, the same broader challenge in a particular context. And that learning is *priceless.* Collaborative philanthropy facilitates that if it is done well because it reduces the burden on grantees to provide multiple applications to multiple partners and to have one more streamlined reporting mechanism.' Sarah Jeffery, Head of Health, Vitol Foundation

CONCLUSION

Philanthropy in Asia has grown immensely and is well placed to play a focal role in addressing the fallout from the COVID-19 pandemic. This growth is reflected in and enabled by how actors across the ecosystem are increasingly looking to learn from each other, share resources, collaborate, and take risks to deliver more impact.

Ecosystem builders lay the groundwork for collaboration between philanthropists and their allies; they are able to convene, and they drive partnerships across the impact space. Being effective enablers of collaboration requires networks to be more than just a passive meeting ground for members. Instead, networks need to leverage their bird's-eye perspective of the ecosystem to amplify impact, taking risks so that philanthropists can be bold.

AVPN's experience as the largest social investment network in Asia shows that being an ecosystem builder is not without its challenges. Ecosystem builders struggle to articulate their true value because their contributions are difficult to account for directly and often go unrecognised. At the same time, by virtue of connecting dynamic spaces, they must adapt rapidly to better serve members, connect with regional markets, and represent their own changing capabilities and goals.

Yet, AVPN's phenomenal success in the face of these challenges also shows the way forward for ecosystem builders. When networks embrace their role as leaders in the space, constantly re-evaluating their own value proposition, taking risks, pivoting, and learning from mistakes along the way, they are able to leverage the complexity and diversity of their environment to amplify their impact.

AVPN continues to iterate on its core value, offers, and identity, adapting the structure of its activities – Connect, Learn, Act – and introducing new ways of collaborating and acting for social investors. In these ways, AVPN has made breakthroughs in Asia. Despite its breadth, AVPN has also established systems to expand its footprint in different local markets in Asia by providing the autonomy local teams need to bring their market-specific expertise to the table.

While AVPN has created a tremendous suite of products to develop the ecosystem over the last few years, its history suggests that the process of iteration, adaptation, and risk-taking will never cease. This is the lesson that stands out for networks looking to achieve great impact: ecosystem builders that lead from the front lines cannot rest on their laurels, they must continue to innovate and change to push the boundaries of what is possible for the ecosystem.

AVPN will continue to grow with ambition, without conflating mere scale with impact. Connect-AVPN will continue to grow the membership, increase the number of markets where it has boots on the ground, and engage thought leaders at C-Suite and board level to support in benchmarking, standard-setting, and best-practice development. Learn-AVPN wants to grow the Academy to provide self-directed learning for thousands of impact practitioners to gain new perspectives, lenses, and frameworks. The network seeks to guide and nurture emerging Asian talent by expanding fellowships to ensure a talent pipeline for the next decade of social investment. Act-AVPN will move beyond influencing impact capital and move more capital towards impact directly through its philanthropic funds. AVPN will also expand the Deal Share Platform to include more impact organisations and impact projects and create mechanisms that support micro-grants to those listed.

AVPN aims to leapfrog transactional philanthropy to transform the ecosystem. AVPN strongly believes in Asia for Asian philanthropy. Its members, partners, and stakeholders are and will continue to be increasingly empowered to transform the region in ways that are astonishing, from committing large amounts of capital to designing and running programmes in the most underserved areas. AVPN's role is to lower the barriers for philanthropy and fuel an ecosystem of creative, dedicated changemakers and innovators. Transactional networks are based on standard operating processes, offering reciprocity but stagnancy. Transformational networks, on the other hand, guide coordination, communication, and cooperation, inspiring others to follow with purpose. AVPN aims to be a transformational network that can lead change in the ecosystem.

AVPN will hold itself accountable. While the network has been intentional about measuring and managing its work and impact, from building its own Theory of Change to conducting post-event assessments, it continues to look for ways to inform and track impact. The network is working to assess the impact of the past decade of work, articulate a strategy for the next ten years, and develop an operating plan to see this vision come to light.

This chapter provides a snapshot of a network that thrived in the face of challenges in being an effective ecosystem builder. The objective is to further catalyse more collaborations and support, both from intermediaries and networks like AVPN, and even more so, from the philanthropic communities themselves. They must be bold, collaborative, and be biased in favour of action. Philanthropists have to leverage the network and collectively build an ecosystem that is strong and adaptive, one that can support post-COVID recovery and impact at scale.

For intermediaries and networks that wish to emulate AVPN's path, the lesson is to maintain the neutrality and breadth of a network whilst leveraging the strengths and expertise of its parts. Ecosystem builders have to be innovative if they are to encourage their members to take risks and see connections made through to execution. The challenges faced by the global population seem insurmountable, but through the sum of our parts, we can begin to chip away at assumptions that preserve and exacerbate inequality. If there was ever a time for networks in Asia to accelerate their pace, it is now.

2 A Model for Promoting Systems-Change Philanthropy by Leveraging Networks

Olivia Leland and Silvia Bastante de Unverhau

INTRODUCTION

This chapter shares insights about promoting higher-impact philanthropy, through the experiences of Co-Impact, a global collaborative that advances inclusive systems change and gender equality through grant-making and influencing philanthropy. The chapter also explores the importance of philanthropic networks to promote collaborative giving and support the advancement of philanthropy across the Global South.

Across its two funds, Co-Impact's goal is to ensure that systems that provide the most fundamental services of health, education, and economic opportunity are more just, inclusive, and effective, resulting in improved outcomes for millions of people across Africa, Asia, and Latin America. Its vision is a world where all people can live fulfilling lives, where systems and societies are just and inclusive, and where all women have the opportunity to exercise power, agency, and leadership.

We at Co-Impact believe that philanthropy has the potential to do more – and do better – and that a crucial element of how we can increase impact is via philanthropic networks. For us, a network is not a loose transactional collection of people and organisations but rather a community of interconnected individuals and organisations that share similar values, which are expressed through their work in philanthropy. We are not referring only to formal or membership-based philanthropy networks but also to the more informal communities that are organically built on overlapping relationships.

Pooling funding towards systems-change initiatives can achieve greater impact because the vision is long term – far beyond a single intervention or year-to-year funding. By coming together and investing in a way that is supportive of Co-Impact's partners, we can make a more impactful and sustainable contribution towards long-term systemic change.

Since 2017, one of Co-Impact's goals has been also to advance collaborative, 'trust-based philanthropy' for systems change and gender equality that both learns from others and generates learning for the broader philanthropic community. Collaboration is at the organisation's core, as reflected in its name. We at Co-Impact bring together various networks and use our collective experience to influence more philanthropy that is larger, longer term, and more flexible, and helps to grow the overall resources available for work to advance gender equality.

Additionally, with respect to philanthropy, Co-Impact has been able to:

- advance a model of collaborative philanthropy which has succeeded in bringing together nearly fifty philanthropists and foundations from seventeen countries (from both the Global North and Global South), who have chosen to support its work across its two funds with hundreds of millions of US dollars;
- demonstrate how philanthropy for systems change can help to unlock additional capital from others, such as influencing public-sector funding and resources, or supporting market-based solutions; and
- advocate for more philanthropy for systemic change and gender equality, promote 'trust-based philanthropy' and better philanthropic practices, and collaborate with various stakeholders to share knowledge, evidence, and best practice.

Co-Impact's significant growth since 2009 has been against a backdrop of scepticism about the viability of collaborative, pooled-funding models, especially for systems-change philanthropy. Co-Impact's founder, Olivia Leland, who spent three years (2014–2017) researching and interviewing over 250 philanthropists and social change leaders to design the Co-Impact model, recalls the type of responses she received at the outset:

> There were so many voices constantly arguing that the model for Co-Impact would not work, including concerns that philanthropists, especially those from the Global North, would not give US $50 million of their own funding for the Global South, and especially not to a new entity that required pooling funding with others and so giving up some degree of control. People raised concerns about the nature of Co-Impact as a collaborative bringing together various existing philanthropic networks. Even the day before launch in November 2017, I was told by a prominent US philanthropist: 'There is no way this will work because philanthropists don't like to collaborate and prefer to do their own thing. No one will want to give into a pooled fund.' Others said: 'why do you need a 10-year fund? Just go in like a SWAT team and do this faster' and 'you need to prove this out first before you can get funding for it. Go do it with one organisation and then you can prove it works.'

CONSTRAINTS THE MODEL ADDRESSES

The Co-Impact model is designed to address the following three constraints in philanthropic practice.[1]

The Type of Giving

Most giving remains small, fragmented, and unaligned with what is required for large-scale and enduring impact; it does not explicitly address inherent power dynamics or gender inequality. Even proven social change leaders struggle to piece together the funding and support to pursue enduring impact at a national, regional, or global scale and must expend extraordinary time and effort. Most grants

---

[1] Some ideas in this chapter have already been presented in the Handbook published on the Co-Impact website in June 2021 (first published September 2019), www.co-impact.org/wp-content/uploads/2021/09/Handbook-2021-ENG.pdf.

are small, of short duration (typically one to two years), restricted, and do not cover the necessary costs related to overheads, monitoring, evaluation and learning, or organisational development. Restrictions on grant use can constrain social change organisations. For example, many small grants with earmarked funding can fragment focus and undermine strategic coherence. This fragmentation often requires the leaders of social change organisations to spend too much of their time – typically upwards of 30 per cent – chasing funds and meeting donor requirements instead of focusing on their core work and developing their strategies for systems-change efforts.

Donor requirements for proposal-writing, due diligence, and reporting can also be overly burdensome, taking away valuable time and energy from doing the core work. Much funding is given with an overall high degree of control by the funders and does not recognise the inherent power dynamics in the sector, nor does it support gender equality with intersectionality.

Furthermore, social change organisations lack reliable access to the kinds of non-financial support that can significantly accelerate systems-change work. For example, funders' influence, networks, and convening power can be extraordinary assets to organisations. Yet relatively few funders offer this kind of holistic support, and few organisations have the resources to secure them on their own.

The Availability of Systems-Change Efforts

Investment-ready systems-change efforts are rare; few social change leaders have built robust strategies, capabilities, and partnerships to drive systems change, although many have the vision and ability to do so. There are examples of visionary social change organisations driving systems change today and throughout history. Yet these are still relatively rare. We at Co-Impact know leaders from organisations who are eager – and have already started – to develop compelling and credible plans and partnerships for systems-change efforts. However, they need flexible support and encouragement from realistic funding opportunities to get their initiatives ready for substantial large-scale investment.

Too often organisations feel that they must tailor their goals to the priorities, funding cycles, and ways of working of their donors. This can consign them into a 'subcontractor' role as a manager of dozens of short-term donor projects, rather than architects and drivers of a deep and strategically coherent programme where each component contributes towards a powerful whole. We believe it should be the other way around: funders should support the structure and rhythm of their programme partners.

Mechanisms for Collaboration

There are not enough efficient mechanisms for funders to find and support high-potential investments, and to collaborate with one another in a meaningful way, especially across borders. Many funders want to make substantial investments to help address the world's most intractable problems. However, the time and expertise needed to set up and staff project, source funding, carry out due diligence, and extend grants means that even foundations with ambitious goals and large asset bases can find it difficult to support efforts to drive results at scale.

Furthermore, funders with varying perspectives on strategy, focus, or geographic preference can pull programme partners in opposing directions. Aligning around one shared vision and approach is often critical to achieving large-scale results. However, with a few important exceptions, philanthropy today remains remarkably siloed and rarely collaborate with other sector actors. While some philanthropic networks exist, they usually focus on knowledge-sharing and discussions, not always on acting differently or working together.

Co-Impact nurtures a model of collaborative philanthropy that seeks to better serve social change organisations and funders by overcoming these constraints. In their support for Co-Impact, its funders take a new approach. This model facilitates the interaction between funders with programme partners in the Global South in a respectful and supportive, rather than directive, way. We at Co-Impact have from the outset worked to make this organisation a global collaborative, where there is cross-learning between different regions of the world, and where similarities and particularities in the way philanthropy is practised can be a source of learning and strength for the collaborative overall. Co-Impact's collaborative model thrives by bringing together different philanthropic networks and strengthening trust-based relationships between funders and programme partners. Furthermore, with nearly fifty philanthropists and foundations in the collaborative, the reach and influence of this model becomes even more significant.

PHILANTHROPY FOR SYSTEMS CHANGE IN THE GLOBAL SOUTH

In the discussion that follows we expand on the key features of Co-Impact's approach to funding to make a meaningful contribution towards long-term systemic change. We at Co-Impact have chosen to work for the Global South because most of our expertise is focused on these regions, comparatively less systems-change funding is available for work in these parts of the world, and fewer established philanthropic networks exist there. Nevertheless, we hope some of our learnings will also be applicable in the Global North.

As funders, we seek to live up to key philanthropic practices which apply both to good funding practice in general and in supporting systems change in particular. The key features of our approach to funding systemic change centre around several areas, described in the following sections, and are a direct response to the constraints that we observed by listening to social change leaders working in their own communities.

Our Approach to Systems Change

- **Addressing power and the political economy**: We support partners to understand and address root causes to problems, particularly political and institutional gender constraints, and other socio-contextual factors that underlie exclusion, inequality, low performance, and lack of accountability.

- **Focusing on key levers that drive change**: Systems have multiple challenges; working on all of them can quickly become unwieldy. Instead of addressing everything, our approach supports partners to identify a few key levers, such as policy, laws, mandates, system financial resources, and/or formal and informal incentives, and to promote accountability, which can improve the functioning of core parts of the system and lead to the adoption at scale or institutionalisation of key innovations.

- **Building effective and powerful coalitions for change**: We support partners in undertaking power analyses and developing relationships that support a coalition of government (or market) leaders that is powerful and focused enough to achieve shared outcomes. Building powerful coalitions inherently relies on networks and relationships between individuals and organisations with a shared purpose.

- **Supporting strategic coherence**: Good strategy sits at the heart of successful systems change initiatives. With the grant-making processes at Co-Impact, we aim to provide programme partners with the time and space needed to clarify their strategic choices. We support their ability to make coherent decisions, including saying no to otherwise good ideas and funding from donors when these do not align well with strategic priorities.

- **Encouraging learning and adaptation**: We neither believe that measurement is something that the 'grantee does for the donor' nor that success comes from adhering to a fixed plan; we encourage programme partners to use data to assess progress and make course corrections. We support a learning orientation across our programme partners and work to generate and disseminate a body of rigorous evidence to contribute to field-building and serve as a global resource about what works at scale.

How Networks Help Build Capacity

- **Funding to coalitions of actors**: Co-Impact has been called 'the network for networks'. This refers to both the fact that it brings together various philanthropic networks into a community of funders and that it supports coalitions of actors that have the capacity to effect significant change. Its funding for systems change rarely supports the work of a single organisation which is not partnering with others, as this would not usually promote systems change. We at Co-Impact mobilise the power of networks and trust-based, meaningful relationships at both the funder level and the programme partner level.

- **Funding for locally rooted, primarily women-led organisations:** We take an intersectional gender approach in the ways that we analyse problems, make grants, and engage with partners. We believe that systems change is only possible when discriminatory structures are consciously addressed and women and other excluded groups can exercise their full share of agency and power. Programme partners that have local roots are best placed to achieve results for the communities Co-Impact seeks to serve. In the organisation's second fund, 100 per cent of the country-level grants focus on Global South-rooted organisations, of which a high percentage will be women-led organisations.

- **More significant, flexible, and longer-term funding**: We at Co-Impact offer grants (up to US $25 million, and up to five years) accompanied by deep, non-financial support. This is rare in philanthropy, where most funding is restricted, with smaller grants typically given for a period of one to three years. It is more challenging for individual funders, rather than a collaborative built on philanthropic networks, to offer both the significant funding and the deep, non-financial, tailored, and flexible support that social change leaders need.

- **Supporting the strengthening of key capabilities**: Systems change requires strong organisations. We invest in both achieving large-scale, sustainable outcomes and in strengthening organisations to become even more powerful and effective. Our major grants include an earmarked amount (typically up to US $500,000 over five years) for strengthening organisational capabilities.

Addressing Inherent Power Dynamics

- **Being programme-partner supportive**: Throughout our work, we see programme partners and governments as the leaders, architects, and drivers of the deep change they seek. We practise 'trust-based philanthropy', supporting programme partners to advance their visions for change.

- **Being outcomes-focused and flexible**: We support programme partners to achieve, and hold them accountable to, key outcomes and programmatic milestones. Instead of demanding a detailed plan and budget, we ask for clear articulations of long-term goals, specific outcomes, and periodic milestones, so that programme partners can deploy funds flexibly towards mutually agreed goals.

- **Valuing partners' time and effort**: To enable programme partners to focus on their work, we make our requirements simple, streamlined, and predictable. We at Co-Impact aim to keep our expectations and processes transparent, through documents such as our Handbook and open calls for concept notes. We encourage single reporting to all funders on a schedule that fits the work rhythm of programme partners.

- **Behaving as true partners**: Given that a true partnership is about mutual respect and trust, we set the agenda together with our programme partners. We listen with intent and curiosity and challenge where relevant, while always striving for empathy. Thus, the nature of our relationships with programme partners is key. We are mindful of the power dynamics in the 'grantor–grantee' relationship and commit to actively work to counter those through mutual respect, listening well, and developing an open, curious, and supportive posture.

HOW NETWORKS SUPPORT SCALING-UP

The Beginning

Given that a pooled fund to support systems change across health, education, and economic opportunity in the Global South did not exist before, when Co-Impact was launched in November 2017 it was set up via a fiscal sponsor (rather than as an independent entity) with the idea that the organisation would review the approach again within three years.

During 2018 we at Co-Impact finalised our first round of systems-change grants within our Foundational Fund, which our team had been working on since early 2017, and brought more philanthropists, foundations, and philanthropic networks together to support the work. In September 2018, we held an in-person gathering with our initial partners and new supporters in New York around the United Nations (UN) General Assembly meetings. That proved a decisive moment to expand our collaborative community. This event provided a unique opportunity for interested funders to meet our team in person and, very importantly, to engage and exchange with each other.

We recognise that bringing funders into a global collaborative and pooling funding for systems-change efforts is not yet the norm. In growing the Fund, we spoke to many funders globally to understand with whom this approach to philanthropy would resonate. Our approach from the early days has been to work with other philanthropic networks and expert practitioners who are working on collaborative giving models.

One of our most important learnings was about the importance of networks for collaborative giving and pooled funds. We would not have been able to develop Co-Impact to where it is now without working with many other philanthropic networks, both formal and informal, in a collaborative way. Philanthropic networks have contributed in many ways to the growth of Co-Impact and the philanthropic community's collective impact. They have:

- enabled supporting systems change at scale by pooling resources;
- contributed their collective local knowledge and expertise, especially those philanthropic networks operating within the regions where Co-Impact works;
- helped to address the power dynamics in giving, which is easier in a community of funders than at the level of an individual funder;
- amplified the call for higher-impact philanthropic practices, as can be seen in Co-Impact's joint advocacy with other philanthropic networks;
- fostered exponential learning across regions, helping to bring together different organisations and groups to share and learn together; and
- supported both the sourcing of systems-change opportunities as well as bringing together funders, especially regional philanthropic networks.

For Co-Impact, collaborating with others and bringing different groups together in ways that mean that the sum is larger than each of the individual parts is in and of itself part of the organisation's reason for being. We at Co-Impact collaborate with funders, programme partners, and philanthropic networks in a way that builds bridges, relationships, and a sense of community so that our collective work can go further. Importantly, members of the philanthropic community must be supportive of each other's goals. We believe it is this focus on trust-based and meaningful relationships that has helped Co-Impact move collectively to action, beyond traditional and transactional 'networking'.

Given Co-Impact's focus on the Global South, it has prioritised collaborating with other philanthropic networks focused on these regions including WINGS and the AVPN. In terms of influencing philanthropic practice, and amplifying other voices, we at Co-Impact have partnered with groups such as Catalyst 2030, a global movement of social entrepreneurs and social innovators from all sectors who share the common goal of creating innovative, people-centric approaches to attaining the Sustainable Development Goals (SDGs) by 2030. Together with them and Ashoka, Echoing Green, the Schwab Foundation for Social Entrepreneurship, and the Skoll Foundation, we published in 2020 a report entitled *Embracing Complexity: Towards a Shared Understanding of Funding Systems Change*,[2] which lays out key shared principles for funding systemic change.

The COVID-19 Pandemic

In 2020, during the COVID-19 pandemic, all over the world health – and other systems – were tested to their limits and in many cases crumbled. We spent time considering how the pandemic was affecting our own team, all our partners, and, in particular, the communities we seek to serve. We believed it was more important than ever that we keep a focus on strengthening underlying systems so that those systems were able to respond to that emergency and recover for the future, while continuing to deliver essential public services. Though all societies were affected, we now know that weaker systems were most affected – and, within those systems, the most disadvantaged, including women, bore the brunt of the burden.

---

[2] Ashoka et al., 2020.

As funders, we leaned into five principles in our work with our programme partners during the pandemic: active listening, showing empathy, being supportive, being flexible, and supporting fundraising. On the last of these, we launched the Co-Impact Systems Response Fund to support two of our programme partners working on health systems who had been called upon by relevant governments to take a leading role in responding to COVID-19 and needed additional flexible funding. We also advocated for funders and other partners to continue supporting the crucial work of strengthening underlying systems. We signed the call to action 'Philanthropy's Commitment During COVID-19' from the Council on Foundations, among other collective commitments by different philanthropic networks.

During 2020, and despite the COVID-19 pandemic, we also attracted numerous other philanthropists and foundations to the Co-Impact collaborative. While the pandemic exposed the levels of systemic injustice and discrimination which led to some increase in giving, establishing new relationships with funders through videoconferencing proved challenging and many funders understandably decided to double down on existing grantees rather than making new commitments. On balance, we would argue that raising philanthropic funding during the pandemic for long-term systems-change efforts was more difficult than in previous years.

Building Funds through Collaboration

In 2020, we reflected on what Co-Impact as an organisation was advancing in the world and within the philanthropic space. While we started the process to create a more permanent set-up for Co-Impact as an independent organisation, we also started working on our second fund: the Gender Fund. This Fund seeks to raise and grant US $1 billion over the next decade to accelerate progress towards gender equality, advancing women's power, agency, and leadership.

The Fund builds on the extensive work of our existing programme partners who continue to demonstrate how integral an intentional focus on gender equality is to achieving sustainable systems change. The Fund benefited from a year-long consultation and development process that included structured discussions with more than fifty leaders, predominantly from the Global South, including women's rights organisations, women's funds, feminist activists and scholars, cross-sector experts, donors, and practitioners working at all levels. The Fund also included a deepening of our approach to supporting systems-change work and benefited from a systematic review of existing evidence. We commissioned reviews focusing on rigorous evidence of scaled initiatives in the Global South that have achieved gender-equitable outcomes in the areas of leadership, education, health, and economic opportunities, which helped to inform the Fund's design.

We also increased support for gender equality work, specifically bringing in funders who may not have typically funded in this space. We aim to deliver significant resources to a historically underfunded space and pave the way towards more equitable, longer-term, flexible funding led by the needs of the organisations driving progress across our operating regions. During 2020 and 2021 we received the first funding commitments to the Gender Fund, in addition to expanded commitments from existing funders. With this Fund we are also reinforcing on our efforts to create a truly global organisation.

We at Co-Impact further partner with local and regional philanthropic networks. For example, we work closely with the African Philanthropy Forum, a strong and vibrant community of partners who foster shared prosperity on the African continent. We partner with them to bring together a group of philanthropists who want to support gender equality in Africa. We have also been working with EdelGive Foundation in India, a grant-making organisation that aims to build a strong, efficient, and high-impact social sector for a better India by funding and supporting the growth of small to mid-sized grassroots non-governmental organisations (NGOs). Through these and other partnerships, we are not only bringing on board many more funders from the Global South but also fostering cross-learning and amplifying our organisations' joint influencing and advocacy agendas.

On learning and training, we at Co-Impact have joined forces with The Philanthropy Workshop (TPW), recently renamed Forward Global, a community of over 450 global leaders committed to solving the world's most pressing social issues and a leader in strategic philanthropy education. Forward Global helps organise the learning agenda for some of the philanthropists we work with and, at the same time, the funders who support Co-Impact gain access to Forward Global's expertise, learning platform, and vast network.

Working with partners and philanthropic networks has been instrumental to Co-Impact's goals, development, and learning, and to increasing its collective impact in the world, and we at Co-Impact are eager to continue to build on and expand these partnerships as our work progresses.

THE VALUE OF POOLED FUNDS

There is much to say about collaborative philanthropy; however, 'collaboration' in philanthropy means very different things to different people. A 2018 global study by the Hauser Institute for Civil Society at Harvard Kennedy School found that while many foundations recognise the importance of collaboration and partnership to achieve impact and scale, such alliances can be difficult to create, manage, and sustain. Only 42 per cent among the 7,364 foundations in thirteen countries and Hong Kong 'indicated that they collaborate with other philanthropic institutions'.[3] Globally (excluding the United States and Australia), more than 50 per cent of foundations operate their own programmes.[4] As Table 2.1 illustrates, collaboration can range all the way from knowledge exchange to a pooled fund.

---

[3] Johnson, 2018, pp. 11, 28. This is a pioneering study that includes data on 94,988 funders from nineteen countries/territories (Argentina, Australia, Brazil, Canada, China, Chile, Colombia, France, India, Ireland, Hong Kong, Mexico, Nigeria, Peru, Switzerland, Turkey, United Arab Emirates, the United Kingdom, and the United States).

[4] Johnson, 2018, p. 33.

Table 2.1 *Collaborative philanthropy and pooled funds*

Knowledge Exchange	Coordinated Funding	Co-investments	Pooled Funding
Funders exchange ideas, knowledge, and experiences. Investments are not pooled nor necessarily aligned. Each funder retains decision-making rights.	Funders agree on shared strategy and invest in aligned causes. They retain individual decision-making rights. In some cases, they share due diligence and reporting.	A funder raises additional resources from other donors for a specific initiative it supports. Or a group of funders co-invest in an initiative and share some decision-making around it.	Multiple funders pool their funding (and in some instances expertise) behind one fully integrated strategy with a specific governance structure. Usually, an independent entity is created which then manages the pooled fund.

⟵————————————————————————⟶

Less Integration   *More Integration*

While any form of collaboration brings some benefits, in our view a pooled fund has significant advantages when supporting systems change. While we advocate for all funders to follow practices such as those we outlined earlier, and while in theory all funders could do this independently, we believe joining a pooled fund makes these kinds of activities more likely and easier in three ways:

- **Addressing power dynamics directly in their giving is more likely when a group of funders comes together**: It is certainly possible for individual funders to address power dynamics in their giving independently; however, this is more likely in a pooled fund, given the fundamental requirement of relinquishing some level of control. At the same time, while addressing power dynamics is more likely in this way, it is also not a given or guaranteed. Collaboratives can still behave in highly controlling ways towards their grantees. Yet we also know that funders likely to join a collaborative tend often to be the more experienced funders, advanced in their own philanthropic journeys, and focused on what they can contribute rather than attribution.[5]

- **Giving more significantly and more efficiently is more likely in a pooled fund**: A pooled fund allows a larger amount of resources to support increasing scale and impact, as multiple funders bring together and further leverage their financial resources. Pooled funding also supports a diversified portfolio that decreases risk for each individual funder. Social change leaders require different kinds of non-financial supports, which are best delivered through the strengths, experiences, and expertise of a variety of funding partners. A pooled fund increases operational efficiency, given all funders involved follow a single process for sourcing, vetting, awarding, and supporting grantees, and simultaneously can minimise the risk of duplicating efforts.

- **Increasing collective voice and mutual learning**: This is arguably more likely when a group of funders come together in a highly integrated way. Pooling funding and living up to certain practices makes for a stronger voice when advocating for others to behave in similar ways, as any advocacy carries more weight when based on lived experience. Advocating for more resources to be made available for inclusive systems change in the Global South and to advance collaborative, 'trust-based philanthropy' is more effective through a collective voice. Often funders increase their own learning and gain access to the knowledge and experience of their peers to inform their individual giving strategies. Our experience is that funders learn more by doing together, not only by discussing or exchanging information.

While we believe collaborative philanthropy that unleashes the power of networks through a pooled fund can have significant impact in the world, we also gathered the following learning and insights, at the level of bringing donors together. These learnings have been informed by multiple funders we approached and interacted with in recent years at Co-Impact.

- **Bringing funders into a pooled fund can be challenging**: Pooled funding necessitates that donors relinquish some degree of control and accept

---

[5] See *Promoting Higher-Impact Philanthropy: What We've Learned*, published in November 2021 on the Co-Impact website, www.co-impact.org/wp-content/uploads/2021/11/Promoting-Higher-Impact-Philanthropy-Nov-2021.pdf.

that the outcomes of the initiatives are prioritised ahead of any specific organisational or individual recognition. It was more challenging than anticipated to bring funders together, despite our having developed the model, having a highly qualified team, and already enjoying the support of some prominent philanthropists. Usually, it tends to be the more experienced philanthropists who are willing to pool their funding with others.[6]

- **Funders want to feel a degree of ownership of the initiative, especially at a significant level**: When providing funding of over US $50 million, funders prefer to be in the 'founding group' and help shape the initiative. We believe the initial group coming together is crucial to raising a significant fund. There is usually a better chance of convincing funders to join before you launch a new philanthropic fund.

- **Having different funding levels can be helpful, but specific and distinct value propositions are important**: In our experience, when offered a range, many funders selected the lowest commitment level. So offering specific amounts, as opposed to ranges, with a clear and sufficiently differentiated value proposition for each level, can be helpful. At the same time, it takes as much effort to raise relatively smaller amounts, for example US $25 million, as to raise larger amounts, for example US $50 million.

- **Most philanthropists are moved to action based on their relationship with the person making the ask**: A key finding from all the studies we have seen and our own experience is that people are moved to action based on the relationship with the person making the ask and that most major gifts build on existing relationships.[7] Some of our funders were motivated to join because they knew and trusted the Co-Impact leadership. It is not exclusively about the relationship, though – the quality of the work, pitch, and materials also matter. If you do not meet quality standards, you can easily lose a potential donor. Given the importance of the relationship with the person making the ask, ideally a philanthropic initiative should be introduced by a peer, with the aim of developing a direct relationship over time.

---

[6] See note 5. Most philanthropists eschew collaboration and start and manage their own efforts. According to a calculation in Wealth-X, 2018, p. 31, over 70 per cent of billionaires that are involved in philanthropic giving have created their own foundations.

[7] Foster et al., 2019.

- **Peer advocacy is crucial as having already prominent philanthropists as supporters can make others hesitant to give**: While being associated with prominent philanthropists is a draw for some, it can also be a detraction for others. It may give the impression that the organisation has all the funding it needs and can be intimidating for funders who are not as experienced to come in at the same level as these prominent partners. It is imperative that your champion funders speak up for your cause or organisation.

- **Emphasize the impact and leverage that a pooled philanthropy fund can have**: The potential for increased impact and leverage motivated many donors to join Co-Impact. Some recognise that collaboration in the form of pooling funding maximises impact. Many donors care about leverage (for example, other funding, both financial and in kind, that the work can attract, influenced by their giving). Leaning into these two things can be a strong motivator for philanthropists and foundations to give more significantly. At the same time, we at Co-Impact realised that there is much confusion with the term 'collaborative philanthropy', as everyone likes to claim that they are collaborative or they collaborate with others; this can refer to a loose collaboration where some knowledge is exchanged, rather than a pooled fund.

- **Few philanthropists have a passion for 'systems change' and it is challenging to tell a simple story around it**: Many philanthropists care about a particular issue area rather than 'systems change'. Some funders simply do not believe in supporting systems change or see it as too complicated or intangible,[8] so framing what can be achieved through this approach as concretely as possible is helpful. However, telling a 'simple and straightforward story' around systems change was challenging and we at Co-Impact continue to work on ways to express the complexity of this work in terms that are more easily understood.

- **Avoid accepting funding from a philanthropist or foundation** where **there is no alignment of values and approach**: This is the most crucial factor for the success of a funding partnership. No matter how much

---

[8] Most philanthropists prefer philanthropic efforts that one can visit, feel, and touch. Longer-term and more intangible outcomes are less popular. Most philanthropy focuses on tangible things; 'big bets' on social causes are infrequent. Bridgespan (2019) states that two thirds of major gifts over US $25 million go to institutions such as hospitals, libraries, and universities. Only about a third of such major gifts go to social causes.

money is on offer, we believe that sticking to your values, principles, and approach is paramount to achieving impact in the longer term. We have declined some funding that did not align with our funder vetting policy which centres on: (1) the source of funds, including both original source of wealth and current business practices or investment policies, (2) the funder's reputation, and (3) alignment with Co-Impact's values and approach.

CONCLUSIONS

Funder collaboratives offer a model to bring together the level of significant funding and additional efficiency needed to support systems-change efforts in the Global South. They are also an effective way for funders to address collectively the power dynamics in their giving because it requires them to relinquish some degree of control. Finally, a collaborative has a stronger voice to advocate and influence others towards better practices and promote mutual learning. Rarely do individual funders behave in this way, and being part of a collaborative makes all these advantages more likely. Building a collaborative, by definition, relies on establishing and nurturing trust-based, meaningful relationships with philanthropists and foundations, and bringing forwards the power of philanthropic networks.

We hope that the establishment and growth of Co-Impact can help to demonstrate how funders should come together to support inclusive, meaningful, and enduring systems change for millions of people. This impact is further amplified when a chorus of voices advocates for more philanthropy for systems change and gender equality, and promotes better philanthropic practices such as 'trust-based philanthropy'. We hope to have demonstrated that this model can work, and we also hope to have shown how important philanthropic networks are for supporting the development of Global South-focused philanthropy.

We believe in philanthropy's power as a catalyst for inclusive, meaningful, and enduring systems change, delivering better outcomes for millions of people. We believe in transforming the system of funding itself, so that philanthropy delivers the capital and additional supports that are truly needed to achieve systemic change. We would encourage any funder to consider joining pooled funds as part of their portfolios and to offer more significant, flexible, and longer-term funding for locally rooted, primarily women-led organisations – and, very importantly, to do so in a manner that addresses inherent power dynamics by being programme partner-supportive, outcomes-focused, and flexible, valuing partners' time and effort. Finally, we encourage funders to join their local philanthropic networks and help to build bridges, relationships, and a sense of community so our collective work can go further together.

REFERENCES

Ashoka, Catalyst 2030, Co-Impact, Echoing Green, the Schwab Foundation for Social Entrepreneurship, and the Skoll Foundation. 2020. *Embracing Complexity: Towards a Shared Understanding of Funding Systems Change.* Ashoka. www.ashoka.org/fr-fr/embracing-complexity.

Bridgespan. 2019. *Unleashing Philanthropy's Big Bets for Social Change.* www .bridgespan.org/bridgespan/Images/articles/unleashing-big-bets-for-social-change/Big-Bets-Supplement_VFinal.pdf.

Foster, W., Perreault, G., and Seeman, B. 2019. *Becoming Big Bettable.* Bridgespan. www.bridgespan.org/insights/library/big-bets/unleashing-big-bets-for-social-change/becoming-big-bettable.

Johnson, P. 2018. *The Global Philanthropy Report: Perspectives on the Global Foundation Sector.* Harvard University's John F. Kennedy School of Government. https://cpl.hks.harvard.edu/publications/global-philanthropy-report-perspectives-global-foundation-sector.

Wealth-X. 2018. *Billionaire Census 2018.* https://wealthx.com/reports/billionaire-census-2023.

3 Building Effective Philanthropy through Strategic Partnerships

A Case Study of the Tanoto Foundation

J. Satrijo Tanudjojo

INTRODUCTION

According to Harvard Kennedy School's *Global Philanthropy Report*, the development and work of institutional philanthropy in the last century have been highly concentrated in the Global North, with 95 per cent of philanthropic foundations currently located in Europe and North America (Johnson, 2018, p. 10). However, the emergence of high net-worth individuals (HNWIs) and families in the Global South in the last few decades has signalled a shift in global dynamics among foundations towards a new discourse that rebalances the predominant power asymmetries between North and South. This shift is accelerated by the growing interest in and rapid development of local philanthropic institutions in developing countries.

In Asia, the growth of philanthropy has outpaced Europe and North America – with the number of billionaires expected to grow another 27 per cent by 2023 (Tang et al., 2020). This increasing wealth is parallel with the increased desire for giving, as well as the potency of giving. The Centre for Asian Philanthropy and Society (2018), for instance, notes that the potential to give in Asia is eleven times more than the amount being donated today. Given that nearly half of the world's most vulnerable communities live in this region and have been disproportionately affected by the COVID-19 global pandemic, the importance of philanthropy towards fulfilling development outcomes cannot be overstated.

The United Nations Development Programme (UNDP, 2014, p. 8) has noted another trend in giving among developing countries, which is represented by the shift from 'common personalised giving (to family, religious institutions, or marginalised communities) to more formalised structures of giving through organised philanthropy'. It is also worth noting that Global South philanthropic institutions leverage their rootedness, adapt the best practices of the once-trodden philanthropic paths, and readily embrace and normalise global frameworks for development to deliver sustainable, scalable, yet contextualised solutions. Global South philanthropic institutions have also increased their international exposure and experience through international partnerships and collaborations.

Indonesia is an example of a country experiencing a rapid growth in the philanthropy sector (CAF, 2021). However, despite the growing trend and increasing numbers of charities, giving in the country is considered scattered and unstructured. While the Charities Aid Foundation (CAF) World Giving Index ranks Indonesians as the most generous people in the world, the country was ranked at the bottom of the Doing Good Index by the Centre for Asian Philanthropy and Society (CAPS, 2018) in terms of philanthropy conduciveness – that is, the existing legal framework results in most giving being unstructured and ad hoc. This observation of Indonesian philanthropy is also not uncommon across other countries in Southeast Asia, where giving is built upon personal and faith preferences instead of the needs assessment of the society.

COVID-19 may have exposed the frailties of the pre-pandemic system in areas such as education, health, and social justice, but it has also created room for philanthropy to play a role in systemically addressing these vulnerabilities. This process has similarly compelled philanthropic institutions to re-evaluate their roles, strategies, and methodologies along the considerations of resiliency, scalability, and sustainability. Such outcomes can only be achieved with more organised and professionally run philanthropy that can address the needs in a post-COVID-19 environment.

This chapter provides a case study of the Tanoto Foundation (TF), a Global South-originated philanthropy, and its contribution to development in Indonesia. It examines TF's transformation into an institutionalised philanthropy, its partnership approach that encompasses both local and international agencies, and how it supports the development of a more sustainable social system and a more resilient community through education. In doing so, this chapter examines how a grounded – yet nuanced – catalysing of partnerships and implementation of scalable human capital development (HCD) programmes bring much-needed focus to the impact of philanthropy on the lived realities of communities in the Global South. By considering the substantial disruption that COVID-19 poses towards education, as much as towards health and the economy, this chapter explores solutions and timely interventions across the region – with institutionalised philanthropy and strategic partnerships as the locus.

INDONESIA'S EDUCATIONAL LANDSCAPE IN THE AGE OF COVID-19

The key towards an 'adaptive, productive, innovative, and competitive' Indonesia based on President Joko Widodo's 2019 re-election slogan is HCD (World Bank, 2020b). This understanding has been ingrained in the Government of Indonesia's (GoI) development agenda since the beginning of the twenty-first century, where it sought to revolutionise the education sector. In the early 2000s, GoI introduced several reforms to improve the quality of education, which included increasing the education budget to a historical high, decentralising the education system, and implementing programmes for improving educator capacities. From 2002 to 2018, a 200 per cent increase in education spending was aimed at making education more inclusive and expanding access, particularly among marginalised children. The country has also made significant headway in ensuring equitable enrolment across different economic, social, and geographic backgrounds – thereby placing an additional 10 million primary and secondary school students into classrooms (World Bank, 2020b). Today, more than 91 per cent of Indonesian children have access to basic education, while lower secondary school enrolment has risen to more than 76 per cent (KEMDIKBUD, 2021).

Nonetheless, managing a sector the size of Indonesia's education system,[1] coupled with the vast geographical spread of the system's operations, remains a complex and challenging endeavour. Learning inequality is observed across schools and regions, with the largest learning gap experienced by students living furthest away from the capital, that is, in the least developed parts of the country. Indonesian students also fall behind their international counterparts: underperformance on PISA (Programme for International Student Assessment) tests show that learning outcomes have stalled in Indonesia,[2] progressive policy-making and a significant increase in funding and investment notwithstanding. This is because student achievement depends highly on teacher quality, school leadership, and early childhood intervention – areas that still require improvement in the Indonesian context. Learning poverty remains one of the most critical challenges facing the country's education sector. According to the World Bank, 53 per cent of Indonesian late-primary age students do not reach the required reading proficiency level, while 49 per cent fail to achieve the minimum passing level at the end of primary school.[3] Another study has shown that the average ability of Indonesian children is equivalent only to 7.8 years of schooling, despite having spent 12.4 years in school (World Bank, 2020b).

The sudden onset of COVID-19 led to some 94 per cent of students globally having to quickly adjust to learning from home[4] – an abrupt transition that has posed a critical challenge to education systems around the world, not least Indonesia's. Learning loss remains a threat, as schools and teachers were unprepared to deliver remote and blended learning syllabi amidst insufficient infrastructural

---

[1] Indonesia has the world's fourth largest education system with around 53 million grade 1–12 students, 6.3 million children in early childhood education, and 8 million students in higher education. The formal education system collectively employs more than 3.3 million teachers (World Bank, 2020b).

[2] PISA tests evaluate educational systems worldwide by measuring the scholastic performance of 15-year-old students in mathematics, science, and reading.

[3] World Bank, 2020a.

[4] United Nations, 2020.

deficiency. Data by the United Nations Children's Fund (UNICEF) shows that 20 months of school closure has impacted more than 60 million students across Indonesia – the highest number in the region.[5] Several factors may further hinder the achievement of desired learning outcomes and/or exacerbate learning losses, including: (1) differing capacities in teaching abilities and methods, (2) differing capacities in providing learning infrastructure and support, and (3) the gap between classroom and home learning environments, coupled with the economic inability of parents to support their children with further educational enrichment.[6] These factors pose a complex challenge to policymakers and educators alike, and will continue to persist in a post-COVID-19 world.

THE IMPORTANCE OF PHILANTHROPIC PARTNERSHIPS

> No one can whistle a symphony. It takes a whole orchestra to play it.

—H. E. Luccock

Even prior to the outbreak of COVID-19, the World Bank (2020b) had made a key recommendation to address Indonesia's education challenges via multi-stakeholder coordination that would ensure coherence and alignment in the education system. These shared challenges, which the pandemic has further unearthed, can only be overcome through partnerships at the national and subnational government levels – and with dependable partners.

Indeed, partnerships have gained a growing importance in development work for their ability to save costs, strengthen programmes, expand value proposition, improve efficiency, utilise complementary skills, and increase leadership skills. Collaboration also improves interpersonal and inter-organisational capacity through shared power and commitments, as well as resources and capabilities. More crucially, partnerships are required to tackle complex problems, which

---

[5] United Nations Children's Fund, 2021.
[6] Alifia et al., 2020.

often have political, social, and technological dimensions (Orfalea, 2015) – such as the educational challenges Indonesia faces.

Philanthropic organisations often play a critical role in strategic partnerships – by virtue of their ability to fill gaps through knowledge exchange, inspiration-sharing, and collaborating with others on social causes. Owing to their neutrality and resources – such as funds, connections, network, information, and knowledge – philanthropic organisations also possess more flexibility to pursue their objectives and more capacity to take risks (Ferris and Williams, 2012). These resources have enabled philanthropic institutions to create innovative solutions that address structural problems, fulfil existing needs, and adapt to the immediate needs in a crisis, such as COVID-19. To this end, philanthropic organisations have a role to play in stimulating efforts to rebuild educational structures, while creating more strategic and sustainable ways to stay resilient amidst the inevitable changes brought about by the pandemic.

BUILDING EFFECTIVE AND STRATEGIC PHILANTHROPY

Whole leaves wrap torn leaves.

—Old Vietnamese saying on giving and helping

The number of billionaires in the world has grown sevenfold in less than 30 years, from about 310 in 1993 to 2,200 in 2020.[7] This multiplication of global wealth, democratisation in the political sphere, the shifting relationship among the state, commercial marketplace, and civil society (Johnson, 2014), along with the swelling desire to give, have transformed the face of philanthropic organisations. Even before the rise of formal philanthropy, however, it should be noted that the tradition of giving is ubiquitous in Southeast Asia, with long-standing roots among many societies.[8] What the recent development in public giving does is

---

[7] Peterson-Withorn, 2020.

[8] This is exemplified by, among others, the spirit of *gotong royong* in Indonesia and *bahaniyan* in the Philippines, the tradition of putting out water jars for thirsty passers-by in Thailand, as well as the long tradition of volunteering in Vietnam.

to signify a new understanding of philanthropy's emerging role in the region. The mushrooming presence of charity-based organisations in the past three decades, for instance, has led to increased public participation in addressing societal challenges. This increased visibility and prominence have been accompanied by efforts across Southeast Asia to institutionalise the charitable practices – reshaping their form into a more structured and organised private giving.

The institutionalisation of philanthropy is defined as 'the set of private initiatives aimed for the public good that are channelled through independently governed organisations' (Rey-Garcia and Puig-Raposo, 2013, p. 1019). Unique individual values as well as localised aspects of philanthropy create new, specific pathways and approaches to institutionalised giving among philanthropists around the world.[9] This thriving trend is also aimed at making philanthropy sustainable without destroying traditional giving motivations and practices– in that while traditional giving is typically associated with emotional impulse, institutionalised giving relies on long-term, end-to-end, systematic solutions.

Today, philanthropy has gone beyond complementing public and private endeavours – known as the first and second sector respectively – by propelling major social advances.[10] In addition to creating external impact, philanthropy allows knowledge and leadership to be cultivated internally, as well as among key stakeholders and across areas where they operate. Furthermore, this 'third sector' provides an avenue for improving organisational capacities to better manage intergenerational wealth while, at the same time, promoting beliefs, values, and good governance. Research by Institut Européen d'Administration des Affaires (INSEAD) and Swiss bank UBS has shown that the inception and operation of philanthropic platforms among family businesses comes from 'the desire to instil values, strengthen family ties, and promote knowledge and leadership'

[9] Johnson, 2014.
[10] Foster, 2019.

(USB-INSEAD, 2011). It was also the emergence of family foundations that set a new epoch for formalised giving in this region, despite more structured philanthropy being a novel concept.

The next section will explore how TF, as a family philanthropy with a financing system and capacity separate and independent from its business group – Royal Golden Eagle (RGE)[11] – created a partnership framework to build effective programmes. While TF operates across three countries, this chapter will only discuss its impact on improving early childhood education and development – including combating the prevalence of stunting, improving educator capacities, and developing future leaders – in Indonesia.[12]

TANOTO FOUNDATION AND ITS STRATEGIC PARTNERSHIPS

> If you want to go fast, go alone. If you want to go far, go together.
>
> —African proverb

The Tanoto family has four decades of involvement in philanthropic activities, beginning with the establishment of the RGE Kindergarten in 1981 to provide underserved children in Besitang, North Sumatra, with a healthy learning environment. Since then, TF's activities have been conducted primarily in areas where RGE operates, that is, in Riau, Jambi, and North Sumatra. Yet, it is arguably the transformation of TF into a full-fledged and independent philanthropic organisation – and its decision to pursue strategic partnerships as its capabilities grew to become more mature and sophisticated – that has resulted in the Foundation's ability to address critical issues at the national level.

The need and decision to transform the Foundation arrived in 2017, the 50th anniversary of Mr Tanoto's entrepreneurship journey. An endowment fund concept was adopted, which kicked off the work of TF as an independent philanthropic organisation. The

---

[11] RGE is a resource-based manufacturing group with global operations.

[12] In addition to Indonesia, TF also operates in China and Singapore. Its other area of focus lies in conducting medical and scientific research.

transformation renewed focus on impact as the cornerstone of TF's philanthropic activities – specifically, how to scale up and scale out its impact. Consulting with multiple like-minded organisations that have assisted TF in developing its strategies and plans, the Foundation arrived at a conclusion to focus more intensively on education to optimise resources, operate not only as an implementer of programmes but also a provider of grants, and engage in strategic partnerships to develop internal capacity, expand reach, multiply impact, and facilitate sustainability. This transformation would also bring systematic change to TF's programme design and delivery which, specifically, must be evidence-based, impact-oriented, and ensure the programme's function as agents for advocacy.

Accordingly, TF seeks to deliver impact through three flagship programmes in Indonesia that aim to develop, institutionalise, integrate, and incorporate best practices for quality long-life learning and education, as follows:

(1) SIGAP (Strengthening Indonesia's Early Generation by Accelerating Potential; 'sigap' also means 'energetic and active' in Bahasa Indonesia) works with relevant stakeholders at the national, subnational and community levels to support early childhood (0–6 years of age) development and nurture school-ready children, through stunting prevention and developmental care.

(2) PINTAR (Promoting Improvement to INnovate, Teach and Reach; 'pintar' also means 'clever' in Bahasa Indonesia) addresses basic education needs by enhancing educator capacities in primary and junior high schools.

(3) TELADAN (TEaching the LeADership, Advancing the Nation; 'teladan' also means 'role model' in Bahasa Indonesia) aims at developing select university students as future leaders, equipping them with the skills required to thrive and to contribute to their communities. It works through scholarships, structured leadership training, exposure to industries, and mentoring programmes.

Because these programmes involve a broad range of stakeholders, collaborative partnerships are critical not only for their effective and sustainable implementation, but also for maximising their impact.

SIGAP: Partnership for Early Childhood Education and Development

Stunting – defined as a condition in which a child's growth and development is impaired due to the lack of nutrition and early stimulation and frequently observed in the child not meeting height-for-age standards – is a major structural challenge across Indonesia that necessitates proper investment in early childhood education and development. One in four children under the age of 5 suffers from stunting and will experience development impediments that result in lower learning capacity and poor educational performance in childhood as well as reduced earning capacity in adulthood.

While the rate of stunting in Indonesia has decreased significantly from 37.2 per cent in 2013 to 24.4 per cent in 2021, its prevalence is still considered high when taken against the World Health Organization's (WHO's) target of a rate not exceeding 20 per cent (BKKBN, 2021).[13] The pandemic posed additional challenges in combating stunting in such areas as access to health care for mothers and children, policy-making and execution, implementation needs and priority, multi-sectoral coordination, and capacity to implement, as well as data availability. Addressing stunting thus requires a multi-sectoral approach that includes both nutrition-specific (e.g., exclusive breastfeeding and food fortification) and nutrition-sensitive (e.g., water sanitation, hygiene, and social protection) interventions. It also requires the effective alignment of strategy and implementation at the national and subnational, as well as community, levels. As such, strategic collaboration with various levels of government, the private sector, local non-governmental organisations (NGOs), academic institutions, and media help to simultaneously increase programme coverage, optimise resource allocations, promote cross-learning, and maximise impact.

TF focuses its stunting-reduction interventions on advocacy, capacity development, and provision of technical assistance to the

---

[13] Faizal, 2021.

national and local governments – to develop, implement, and evaluate stunting-reduction strategies. For example, the Ministry of Social Affairs (MoSA), with the largest budget allocated to stunting reduction,[14] specifically targets lower-income households whose children are at higher risk of stunting. This is accomplished through a conditional cash transfer social assistance programme that employs around 39,000 frontline social workers to assist 10 million households. In collaboration with TF, MoSA developed a stunting-prevention module using a training-of-trainers approach to build capacity for master trainers across the country. In turn, these trainers equip social workers with skills that promote better dietary habits, sanitation, and hygiene behaviours, as well as good child-rearing practices, in families.

At the subnational level, TF works closely with the government of DKI Jakarta, Central Java and Riau provinces, and the government of Kutai Kartanegara and Pandeglang regencies. This involves an initial financial investment by TF in the establishment of parenting and early learning centres – Rumah Anak SIGAP – to improve the caregiving practices to children from birth to 3 years of age, which are the most critical years in a child's development. Such an arrangement is predicated upon the local government and community taking up ownership, management, and financing of these centres in the long term, while adopting and replicating them in the other villages in the region. As such, the interest, commitment, and readiness of these partners are key factors for ensuring effective programme design, implementation, and scalability.

To advocate for the better alignment of multi-sectoral programmes, systemic changes, and effective implementation of national-level initiatives, TF has also established strategic partnerships with the Office of the Vice President, Coordinating Ministry of Human Development and Cultural Affairs, Ministry of Health (MoH), Ministry of Home Affairs (MoHA), Ministry of Education,

---

[14] The budget was IDR 26.9 trillion (or $1.86 billion) in 2021.

Culture, Research, and Technology (MoECRT), Ministry of Women Empowerment and Child Protection (MoWECP), and the National Population and Family Planning Agency.

Furthermore, TF works with non-state development partners to support GoI's stunting-reduction programme. These partnerships have enabled the Foundation to achieve greater impact by taking stunting intervention measures nationwide. In 2019, TF became a founding member of the World Bank's Multi-Donor Trust Fund (MDTF) for Indonesia Human Capital Acceleration (IHCA), which finances activities aimed at supporting and accelerating stunting-reduction efforts. Specifically, the MDTF helps to realise the GoI's long-term vision in improving human capital results in the areas of leadership development, improving the quality of spending at the local and national levels, enhancing sector and local performance, as well as empowering citizen engagement in frontline service delivery. TF also partnered with UNICEF to support Indonesia's adoption of globally recognised early childhood development measurement instruments – the Early Childhood Development Index (ECDI) and Caregiver Reported Early Development Instrument (CREDI). The collaboration with UNICEF has also been instrumental in helping provincial governments develop operational guidelines aimed at implementing behaviour-change communications towards stunting prevention.

PINTAR: Partnership for Basic Education

Basic education comprises a major part of TF's work in Indonesia and constitutes the Foundation's largest programme to date. Despite having the flexibility to deploy resources through piloting, modelling, research, and documentation, TF acknowledges its limited ability to conduct intervention outreach and ensure programme sustainability on its own – factors that are important to supporting the basic education ecosystem in Indonesia. To mitigate this, TF operates across twenty-five districts in five provinces, modelling innovative intervention in select schools that serves as centres of excellence and working alongside government partners to plan and disseminate these programmes to even more schools.

This arrangement enables TF to function as a cog in the broader wheel of Indonesia's education system, by addressing implementation gaps on the ground. This includes areas like quality assurance, training, and content provision, as well as strategic planning, which are conducted by different agencies within each district. By employing a piloting and monitoring methodology, PINTAR provides capacity-building for teachers, school principals, and teacher training institutes (teacher colleges) to raise pedagogical standards that can optimise learning outcomes.[15] Being present in the field also allows TF to better understand, document, and advocate around the actual challenges of policy implementation in the classrooms.

Partnership with the government at all levels enables several objectives to be met. At the subnational level, district governments are key partners for the effective delivery of the PINTAR teacher training programme in schools, while ensuring programme scale, continuity, and sustained impact. As a case in point, TF reached a total of 8,490 teachers directly between 2018 and 2021, and 44,306 teachers – a five-fold increase – through the Foundation's partners.[16] Indeed, the key to successful programme dissemination lies in proper documentation and use of data, both of which build credibility and ensure confidence when investing in best practices. On the other hand, strategic collaboration with the national government opens the door for TF to inform policy based on lessons learned from the field as well as obtaining first-hand information about new initiatives that can be further conveyed to its government partners at the subnational levels. Operating at both levels of government also places the Foundation in a unique position to facilitate the central–local communication and coordination, thus closing the feedback loop in an effective manner.

---

[15] www.tanotofoundation.org/en/program/learning-environment/basic-education/pintar/.
[16] www.tanotofoundation.org/en/publications/annual-report/.

When COVID-19 struck the world, TF was able to transform the delivery approach of its programmes from a conventional face-to-face setting to digital-based training. Some 2,751 teachers were trained around the themes of digital active learning, while an additional 445 principals were trained in school management. These training materials have since been integrated into several existing or newly built government-owned digital platforms, which have then been made accessible for all teachers within a district and beyond. This bodes well for programme sustainability. The success has also culminated in the official launch of e-PINTAR – an open and free online teacher training programme through which participants can enrol in selected courses, self-learn through structured materials, and be mentored virtually by facilitators.

The impact of PINTAR is borne out by statistics. Since the implementation of PINTAR in 2018, the percentage of principals implementing best management practices has risen significantly: by 26, 30, and 27 percentage points respectively, for making scheduled classroom supervision visits and involving the community in school planning, as well as implementing reading programmes as part of the school's annual lesson plans in 2021. In primary schools, the number of teachers implementing best practices have risen by 12 and 26 percentage points for reading and mathematics at the upper grades, and by 49 and 16 percentage points at the lower grades. These results must also take into context the disruption to classroom activities caused by the outbreak of COVID-19. In PINTAR schools, the learning loss that resulted from school closures was practically negligible.

At the same time, TF acknowledges the importance of building strategic partnerships with like-minded organisations to drive and sustain impact through knowledge-sharing, information dissemination, and policy advocacy. The Basic Education Working Group (BEWG) comprises organisations that address structural issues in basic education, such as the World Bank, UNICEF, The Department of Foreign Affairs and Trade (DFAT), and The Abdul Latif Jameel

Poverty Action Lab (JPAL). These organisations employ different models and approaches, from giving grants and informing policy, to conducting research and building infrastructure. Through the BEWG, TF connects with like-minded development partners in basic education to collaborate in realising GoI development goals.

Finally, TF employs the partnership model of grant-making together with the Global School Leaders (GSL), Djarum Foundation, and TAP Agri through the INSPIRASI Foundation, an initiative that supports school principals and administrators to improve the quality of learning. This mechanism allows TF to trial, and prove the effectiveness, of innovative ideas on a smaller scale before integrating them into the Foundation's flagship programmes, which helps to mitigate risks.

TELADAN: Partnership for Leadership Development

TF's leadership development programme is carried out in partnership with nine public universities.[17] TELADAN is designed to produce future leaders through the provision of training, mentoring, and experiential learning activities for university students. In addition to financial support via scholarships, students are put through soft skills-building, internships, and apprenticeships, as well as community development programmes.

With the short-term goal of enabling these scholars to be successfully absorbed into the workforce, partnerships with industries and alumni are important programme components. TF works with more than 67 companies that provide these scholars with internship and career placement opportunities, in addition to some 100 industry professionals who volunteer their time and expertise as mentors. To better develop leadership capabilities, scholars are expected to mentor first-year students upon reaching their final year in university.

---

[17] These are Bogor Agriculture Institute, Bandung Technology Institute, Andalas University, Brawijaya University, Diponegoro University, Gadjah Mada University, University of Indonesia, University of North Sumatra, and University of Riau.

That scholars are placed at the centre of TELADAN's programme development is recognition of the role they can play in programme delivery and impact measurement. Once admitted into the programme, scholars are at liberty to determine their learning and growth journeys, supported by a strong network and a direct feedback channel to TF. It is through this feedback and consultation channel that the Foundation can identify concerns among its scholars on a host of matters, including burnout, remote learning, and socio-emotional care – and re-synthesise the programme accordingly.

In the same vein, TF has acknowledged that a top-down approach is dated and no longer tenable for a scholarship programme that wishes to accommodate a heterogeneous set of growth trajectories and talents. This recognition has encouraged the TELADAN team to collaborate more closely with university partners to achieve scholar-centric development goals. Thus far, results have been promising. In 2017, 68 per cent of TELADAN scholars successfully found employment within six months. That number has since risen to 100 per cent in 2021.

Fostering South–South Philanthropic Partnerships

As the number of wealthy individuals continues to grow exponentially, private giving and institutionalised philanthropy will continue driving sustainable development in the region.[18] The increasing number and financing capabilities of philanthropic organisations in Indonesia and across Southeast Asia have also allowed cross-cutting collaboration among institutions and countries. TF adopts the South–South Philanthropy Partnerships model with Filantropi Indonesia (FI), Asian Venture Philanthropy Network (AVPN), and Asia Philanthropy Circle (APC).

---

[18] According to the Asian Development Bank, private philanthropic giving and its impact on accelerating poverty alleviation and other Sustainable Development Goals (SDG) efforts is gaining more salience in the Asia-Pacific, and has already helped 1 billion people exit poverty.

FI aims to strengthen the philanthropy network and amplify its impact across Indonesia. It leverages the complementing power of its members to work on social justice and sustainable development agendas through three programme pillars – advocacy and facilitation, communication and partnerships, as well as research and education. As the coordinator of the Education Cluster at FI, TF serves as a catalyst and forges cross-sectoral partnerships for knowledge-sharing, best practices, philanthropy capacity-building, and policy advocacy in the education sector.

At the regional level, TF has partnered with AVPN, a social investment network which builds collaborative ecosystems aimed at increasing capital flow for effective and impactful resource allocation across Asia. Through AVPN, members connect and learn from each other while driving systemic changes through capital mobilisation. They also impact community-building, resource and tools development, learning, and best practices. The Foundation's support for the AVPN Southeast Asia Summit reflects how philanthropic organisations can tap into network associations to drive collaboration and knowledge exchange.

TF has also partnered with APC, a platform for philanthropic organisations in Asia, to catalyse and grow the impact of their work. The platform aims to foster an innovative, forward-looking, and respected community of progressive givers through knowledge exchange and collaboration. In 2017, TF and APC published the *Education Giving Guide for Indonesia,* based on a study by McKinsey & Company and AlphaBeta (APC, 2017). The guide provides analysis of the education landscape in Indonesia and the opportunities it presents for philanthropic institutions to effectively review and adapt their efforts. It was also through APC that TF and its partners developed the INSPIRASI Foundation initiative.

The above examples demonstrate how Global South philanthropic institutions can synergise and collaborate to accelerate the improvement of quality education, while also positively influencing government policy.

Partnership with Government in an Emergency Context and Beyond

Besides addressing systemic challenges to development, the partnership between philanthropic organisations and state agencies supports pressing needs, especially in areas of disaster mitigation and relief and other emergencies. When Indonesia faced a shortage of personal protective equipment, face masks, and oxygen masks during the COVID-19 outbreak, the public–private partnership between TF and GoI expeditiously facilitated the delivery of life-saving equipment to hospitals and communities in need. As the pandemic abated and schools started to reopen, TF mobilised vaccination for teachers and principals in partner districts, while also helping to supply temperature-checking equipment. This has enabled schools to meet the minimum health and safety protocol requirements that are necessary for conducting physical lessons.

Philanthropic partnerships with the government also accelerate and support the government's work in dealing with the barriers to sustainable development. According to UNICEF (2020), programme implementation, along with monitoring and evaluation, are among the challenges to realising Indonesian children's developmental needs. Recognising this, TF has invested in leadership and capacities-building for public service officers through partnerships with the State Administration Agency (Lembaga Administrasi Negara, LAN) and the SDG Academy Indonesia. The latter is a product of TF's collaboration with the UNDP and the Ministry of National Development Planning (Bappenas),[19] and serves as the country's first comprehensive capacity-building programme for SDGs targeted at stakeholders across the public, private, and people sectors. In April 2021, the Academy further launched an SDG Leadership Programme to empower leaders in various sectors by enriching their knowledge of development within the SDG framework. To sum up, these

---

[19] Kementerian Perencanaan Pembangunan Nasional Republik Indonesia/Badan Perencanaan Pembangunan Nasional (Kementerian PPN/Bappenas).

partnerships provide stewardship and agility to the development agenda – by leveraging the leadership, resources, and networks of government, and with the support of subject matter experts from the philanthropic and research networks.

Pushing the Agenda of SDGs

In the 2021 SDG Index – which measures performance based on progress towards achieving the 17 SDG goals – Indonesia's rank increased from 101 out of 166 countries to 97. These goals continue to provide a common language for deeper public–private collaboration and an impetus to drive meaningful change on the ground. To this end, TF has partnered with local and national government bodies, international development organisations (e.g., UNDP, World Bank, UNICEF), philanthropy organisations both local (e.g., FI) and overseas (e.g., GSL, Bill & Melinda Gates Foundation (BMGF)), and business entities (e.g., APRIL Group).

TF strives to ensure that its philanthropic programmes are aligned with both the GoI's national priorities as well as the United Nations (UN) SDGs. For instance, stunting reduction is aligned with SDG Goal 2, Target 2.2,[20] while the Rumah Anak SIGAP programme that aims to ensure early childhood development, care, and pre-primary education is aligned with SDG Goal 4, Target 4.2.[21] Similarly, the adoption of ECDI – a population-based measure used in UNICEF surveys – is critical to the GoI improving data collection and performing analysis on the well-being of children and women. These actions, in turn, drive policy decisions, programme interventions, and public outreach. It is worth noting that prior to the adoption of ECDI, Indonesia did not possess any metadata to understand

---

[20] Target 2.2 aims to end all forms of malnutrition by 2030, including achieving, by 2025, the internationally agreed targets on stunting and wasting in children under 5 years of age, and addressing the nutritional needs of adolescent girls, pregnant and lactating women, and older persons.

[21] Target 4.2 aims to ensure that all girls and boys have access to quality early childhood development, care, and pre-primary education so that they are ready for primary education, by 2030.

the state of early childhood development or to provide any indicator report related to SDG progress.[22] Today, the index has been successfully integrated into SUSENAS, the national survey conveyed by Indonesia's National Bureau of Statistics.

Thus, TF's approach brings a range of benefits that includes the harmonisation of data-collation methodologies at the national level, the sharing of newly codified knowledge from its HCD work, and growing solidarity among like-minded public and private-sector partners. These are the outcomes of impact-driven institutionalised philanthropy which, through strategic partnerships, drives stakeholders to look at transforming systemic vulnerabilities into new launch pads for HCD.

LONG-TERM CHALLENGES TO IMPACT DELIVERY

While SIGAP, PINTAR, and TELADAN have made considerable progress in the respective areas of stunting prevention, improving basic education, and leadership development, longer-term challenges remain that may affect the Foundation's ability to further its impact across Indonesia.

The first challenge lies in quantifying progress, which is key to evaluating the success of programmes across the development world. With an ambitious GoI target of lowering stunting rates to below 20 per cent by the end of 2024, the acceleration of prevention programmes has become more crucial. But while the national rate of stunting has accelerated in the three years since the implementation of SIGAP,[23] it may be difficult to attribute exactly how much the programme has contributed to overall progress in and of itself. This is a challenge faced not only by TF, but by all organisations with development as their raison d'être.

---

[22] The SDG 4.2.1 indicator looks at the proportion of children aged 24–59 months who are developmentally on track in health, learning, and psychosocial well-being, by sex.

[23] Stunting decreased from 37.2 per cent to 30.8 per cent between 2013 and 2018, that is, over a span of five years. From 2018 to 2021, the rate of stunting fell from 30.8 per cent to 24.4 per cent – marking a quicker acceleration rate over three years, and despite ground operations being disrupted by the COVID-19 pandemic.

The second resides in the replicability of TF's programmes. Doing so requires more than merely an acknowledgement of the Foundation's work by the GoI, but the political will to advocate that these best practices be adopted elsewhere. The heterogeneity of Indonesia necessitates the localisation of training content and poses challenges to successful programme replication. Taken in this light, the stunting-awareness module developed to train frontline social workers may not necessarily be replicable across Indonesia. While digital PINTAR represents a cost-effective and scalable means of bringing quality professional development content to Indonesian teachers outside TF's partner districts, its successful adoption may depend on factors beyond the Foundation's control.

The third relies on TF's ability to continue identifying areas of intervention that it can leverage partners to either match or add to, in terms of funding. For example, TF has contributed $2 million to the World Bank MDTF to support GoI in executing the national stunting-prevention acceleration strategy, while enabling other partner organisations to contribute and expand the reach of the programme. The BMGF has committed $4.45 million, and the German Development Bank has committed €800,000 – effectively tripling the amount of funding to the MDTF. As with any organisation involved with development work, TF needs to ensure that it can continue to achieve the greatest impact and multiplier effect with its limited resources.

DISCUSSION: FROM CASE STUDY TO THE PHILANTHROPY REALM

The transformation journey towards becoming a more strategic philanthropy has shaped how TF establishes its strategic partnerships. There are several key learning points to note.

First, the institutionalisation process plays a key role in shaping strategic and effective philanthropy. For philanthropic institutions in the Global South, the institutionalisation process is critical to facilitating a move towards structured giving that fulfils public needs and, more strategically, avoids ineffective social investments while grounding giving in evidence and partnerships. As institutionalisation often means being independent and free-standing, it provides a stronger impetus for an organisation to apply systematic interventions and giving. Institutionalisation also facilitates the internal restructuring that is often necessary to optimally align with the lived daily realities of beneficiaries. More importantly, it allows the organisation to effectively define a strategy that goes beyond just charitable giving, and that is focused on sustained and replicable impact. Indeed, the transformation of TF into a full-fledged philanthropic organisation has allowed the Foundation to address nationwide issues of stunting prevention, alleviating learning poverty and developing future leaders at a holistic level – as opposed to focusing its philanthropic activities only in the areas where RGE businesses operate.

Secondly, a strong strategic partnership requires alignment of vision and values, shared commitment to consolidate resources, ownership of issues, and the readiness of all partners to act. How effective a partnership turns out is largely dependent on partner selection and the organisation's ability to build effective partnerships with them. Strategic partnerships must remain sufficiently flexible and agile to adapt to the needs and contexts of stakeholders and beneficiaries.

Thirdly, there is no one-size-fits-all approach to strategic partnerships. The partnership strategy, approach, and model depend on the objective of the partnerships, the interconnectivity among stakeholders, issues that are addressed by the programme, as well as the type and stage of partnership-building. It is thus imperative to carefully determine the needs, shared values, and the sets of objectives expected from the intended collaboration.

Equally, the nature of the issues, flagship programme, and local context are important considerations when determining the partnership model. For example, PINTAR deals with the quality of learning through building capacity for teachers and school administrators. SIGAP addresses the stunting issue, which requires the deployment of interventions across multiple vulnerable areas. TELADAN works with the higher education system, a domain comprising institutions that are comparatively established. These differing contexts influence the partnership models that a philanthropic organisation like TF must carefully review and adapt to.

Fourthly, establishing a strategic partnership with the government is central to philanthropic work, and is particularly critical to scaling up intervention programmes. *Strategic* philanthropy must take into consideration various aspects of public policy and government funding (Bridgespan Group, 2021). In its transformation journey to becoming a more strategic organisation, TF recognises the importance of working closely with the government at the local and national levels, on a more formal and continuous basis. With respect to the programmes mentioned in this chapter, the aim of TF lies in enabling their eventual ownership and sustenance by the GoI. Hence, the Foundation has a clear entry-to-exit strategy, with clearly defined roles for TF and the GoI – such that for every role TF occupies at the district level, a government counterpart also exists. This enables the Foundation to better address pressing public problems while also ensuring social impact that is sustainable and lasting.

Fifthly, building an effective partnership and maintaining its dynamic is a process that requires time. An effective partnership must possess several elements, including shared values and agreement on the levels of commitment and contribution. To deliver impact, discipline is necessary both to identify partnership needs and to navigate the diverse perspectives of multiple stakeholders and characters. When partnering with the local government, it is crucial to engage local leaders to holistically influence systemic changes via policy and programme replication. It is equally important to engage the various levels of leadership within a government organisation, to garner trust and establish robust relationships at the institutional level. All of these constitute processes that demand time.

CONCLUSION

As Asian philanthropic institutions continue to flourish and thrive, private giving has the capacity to help both governments and markets address emerging societal challenges. The rise of Global South philanthropy has presented opportunities for a more effective philanthropic contribution. These philanthropic organisations' unprecedented exposure to global partnerships, while maintaining rootedness in addressing local community issues, should be considered strengths in a modern world that demands contextualised solutions to complex challenges.

Through a more institutionalised and structured private giving model, TF has transformed itself from a charity-based organisation that provided improved access to education, to an impact-seeking philanthropy aiming to uplift lives through a more structured approach. This transformation is crucial in view of TF's mission to continuously unlock the potential of people through the provision of quality education; more so in a milieu that will inevitably entail navigating the long-term effects brought about by COVID-19 to the education sector.

With learning poverty remaining one of the most critical challenges facing Indonesia's education sector, a more exhaustive, well-targeted, and sustainable approach involving diverse sectors and multiple actors is required. Improved partnerships in the TF's programmes – SIGAP, PINTAR, and TELADAN – have enabled the Foundation to strengthen programme planning and deliver better implementation. Partnering with both national and local governments, like-minded organisations, and beneficiaries have allowed the organisation to expand its value proposition and improve knowledge and leadership within and between organisations. Both the partnerships, and the improved organisational qualities they bring about, are expected to serve TF well as it continues to expand its philanthropic mission in a post-COVID-19 world.

As the pandemic crisis continues to expose vulnerabilities in our social system and uncover areas for improvement that only cross-sectorial partnerships can address, private philanthropic institutions will feel a continued impetus to reflect upon and improve their roles and methodologies in giving. Such a process will not only enable philanthropic institutions to solve the immediate needs brought about by the most pressing global health crisis of our time, but also place them in a stronger position to address systemic shortcomings and achieve development goals in the longer term.

Finally, the presentation and discussion regarding TF's approach in building partnerships are not intended as a model. After all, the world is too diverse for only a single model to suffice. However, the approach can serve as a source of inspiration – with many practical solutions that may be applied to similar challenges that philanthropic organisations face.

REFERENCES

Alifia, U., Barasa, A. R., Bima, L., Pramana, R. P., Revina, S., and Tresnatri, F. A. 2020. Learning from Home: Portrait of Teaching and Learning Inequalities in Times of the COVID-19 Pandemic. *Smeru Research Institute*, 1(1), 1–8. https://smeru.or.id/en/publication/learning-home-portrait-teaching-and-learning-inequalities-times-covid-19-pandemic.

APC (Asia Philanthropy Circle). 2017. *Catalysing Productive Livelihood: A Guide to Education Interventions with an Accelerated Path to Scale and Impact.* www.edumap-indonesia.asiaphilanthropycircle.org/.

BKKBN (Badan Kependudukan dan Keluarga Berencana Nasional). 2021. *Indonesia Cegah Stunting*, 17 February. www.bkkbn.go.id/berita-indonesia-cegah-stunting#:~:text=Dalam mengatasi stunting%2C BKKBN siap,usia subur sebelum proses kehamilan.

Bridgespan Group. 2021. *A Philanthropist's Guide to Working with Government and Local Communities*, 15 January. www.bridgespan.org/insights/library/philanthropy/philanthropists-guide-working-with-government.

CAF (Charities Aid Foundation). 2021. *World Giving Index* (Issue June). www.cafonline.org/about-us/publications/2021-publications/caf-world-giving-index-2021.

CAPS (Centre for Asian Philanthropy and Society). 2018. *Doing Good Index 2018: Maximizing Asia's Potential.* http://caps.org/our-research/doing-good-index-2018/.

Faizal, E. B. 2021. Indonesia Races Against Time to Meet Child Stunting Target. *The Jakarta Post*, 16 March. www.thejakartapost.com/academia/2021/03/15/indonesia-races-against-time-to-meet-child-stunting-target.html.

Ferris, J. M., and Williams, N. P. O. 2012. *Philanthropy and Government Working Together: The Role of Offices of Strategic Partnerships in Public Problem Solving.*

Los Angeles: Center on Philanthropy and Public Policy/USC. https://cppp.usc
.edu/download/?file=Philanthropy and Government Working Together_ The
Role of Offices of Strategic Partnerships in Public Problem Solving.pdf.

Foster, W. 2019. Introduction to Unleashing Philanthropy's Big Bets for Social Change.
Stanford Social Innovation Review (SSIR), Spring. https://ssir.org/articles/entry/
introduction_to_unleashing_philanthropys_big_bets_for_social_change.

Johnson, P. D. 2014. *Global Institutional Philanthropy: A Preliminary Status
Report Part One*. https://tpi.org/resource/global-institutional-philanthropy-a-
preliminary-status-report-part-one/.

Johnson, P. D. 2018. *Global Philanthropy Report*. Harvard Kennedy School.
www.ubs.com/global/en/wealth-management/uhnw/philanthropy/shaping-
philanthropy.html%0Ahttps://cpl.hks.harvard.edu/files/cpl/files/global_phil
anthropy_report_final_april_2018.pdf.

KEMDIKBUD. 2021. *APK/APM KEMDIKBUD dan KEMENAG*. https://apkapm
.data.kemdikbud.go.id/index.php/cberanda/apkapmsekolahmadrasah?kode_
wilayah=000000&tahun=2021.

Orfalea, N. 2015. Where Two Rivers Meet, the Water Is Never Calm. *Stanford Social
Innovation Review (SSIR)*, 13(4), A3. https://doi.org/10.48558/ARY1-NX51.

Peterson-Withorn, C. 2020. The World's Billionaires Have Gotten $1.9 Trillion
Richer in 2020. *Forbes*. www.forbes.com/sites/chasewithorn/2020/12/16/the-
worlds-billionaires-have-gotten-19-trillion-richer-in-2020/?sh=1c062d0a7386.

Rey-Garcia, M., and Puig-Raposo, N. 2013. Globalisation and the Organisation of
Family Philanthropy: A Case of Isomorphism? *Business History*, 55(6), 1019–
1046. https://doi.org/10.1080/00076791.2012.744591.

Tang, H. W., Yip, M., and Ooi, V. 2020. Philanthropic Structuring: The Asian
Context. *Research Collection Yong Pung How School of Law*, 1–20. https://
ink.library.smu.edu.sg/sol_research/3184.

UBS-INSEAD. 2011. *UBS-INSEAD Study on Family Philanthropy in Asia*. https://
thegiin.org/research/publication/ubs-insead-study-on-family-philanthropy-
in-asia.

UN (United Nations). 2020. *Policy Brief: Education during COVID-19 and
beyond*, 1–26.

UNDP (United Nations Development Programme). 2014. Philanthropy as
an Emerging Contributor to Development Cooperation. *International
Development Cooperation: Trends and Emerging Opportunities – Perspectives
of the New Actors*, Istanbul, June, 1–30.

UNICEF (United Nations Children's Fund). 2020. Situasi Anak di Indonesia – Tren,
peluang, dan Tantangan dalam Memenuhi Hak-Hak Anak. *UNICEF Indonesia*,
8–38. www.unicef.org/indonesia/id/laporan/situasi-anak-di-indonesia-2020.

UNICEF (United Nations Children's Fund). 2021. *Towards a Child-Focused COVID-19 Response and Recovery: A Call to Action.* August, 1–14. www .unicef.org/indonesia/reports/towards-child-focused-covid-19-response-and-recovery.

World Bank. 2020a. *Indonesia Learning Poverty Brief.* https://documents.worldbank .org/en/publication/documents-reports/documentdetail/579771624553117186/ indonesia-learning-poverty-brief.

World Bank. 2020b. *The Promise of Education in Indonesia.* https:// openknowledge.worldbank.org/handle/10986/34807.

4 Forging Multi-Stakeholder Partnerships

Global South Governments, the Private Sector, Philanthropists, and Civil Society

Natasha M. Matic

> The issues we face are so big and the targets are so challenging that we cannot do it alone. When you look at any issue, such as food or water scarcity, it is very clear that no individual institution, government, or company can provide the solution.

Paul Polman, Former CEO, Unilever

INTRODUCTION

Yes, we are still talking about partnerships. For years, global development and the philanthropic community have been working to find the best ways to partner effectively for social development. The global community unanimously agreed to dedicate Sustainable Development Goal (SDG) number 17 to the issue of partnerships, and yet we still struggle to understand what it means, why partnerships are important, and how to do them right. Many stakeholders find partnerships daunting; organisations are still largely ego-driven, and many don't put enough value on creating a shared vision in order to address the myriad issues facing the world. This is especially the case in the growth markets and the Global South. The question is, why?

The reasons are many – lack of trust, insufficient role models, not knowing how to partner or being unable to see the benefits. Whether in the North or the South, impactful partnerships are essential elements of effective philanthropy and crucial for creating systems change. Only through systems change can we challenge many of the old structures and models that got us here in the first place – be they climate change, inequalities, or injustice. Whether we are a business or a foundation, we must transition towards integration and alignment with others in order to be bold and create new systems.

The year 2021 glaringly underscored the reality that government entities lack resources and agility to support the wide variety of services and efforts critical for social development. On the other hand, increasingly, the private sector is becoming engaged in philanthropic and sustainability efforts while civil society still struggles to find lasting solutions. Everyone works hard in their own bubble creating a situation where – despite all efforts – innovative solutions, achievable climate commitments, and funding for the 2030 sustainability agenda are still lacking.

To achieve this, we must change our mindsets, and recognise our interconnectedness to each other and to nature, and that only collectively can we make this shift. If our philanthropic efforts are aimed at truly sustainable and scalable impact or change, we must explore how to join forces and leverage global multi-stakeholder partnerships for impact. While there can be numerous factors that present challenges to partnering, and collaborations are often difficult to navigate, only by forging partnerships can positive, lasting, systemic change and progress be achieved.

This chapter explores partnerships in the growth markets through lessons learned from Riyadh-based King Khalid Foundation's (KKF's) philanthropic partnerships journey. It provides insights and practical tools to identify key elements that will help us effectively work in partnership with others. The chapter delves into how to initiate, develop, and sustain high-impact partnerships over time between governments, the private sector, and philanthropists, as well as the steps needed for a successful partnership.

BACKGROUND

In 2011, when KKF reached out to other stakeholders in the Kingdom of Saudi Arabia (KSA) and started talking about its willingness and interest to partner, it encountered raised eyebrows and confused looks. 'Why would a royal foundation need to do that, don't you have enough resources to do it yourself?' 'What exactly are your motives for asking us to partner?' These distrustful questions are most likely the outcome of parties' lack of knowledge on what partnerships really mean, how important they are, or how to partner effectively. Many are also still reluctant to see or accept that our collective knowledge and experience is necessary to find new solutions.

Despite tremendous amounts of money spent on development in many growth markets, these countries still need to solve many of their core systemic issues, and solutions mostly focus on fixing the short-term or ongoing problems. Why? Because we lack alignment, perspectives, cohesion, and we suffer from short-term views and no shared vision. Leaders in philanthropy are taking on complex and challenging problems in ever-changing and volatile social, political, environmental, and technological conditions. To achieve real impact and deliver innovative solutions, all stakeholders must explore better-aligned, constructively engaged, and jointly impactful efforts. Working in coordination, sometimes even with non-intuitive partners, is the essential element of resiliency, systems change, and impact.

Historically, the philanthropic sector in growth markets in general has been largely siloed, with only a few foundations or non-profits working together and even fewer engaged in multi-sectoral collaborations. All too often, philanthropists are reluctant to embark on joint efforts because of the perception that their contributions and recognition could be diluted or diminished. In some cases, philanthropists are convinced that they know best the issues in their geographic area or field and that engaging partners is simply not worth the effort. This is especially the case if funding is not an issue, so many philanthropists and business leaders just can't see the benefit. In case of partnerships with governments or the private sector, sentiments like 'governments are bureaucratic and will slow us down' or 'businesses don't really care about social impact, they are only doing it for their branding' are very common. Moreover, many in the corporate world still don't see the benefit, as they consider their social or even environmental engagement just as a necessary box-ticking exercise to protect their brand. There is a great deal of distrust and reluctance to even try.

Since the early 2010s, there have been very few examples or role models of effective multi-stakeholder philanthropic partnerships in the South, especially in the growth markets. Businesses are still driven by profit and not by shared purpose. While profit and purpose shouldn't necessarily be at odds, trying to retrofit a profit model into a purpose model does not work. If we all agree that there is a need to change, we would then be able to create new systems and models together and address the root causes of problems in addition to finding new, bold solutions together. We must first move towards collective consciousness and then to collective action. The only question businesses, governments, or philanthropists need to ask themselves is: 'is this in service to the people and planet?' If not, then don't do it. Purpose and profit can exist but elevating profit as the sole purpose is currently not working and the systems behind profit and fast growth have become the centre of the problem. This is one of the reasons why partnerships are so difficult with the business community.

Another major issue has been that for many in the growth markets, the idea of 'partnerships' may sound attractive but the details of 'how', 'why', and 'with whom' makes action very daunting. Instead of 'what will I lose in the process', the question should be 'what will we do better together and how beneficial will collective action be for my organisation?' In a world where quick action, short-term thinking, more offerings, and more profit are a priority, finding consensus becomes difficult; as a result, partnerships remain very complicated, requiring enormous effort and often slowing things down. Even well-intentioned efforts and resources have been misaligned, or worse, wasted, leading to unmet challenges.

EMERGING TRENDS

The COVID-19 pandemic exposed that silos created many of the systemic issues we now face; however, it is possible that systems issues created those silos in the first place. Regardless of which one came first, in order to survive and thrive we must find lasting solutions rather than quick fixes. 'The COVID-19 crisis will have a profound impact on philanthropy through forging more active collaboration and ensuring more equitable responses. Scale and urgency of the pandemic has prompted philanthropists to engage in more active collaboration, not only with businesses and government but also with each other,' remarks Bill Gates in a video interview conducted by Badr Jafar, the founding patron of the Cambridge Centre for Strategic Philanthropy.

Thankfully, many growth markets' philanthropic organisations are finally indicating a desire to significantly recalibrate traditional industry practices. Mindsets are starting to change, philanthropy is slowly adapting, and our world is changing even faster. Global South practitioners are expressing an appetite for multi-stakeholder partnerships and South–South collaboration, with a view to scaling impact, building strong peer networks, knowledge-sharing, and collaborative initiatives. The United Nations (UN) SDGs have become more accepted and integrated, making it easier to share a common language, identify issues, and create frameworks.

The adoption of the SDGs and their widespread promotion since 2016, as well as the COVID-19 pandemic, have had a significant impact on the concept of partnerships in the Global South. The SDGs provide common language and definitions while explicitly acknowledging the interconnectedness of the prosperity of business, society, and the environment. They also provide clear roadmaps and targets. The SDGs further represent a fundamental shift in the approach, naming all societal sectors as key development actors, and requiring an unprecedented level of cooperation and collaboration among civil society, business, government, non-governmental organisations (NGOs), and foundations for their achievement.

LET'S START WITH DEFINITIONS

There are numerous names and definitions for multi-stakeholder partnerships or philanthropic partnerships. But whether we are talking about multi-stakeholder partnerships or public-private partnership for development, cross-sector collaboration, or collective action, they are all vehicles through which interested players work together to create new solutions and systems to achieve greater impact than they could achieve alone.

> Multi-stakeholder partnerships involve organisations from different societal sectors working together, sharing risks and combining their unique resources and competencies in ways that can generate and maximise value towards shared partnership and individual partner objectives, often through more innovative, more sustainable, more efficient and / or more systemic approaches.[1]

Much like a business discussion about developing a new product or entering a different market, partnerships require a strategic process and joint approach. This applies to all stakeholders, no matter whether you are a CEO, non-profit manager, philanthropist, or public servant. The key question is: How can partnerships be done well?

Partnerships are usually voluntary efforts operating under their own principles, which must be developed and agreed to by all sides. They are highly context-specific, building on the interests, capacities, resources, and leadership of all parties involved. However, they only succeed by having a common, shared vision and a willingness to take risks by adopting creativity and flexibility towards achieving that vision. They represent a different way of doing development, requiring new skills and mindsets. Older, ego-driven practices and systems must be left at the door.

The process of creating a partnership also starts with a well-defined and agreed-upon problem being solved. Deciding on the key problem or issue may seem straightforward, but is actually one of the main reasons problems arise from the start. Spending time to identify the problem together in detail must be one of the first steps in any partnership. Then comes a shared vision. After that, start

---

[1] 'An Introduction to Multi-stakeholder Partnerships'. Briefing document for the GPEDC High Level Meeting, November 2016; The Partnering Initiative (partnerinit.org).

addressing the more practical questions such as: Who are the stake-holders and what role do they play? What do they do well and/or what do they need to succeed? Where are the capability gaps and agreements on primary obstacles? Finally, what is the specific part-nership's contribution and what are the metrics to assess project success and impact? These initial assessments are critical for any successful partnership.

Numerous studies have been conducted on the topic of part-nerships and most of them identify the following key elements of success:

- shared vision
- alignment on the issue the partnership aims to solve
- proper coordinated planning and processes (including exit strategy)
- collaborative definition of success and social-impact performance metrics
- alignment on interests, values, and goals
- clear roles and responsibilities
- leveraging each stakeholder's strengths
- a sense of trust between partners
- transparency and continuous communication
- successful role models.

Using this list will, at a minimum, ensure that your organization is off to a good start.

KING KHALID FOUNDATION'S PARTNERSHIP JOURNEY

Supported by the family of the late King Khalid bin Abdulaziz Al Saud, KKF was established in 2001 as an independent, private foundation dedicated to supporting the creation of a more equitable Saudi society. As a renowned and impactful organisation, the Foundation has been working on building a social-sector ecosystem to create equal oppor-tunities for a thriving Saudi Arabia. The Foundation applies grant-making, capacity-building, partnerships, and advocacy to address inequality, provide economic opportunities, and promote prosperity.

What helped KKF stand out from the outset is its approach to creating a basic social-sector ecosystem and working collaboratively to solve Saudi Arabia's most complex challenges. It partnered mostly with international entities, from academia, philanthropy, the corporate sector, and governments to make this happen. Local multi-stakeholder partnerships are also becoming a reality in recent years. Those involved never wavered in their intention to achieve success through collaborative impact, and learned a great deal throughout this journey.

PHILANTHROPY IN SAUDI ARABIA

The KSA, the birthplace of Islam, has long been one of the world's most generous countries, with charitable giving serving an integral part of the nation's Muslim heritage. *Zakah*, one of the five pillars of Islam, obliges the giving of charity while *saddaqah*, a voluntary form of charity, is also a key Islamic concept. 'Philanthropy in the Arab region is embedded in its culture,' maintains Dr Atallah Kuttab, founder and chairman of SAANED, a philanthropy advisory in the Arab region. 'It has a long history, tied to religious giving. Ours is a giving society.'[2]

By 2019, despite a culture of giving and the sector becoming a part of the Saudi Vision 2030, the ratio of non-profit sector organisations per capita in Saudi Arabia remained considered low, with one organisation for every 10,000 inhabitants.[3] Professionalisation of the sector, while growing, still had a long way to go, with existing non-profit organisations (NPOs) having limited capacity. Additional knowledge and expertise were needed to create truly scalable and sustainable programmes.

Most NPOs in Saudi Arabia were only created since around the late 2010s,[4] and therefore lack significant training and expertise. In this climate, capacity-building became crucially important. Though, many believed that even if the capacity within the sector was there, corporations and other partners still may not be ready to partner for their philanthropic giving due to the sectoral lack of experience and impact.

[2] www.alliancemagazine.org/blog/key-issues-philanthropy-arab-region/.
[3] https://kkf.org.sa/media/ctbb4fi5/4-saudi-nonprofit-trends-report-2018.pdf.
[4] Ibid.

Various sectors collaborating with civil society is still a rarity in Saudi Arabia and co-creating programmes requires significant time and effort. From the outset, persuading corporate partners to work with the social-development sector and invest in scaling programmes requires significant effort and time. Equally, many corporations still consider philanthropic investment an offshoot of their broader marketing and communications activities, which primarily serve to build brand and reputation.

Non-profits had historically helped fill some of the gaps in society left by other sector actors; however, in Saudi Arabia the government traditionally provided most of the services and has only recently started to open opportunities for social development organisations to take their place in this regard. Indeed, there is still a continuing search for ideal balance and compromise between the marketplace, the centralised state, the social sector, and community realms.[5]

In a survey of non-profit leaders in Saudi Arabia, almost all interviewees pointed out the need for governmental support for growth of the non-profit sector and greater professionalisation.[6] Legitimacy of leadership in the non-profit sector also comes from state recognition. The government not only made laws and set expectations on NPOs using legal instruments, but it also supported the sector implicitly in the hope of achieving its own goals.

PARTNERING WITH THE GOVERNMENT

Since 2008, KKF has been instrumental in lobbying for the inclusion of the social-development sector within the national strategy for building the non-profit ecosystem. The Foundation's impactful efforts since 2016 facilitated the adoption of the national strategy entitled Vision 2030, and since then the Saudi government has been sending a strong signal that it considers the social-development sector an important partner in the country's overall development. Prior

[5] Ibid.
[6] Ibid.

to the adoption of this visionary strategy, the non-profit sector was never part of any national initiatives, nor was it considered a significant contributor. Adoption of this document and its major focus on social-sector contribution to the government's future plans represented a significant shift.

Based on our experience, trust, quality, and reputation are key factors when working with the government. KKF is a Saudi foundation working on improving the lives of ordinary Saudis and it has a significant, impeccable record of successful programmes and impact. As a result, it comes to the government with substantial knowledge and experience that politicians can use to their benefit. As an example, the Foundation had great success working with the government on poverty reduction. Prior to KKF's work on this issue, the 'poverty line' was something that not only the government but also wider society would not talk about. For years, KKF has been pushing for policies to reduce the number of people living under the poverty line. KKF shared our findings with the government every step of the way, we were transparent about our aims, and we invited them to witness the situation, especially in rural areas. These initiatives and data collected made it possible for the leadership to be more open about the fact that there is poverty in the country that needs to be addressed. Together, we were able to start concentrating on these problems without placing any blame or pointing fingers.

The key to KKF's approach with the government is not that dissimilar to working with the private sector: identifying a problem in as much detail as possible (broad scope and vague indicators do not work), understanding governments' goals and plans for the specific issue, ensuring that the Foundation's goals are fully aligned, and showing clearly how working together has a more significant impact. Making government officials' lives easier is also a plus!

KKF usually reaches out to the government when there is a specific policy that needs improvement or when we can recommend a policy for a specific issue. Working on policies is the essence of the government's work; therefore, if we can find ways to support them in this process it can be mutually beneficial. KKF also comes to the government with very specific options. This allows for a focused discussion and gives government entities the ability to choose how and what to work on. When partnering with the government, it is important to allow for more time and a slower pace. That said, KKF's partnership between NPOs and the government are still limited with plenty of room to grow because partnerships are very new for the government and therefore, even with the best of intentions, it is not something that comes easily nor can it be done quickly.

CHALLENGES AND LESSONS LEARNED

KKF has partnered with a number of philanthropic, corporate, and government entities. They each brought with them a different set of challenges and opportunities. The Foundation's partnerships included collective grant-making, programme co-development and implementation, and co-funding. However, its main aim was always to engage with partners for the long term, on multiple levels, and make sure that all sides have ownership of the project and contribute in a variety of ways.

As we discussed at the beginning of this chapter, there are a number of challenges organisations can face on their partnership journey. Early in our experience, KKF fell into partnerships organically with anyone who wanted to partner with it but as members gained experience, we learned to be more intentional and deliberate.

From KKF's experience, one of the obstacles to impactful partnerships lay in the fact that many companies' philanthropic departments were managed by the communication department, which had marketing-oriented goals focusing on client retention or accessing new markets and developing new products. Instead of incorporating social responsibility considerations in their overall sustainability strategy and aligning it with their core business, sustainability was often seen as a random, 'bolted-on' effort and expense rather than a 'built-in' addition that will open markets, strengthen communities, and expand the business.

Initially, KKF had more success partnering with international entities, be they foundations, academic institutions, or companies, rather than local ones, because international partners had more experience with collaboration and collective impact. The Foundation decided to pursue these partnerships to use them as models for local efforts and learn from them. Many of these partnerships have been highly successful and helped KKF learn from all the challenges and opportunities. KKF also used every opportunity to publicly speak about them at conferences and on social media so others could learn from our experience.

Through this process KKF learned that organisations must screen partners, as this was crucial for KKF's reputation and ethical code. KKF had once worked with a company that sold food and beverages, so it cooperated with them on a programme that targeted poor families to improve their financial budgeting skills. The main goal was to help these families manage their personal finances better, and during the workshops and events, the company would have the right to do product placements. But because many of the products provided by the company had high sugar content, KKF decided not to go ahead with this collaboration. KKF leadership realised that while such a programme may have positive impact on beneficiaries' financial skills, it would negatively impact their health and well-being. It is important to think about both direct impact and indirect impact, along with other potential consequences.

Another example of KKF's failed attempt to form working partnerships was its experience with a technology company. KKF staff were working with this entity to help its grant recipients improve their technology literacy and teach them to use computers and smartphones. We reached an agreement where only the technology company's products would be used. However, the company was not willing to provide enough smartphones to make a real impact, so we suggested bringing a second technology company on board. They refused and requested KKF buy additional smartphones to meet the goal.

Financial and marketing considerations were still the most crucial factors dictating the success of a partnership, but quick wins rarely delivered sustainable long-lasting social impact. Companies that had a greater awareness of sustainability were more inclined to consider long-term development programmes and understand KKF's rationale. On this basis, successfully forming meaningful partnerships with companies required the Foundation to be very clear about its underlying philosophy of creating social impact at scale. Philanthropy was about creating real long-term change and simply throwing money at challenges was not the solution.

KKF's partnership journey included many questions and challenges:

1. Convincing corporations about the value of forming philanthropic partnerships: How could KKF build a business case that outlines to potential private-sector partners the value of engaging with the Foundation to increase social impact? This business case needed to outline the benefits while also building an understanding that philanthropy is not a marketing 'quick win' but rather a long-term ambition. Moreover, it was a goal that would necessarily require financial but also non-financial input to create truly effective and sustainable partnerships, and ideally needed to be aligned with corporations' core business rather than based on random, marketing-driven interests.

2. Leveraging strengths specific to engaged parties: KKF chooses partners whose knowledge, capacity, and experience are complementary and targeted to achieving the desired outcomes, and who are willing to learn and make adjustments along the way. It leverages existing strengths, builds new skills, provides educational opportunities, and builds pathways to success for beneficiaries by accessing current data and resource experts to build on the overall stakeholder body of knowledge.

3. Building much stronger brand recognition while adhering to the tenets of conservative Islamic culture: While Islamic culture praises humility and keeping a low profile around philanthropic giving, non-profit entities need to have sound reputations to build partnerships and a solid track record in effective giving. To build this, they inevitably must talk about their approach and their achievements to ensure they have a robust brand strategy that supports their reputation. This helps aggregate social and financial capital while also promoting strong aligned internal cohesion around an organisation's core values. KKF must design its branding

strategies to enhance its brand as a platform for nurturing corporate partnerships.

4. Securing government endorsement: KKF needed to ensure that its core stakeholders, and notably government entities, understood its ambitions around creating partnerships with private, for-profit entities and that these partnerships would support rather than compete with the national plans of the state. The government would also need to facilitate such partnerships by ensuring a conducive regulatory framework that allowed them to develop. This was still an area of development in KSA as the country, along with other countries in the region, sometimes regarded philanthropy with suspicion and struggled to regulate it.[7] KKF needed to be very transparent about the objectives behind this plan, be able to showcase how the broader state can benefit, and demonstrate how it will align with specific government objectives and the UN's SDGs.

What KKF Learned:

- The primary lesson learned is that effective partnerships don't just happen – they need to be planned, designed, monitored, adjusted, and facilitated. They take time because building trust and a relationship between parties is very important.
- Careful planning needs to go into the initial first steps. We found that in order to initiate a partnership we need to be clear on what the goal will be and why a collaborative effort will lead to outcomes that might otherwise be unattainable. Then jointly we must tackle a variety of important questions: Should the partnership include other funders? Which non-profits, educational institutions, NPOs, or government agencies need to be involved? What qualities do participants need? What are the potential deal breakers? What 'red flag' threats would rule out a potential partner, or signal that a partner would need to be monitored?[8]
- Effective collaborations start with a discussion about values and mission statements, and agreement on operating principles that will govern and

---

[7] One regional practitioner noted that regional governments sometimes treat 'the civic sector as guilty until proved innocent' according to *Alliance*'s *Philanthropy in the Arab Region* report.

[8] Mitchell, L. and Karoff, P. 2015. Accepting the Challenges of Partnerships. *Stanford Social Innovation Review*, Fall. https://ssir.org/articles/entry/accepting_the_challenges_of_partnership#.

guide the work. In those early talks, it is key to spend time identifying the problem being addressed in detail. It is helpful to cover topics such as: ground rules for discussions, planning, and decision-making; metrics for the ongoing assessment of progress; and planning for the inevitable unintended consequences and 'unknown unknowns'.

- Potential partners also must explore various types of collaborative structures in order to ensure effective leadership, and in some cases they need to provide for different types of leadership at specific levels of the partnership or network. The structural planning exercises we have found most helpful include: documenting each partner's conditions, needs, assets, and strengths; developing a process that ensures active engagement; and identifying resource needs to support planning, implementation, evaluation, and other elements. If partners do not pay attention to these specifics up front, relationships are likely to become unnecessarily strained.

SUSTAINING PARTNERSHIPS OVER TIME

- As important as it is to initiate partnerships and set them up well from the beginning with an effective framework for collaboration, design alone is not enough. Several additional elements are also important: ensuring that all participants have a legitimate voice; creating a comprehensive plan of action that all parties embrace broadly and deeply; committing to reviewing evolving leadership needs and adjusting; reviewing and reworking partner roles as needed; and identifying appropriate metrics to measure progress, improve, and capture evidence of concrete success.
- Partners must be resilient in the face of inherent tensions and inevitable conflict. Establishing clear rules of engagement does not eliminate the conflict inherent in a relationship, but doing so will mitigate the most damaging effects and help build trust. Your partner will frustrate you. In turn, you will frustrate your partner. Your partner may let you down or you may let your partner down. Accept the challenges of partnership because together you are stronger, smarter, and have a much better chance of achieving your goals. The old Ugandan proverb says, 'Where two rivers meet, the water is never calm.' But doesn't philanthropy stir things up to enhance and improve life for everybody?[9]

---

[9] Ibid.

If we look at KKF's journey, the success of our partnerships is due to several fundamental aspects:

- Trust built between leadership and staff of both organisations with a genuine commitment to a shared agenda and focus on delivering the best possible outcomes for programme beneficiaries.
- The complementary expertise and experience that each party brings to the table – KKF with intimate familiarity of the local Saudi development context and history of social impact work, and its partners with deep ESG (Environmental, Social and Governance) content knowledge, a focus on strategy, and global experience with industry leaders, standards, and frameworks.
- Active, transparent, and honest communication throughout project lifecycles with clearly defined roles and responsibilities, all of which enable the accountability and collaboration required for successful joint delivery and innovation.
- Commitment to explaining what was accomplished so others may take up the challenge in their own communities. We are open to honest assessments of what works and what doesn't, and to making improvements along the way.
- Adaptability in the face of unexpected circumstances. The COVID-19 pandemic presented new and significant challenges to KKF and its partner programmes, which were historically planned around in-person engagement with programme beneficiaries. Due to the strength of the partnership, programmes were not only adapted to be successfully delivered virtually, but strategic decisions were also taken to capitalise on the circumstances by reallocating time, resources, and efforts.

If we summarise what successful partnership requires from participants, it would come down to the following areas:[10]

1. Recognising and relishing diversity as an asset rather than a problem.
2. Properly valuing the many different contributions each partner brings.
3. Developing new skills in partnership-building, collaboration-brokering, and collective leadership.

---

[10] Ros Tennyson, Partnership Brokers Association.

4. Identifying and describing potential barriers to partnership success and how to overcome them.
5. Understanding the systems and contexts in which partnerships operate.
6. Applying the highest standards, rigour, and accountability to all partnering endeavours.
7. Investing in the partnering process in order to optimise engagement and create the conditions for efficiency, innovation, and sustainability.
8. Commitment to the attainment of visible, measurable results. KKF works with its partners to develop a continuous improvement cycle, in which all partners use both data and empirical observation to refine strategies and assess progress.

CONCLUSION

No doubt, partnerships are hard – expect delays, rough spots, and misunderstandings, and prepare for them by always keeping in mind that collaboration offers numerous benefits. Governments gain access to much-needed additional capital and social innovation, and businesses are able to align profit with purpose, improve their practices, and attract new talent without having to build their own philanthropic institutions. NPOs and grant-makers have an opportunity to gain access to more funding, align with national development policies, and scale up proven initiatives faster.

Most importantly, partnerships build trust and help create shared prosperity. When partnerships are done well, they lead to more equitable and inclusive solutions where leaders can see and calculate the impact of their decisions for society over the long run. In turbulent and conflicted times, these elements provide a starting point for leaders of all kinds to find commonality in purpose and direction. It takes an effort but it's a win-win in the end.

5 The Whole Is Greater than the Sum

Forging and Sustaining Multi-Stakeholder Philanthropic Partnerships in Africa beyond the Pandemic

Sahra Noor

INTRODUCTION

African philanthropy and the culture of 'giving' are not new phenomena. They are ingrained in the fabric of African societies and how these communities sustain themselves. For centuries, before colonialism, aid agencies and development partners arrived in Africa, grassroots philanthropists and associations mobilised resources to address relevant issues and problems at the individual and community levels (Schwier and Holland, 2020). Religious giving, individual or institutional donations, mutual aid, diaspora remittance, and revolving fund organisations are various forms of grassroots philanthropic activities that continue to exist on the continent.

Philanthropy, however, does not exist in a vacuum. It is influenced by historical, social, and political events. Colonialism and the introduction of modern forms of philanthropy in Africa have made African giving invisible and created an image of dependency while perpetuating societal inequalities and social problems.

Peter Buffet, the son of billionaire investor Warren Buffet, has called mainstream philanthropy a 'philanthropic colonialism' (Buffett, 2013). In an editorial letter titled 'The Charitable-Industrial Complex', Mr Buffet discussed how capitalism and the legacy of colonialism shape modern giving, and the moral and ethical issues associated with it: 'As more lives and communities are destroyed by the system that creates vast amounts of wealth for the few, the more heroic it sounds to "give back". It's what I would call "conscience laundering" – feeling better about accumulating more than any one person could possibly need to live on by sprinkling a little around as an act of charity.'

This colonial mindset with regard to philanthropy is rooted in imperialism and the 'saviour' complex, and has been harmful to Africa in many ways. It not only transplants Western solutions to African problems with little regard to its local political contexts, culture, or societal norms. It also bypasses government institutions and marginalises local expertise and civil society organisations (CSOs).

For example, a research study commissioned by the Vodafone Foundation found that only 50 per cent of bilateral aid reaches Africa, and it is given to Western intermediary organisations to implement projects instead of local CSOs or institutions (Moyo and Imafidon, 2020).

Mainstream media and fundraising television ads by Western donors and non-governmental organisations (NGOs) (i.e., the United Nations Children's Fund (UNICEF), Save the Children) continue to portray Africans as needy and vulnerable people who have no sense of agency or the capacity to address their own problems. In the age of social media, these widespread images showing sickly African women and children who live in extreme poverty contribute to this representation. Most people associate Africa with poverty, disease, and vulnerability, not the wealth, cultural, and environmental diversity of its 1.2 billion people. Nor is there an understanding of the thriving African philanthropy ecosystem that is driven by generosity, solidarity, and unity between local and diaspora Africans.

Global philanthropy has been at a critical junction in recent years. The debate started by Mr Buffet and movements to localise aid and decolonise wealth have led to some reckoning within the sector. Leaders in Africa are demanding reforms, implementing bottom-up approaches to solving problems, and using financial resources to strengthen systems and institutions, and build power within communities.

In 2020, the pandemic and the killing of George Floyd in the United States, which sparked a global movement for racial and socio-economic justice, also brought greater scrutiny of charitable funds. More attention is being paid to how philanthropists address racial and societal inequities that have long existed but are now exacerbated by these recent events.

The 2014 Ebola outbreak and the resulting public health and economic crises in West Africa were turning points for the continent. It profoundly shifted the African Union (AU) Commission's role in addressing regional and continental public health issues, and forced it to take a visible part in the response efforts.

The AU sent a humanitarian mission and forged multi-sectoral partnerships to mobilise millions of dollars to curb the outbreak and protect the health and livelihoods of its fellow Africans (Musabayana, 2014). Though devastating, the crisis effectively put public health on the top of the political agenda for all AU member states.

This chapter explores the importance and impact of AU's strategic leadership and multi-sectoral partnerships in advancing the continent's health and economic agenda, the challenges inherent in sustaining and scaling these alliances in Africa, and the path forward.

BUILDING AN AFRICA-WIDE STRATEGY

During the Ebola crisis in 2014, AU and its member states began to play a leadership role in forging partnerships for public health. The AU organised its executive councils to authorise the deployment of civilian and humanitarian missions to curb the disease (Musabayana, 2016). African business leaders also partnered with AU and the Development Bank to establish an 'Ebola Crisis Fund', which raised over $28 million (BBC, 2014).

For the COVID-19 pandemic, the hoarding of diagnostics and personal protective equipment (PPE) by wealthier nations has forced many African governments, philanthropists, and business leaders to seize this as an opportunity to look inwardly for system-building and support. It dramatically increased African-led giving for pandemic responses at local and continental levels on a scale never before seen (Schwier and Holland, 2020).

The Commission organised the 'AU COVID-19 Response Fund' to mobilise up to $400 million to support a sustainable response to the pandemic. Several wealthy Africans from the private sector were recruited and appointed as AU special envoys to mobilise resources and advocate for debt relief. Debt relief was an essential component of this effort because it would allow African governments to redirect their resources towards combatting COVID-19 instead of servicing debt.

A NEW PUBLIC HEALTH ORDER

After the Ebola outbreak, AU was committed to setting up continental structures to mitigate and prevent similar public health emergencies. To achieve that goal, the AU established the Africa Centres for Disease Control and Prevention (Africa CDC) in January 2016. Africa CDC is a continental public health agency with the mandate to strengthen the capacity of each member state to prevent, control, and respond to emerging public health threats.

Less than two years after Africa CDC was formed, in July 2017, African heads of state and governments issued a commitment to accelerate the implementation of the 2005 International Health Regulations (IHR). IHR is a global legal agreement that aims to prevent and respond to the spread of diseases before they become international crises. This declaration was dubbed a 'new public health order' for Africa. Nkengasong et al. (2017) suggest the declaration 'offers a momentous opportunity for renewed engagement for strengthening health systems to accelerate the implementation of the IHR and other commitments using a broader multisector approach including public-private philanthropic partnerships'.

PARTNERSHIPS FOR PUBLIC HEALTH

The establishment of the Africa CDC and issuing a declaration and commitment to accelerate the implementation of the IHR meant that African governments were serious about investing in the development of health systems and establishing robust surveillance and data infrastructures for health.

Within a short period of time, the agency set the public health strategic direction of the continent by creating emergency operations centres, laboratory systems and networks, and several divisions dealing with topics ranging from policy, health diplomacy, surveillance and disease intelligence, to training and research (Africa CDC, 2016). These nascent systems and structures were instrumental in preparing the continent better to manage the COVID pandemic (Kapata, 2020).

As soon as the first case of COVID-19 was announced in China, Africa CDC developed an 'Africa Joint Continental Strategy for COVID-19 Outbreak' to curtail the virus and prepare the continent for pandemic response and recovery (Africa CDC, 2020). The agency's leadership in setting this continental direction was transformational. Its director, Dr John Nkengasong, has been recognised for his pandemic leadership and advocacy with numerous awards and accolades, including the 2020 Global Goal Keeper Award from the Gates Foundation (BMGF, 2020).

The Centre partnered with the AU envoys, philanthropic entities, and the private sector to launch several initiatives to strategically direct donor funds towards programmes that would strengthen Africa's public health systems and are well aligned with its strategy.

To mobilise resources for its continental strategy, Africa CDC operationalised a new charitable foundation, the Africa Public Health Foundation, in April 2020. The Foundation's sole purpose is to raise money for Africa CDC, and Sahra Noor (the author of this chapter) served as its founding director. It works as a platform for philanthropists and other partners to support Africa CDC's strategic objectives without going through the AU or other intermediaries. During the pandemic, the Foundation partnered with Africa Donor Collective (ADC), a donor group with representatives from twenty foundations, including the BMGF, the Rockefeller Foundation, and Skoll Foundation. According to the June 2021 progress report, the Foundation has a fully functioning governance body and secretariat. It raised $25 million from the ADC group to support pandemic-related activities in fourteen countries and disbursed 70 per cent of all funds received (APHF, 2021).

The Partnership to Accelerate COVID-19 Testing (PACT) was an initiative set up by the Centre to reduce COVID-19 transmission in Africa by mobilising experts, community workers, supplies, and other resources to identify and treat cases in a timely manner. PACT has enabled over 47 million tests to be taken across the continent (Mastercard Foundation, 2021a).

Seeded by a $1.5 billion donation from the Mastercard Foundation, the 'Save Lives, and Livelihoods' project supported the acquisition and delivery of vaccines to at least 50 million people while also 'laying the groundwork' for vaccine manufacturing in Africa (Mastercard Foundation, 2021b).

The Africa Pathogen Genomics Initiative (Africa PGI) is a $100-million, four-year partnership to expand access to next-generation genomic-sequencing tools and expertise designed to build the capacity of public health surveillance and laboratory networks. The initiative will help identify and inform research and public health responses to COVID-19 and other epidemics and endemic diseases like AIDS, tuberculosis, malaria, and cholera (Ayodele, 2020).

The Rise of African High Net-Worth Individuals

Africa's economy has grown exponentially since the 1990s. Subsequently, the continent has approximately 170,000 millionaires with more than $660 billion combined net wealth holdings. From 2000 to 2013, Africa's wealthiest individuals increased by more than 150 per cent compared to the worldwide growth rate of 73 per cent (Tendai, 2018). The number of Africans with more than $30 million in assets is projected to double by 2025, representing a growth of 59 per cent compared to the global figure of 34 per cent for the same period (Tendai, 2018).

This economic growth and rise of wealthy Africans offer a new path for the continent to harness the potential of its people and local resources. Some of these high net-worth individuals (HNWIs) are active philanthropists operating family foundations and supporting various sectors such as health, education, entrepreneurial development, and infrastructure. The most notable wealthy Africans are from affluent countries, including South Africa, Nigeria, Egypt, and Kenya. They include Aliko Dangote, Nicky Oppenheimer, Patrice Motsepe, Mohammed Dewji, Strive and Tsitsi Masiyiwa, Olajumoke Adenowo, and Ndidi Nwuneli (Sieff, 2018).

AFRICAN-LED GIVING

According to research by the Bridgespan Group, African philanthropists gave seven times their annual average number of major gifts to help the continent respond to the COVID-19 pandemic. Among the giving, the Bridgespan Group found that forty-five large donations between March and December 2020 in three countries totalled roughly $269 million in value compared to sixty-four large gifts of $1 million or more than the group identified between 2010 and 2019 (Schwier, 2020)

According to a new survey developed by Dalberg in partnership with the African Philanthropy Forum, 71 per cent of philanthropists who are focused on the continent have either increased their giving as a share of endowments or are considering doing so in response to COVID-19. Their contributions primarily target health care, economic recovery, and food security issues (Mwangi, 2020).

This African-led giving falls into two categories: (1) cash donations and in-kind items intended to strengthen the ability of private and public health-care providers to respond to the crisis, and (2) investments in start-ups and existing businesses that aid in addressing the economic fallout caused by mandatory lockdowns and other measures instituted by different national governments to slow the spread of the virus (Mwathi, 2017).

IMPACTFUL LOCAL PARTNERSHIPS

Beyond projects initiated or led by AU and Africa CDC, various multisectoral approaches are used to fund COVID-19 response activities in local communities to manage and recover from the pandemic. These initiatives have been facilitated through locally led philanthropic funding and implementation.

South Africa's Solidarity Fund was created as a fundraising and rapid response platform to help the government, philanthropists, the private sector, and the general public collaborate and coordinate efforts to fight the pandemic. The Fund has supported multiple health and humanitarian projects, including refurbishing hospitals, paying health workforce salaries, distributing PPE to health-care workers, and rolling out vaccination campaigns across the country. As of December 2021, the Fund had raised 45 billion South African rand, equivalent to 3 billion US dollars (Solidarity Fund, 2021).

Amref Health Africa, the most prominent African charity focused solely on health development, has partnered with the different Ministries of Health (MoH) in East Africa to improve surveillance and early detection of the virus. In Kenya, the MoH has partnered with Amref Health Africa to launch a campaign to educate health workers on COVID-19 by leveraging an innovative mobile network technology known as Leap mHealth. The Leap platform equips health workers to identify, isolate, and refer suspected cases and prevent possible transmission through community education and other prevention measures (Ntonjira, 2020). Amref onboarded over 74,000 community health workers onto the platform.

In Somalia, the Hormuud Salaam Foundation, the charitable entity of two of the largest corporations in the country, formed a partnership with the government and other private-sector leaders to fund COVID-19 response efforts. The Foundation alone funded the dissemination of health awareness messages, refurbished hospitals, and built Somalia's first public oxygen plant (*ADF Magazine*, 2021).

Somalia is one of twenty-two out of the fifty-five African countries classified in 2021 as 'fragile or conflict-affected countries' by the World Bank.[1] These countries face unique governance, political,

---

[1] www.worldbank.org/en/region/afr/overview#1.

and economic challenges not shared by wealthier, more stable countries on the continent. For example, they have populations that live in extreme poverty, and their governance and health systems have been decimated by war and civil conflict, yet the flow of money is inhibited by threats of violence, terrorism, and international sanctions. Local private-sector leadership and philanthropic funding partnerships are essential in buffering the economy. They also help fill institutional gaps and strengthen the government's capacity to curb the disease and save lives.

TRANSFORMATIONAL PLATFORM

The COVID-19 pandemic posed a significant threat to the supply chain of medical commodities, products, and pharmaceuticals. To help African countries procure pandemic-related medical supplies and equipment, the AU launched the African Medical Supplies Platform (AMSP), the world's first continental digital procurement platform.[2]

This game-changing platform was developed by the AU and its Special Envoy, Zimbabwean billionaire Strive Masiyiwa. It is powered by Janngo, an African-led social enterprise that invests in pan-African digital companies. Funding partners include the African Export-Import Bank (Afreximbank), the United Nations (UN) Economic Commission for Africa (ECA), and leading institutions, foundations, corporations, and multilateral partners (Gachenge et al., 2020).

AMSP is anchored in the African Continental Free Trade Agreement (ACFTA). This trade agreement is embedded in the Agenda 2063 of the AU, signed by fifty-four countries. It requires members to remove tariffs from 90 per cent of goods, allowing free access to commodities and services (Kelleher, 2021). To level the playing field between public and private health sectors, purchases made through AMSP are restricted to governments, national health systems, NGOs, and donor organisations (Gachenge et al., 2020).

---

[2] https://amsp.africa/about-us/.

The AMSP has revolutionised Africa's response to the pandemic, and its impact on leveraging Africa's bulk-purchasing power to secure COVID-19-related medicines, vaccines, and supplies was felt immediately.

Pooling continental demand ensured price competitiveness, improved quality and availability of products, simplified payment processes, and reduced logistical bottlenecks. The platform now offers a wide range of health supplies and equipment to meet the needs of Africa's health sector beyond the pandemic (Crone, 2020).

AMSP's plans include an aggressive vaccine procurement effort to help the African Vaccine Acquisition Task Team (AVATT), established by the AU chairperson. AVATT has secured 570 million doses from Pfizer, Johnson & Johnson, AstraZeneca, and Sputnik V (Donnenfeld, 2021). It also facilitates the supply of medicines and vaccines from the Novartis Pandemic Response Portfolio to the AU member states.

As an e-commerce platform, AMSP has bigger ambitions to address historical and emerging procurement challenges. The platform's future plans include boosting indigenous pharmaceutical production by establishing an open licence for enlisting local manufacturers and featuring 'Made in Africa' options on the first page. Such incentives could motivate the diversification of operations by African companies to address the demand and supply mismatch for protective equipment and COVID-19 supplies in Africa (Ramaphosa, 2020).

RISKS AND CHALLENGES

While generosity and informal philanthropy are substantial on the African continent, some significant risks and constraints must be overcome to sustain and grow Global South–Global North philanthropic partnerships. Corruption, lack of tax incentives and other enabling environments, and political instability in some parts of Africa pose a great risk to the continent's ability to attract local and global philanthropic and development resources.

Corruption and Lack of Enabling Environments

Historical events, including international sanctions, anti-terror, and anti-money laundering policies have limited inter-continental money flow (Messick, 2020) and continue to fuel donor apprehension.

Rampant corruption, money laundering, and a lack of transparency harm Africa's image and ability to build trust among diverse stakeholders and shepherd these fragile alliances (David, 2021). Admittedly, this issue is often hyped by the media and international donors and is used to stigmatise and marginalise the continent. However, there is strong evidence to suggest it exists, and it must be curtailed for the sake of Africa and its people. Given the public perception and its pervasiveness, it is difficult for multisectoral partnerships to thrive without curbing public and private corruption.

Limited tax policies and a lack of regulatory frameworks that meet global standards, promote and incentivise giving, and facilitate the cross-border flow of money are also challenging. Some countries impose burdensome bureaucratic and procedural requirements for foreign donations or require mandatory routing of foreign funding through government channels.

Stewardship and Transparency

During crises, it's normal to see donor enthusiasm increase contributions, but this can overwhelm and potentially collapse the systems they are intended to support. This can also lead to or at least incentivise increased corruption and misappropriation of funds. Identifying the sweet spot where adequate donor funds flow unrestricted and reach the target beneficiaries is critical. Continuously assessing capacity and supporting government and CSOs' accounting systems can improve transparency and accountability. Trust is a precious commodity in philanthropy, and collaborative decision-making can facilitate communication on how, when, and where funds are spent.

Systems Change versus Incremental Change

Global colonial philanthropy tends to entrench African governments and communities in survivalism and competition while preventing a radical change in the name of pragmatism. It hasn't worked and perpetuates inequities and mistrust. To advance more just and equitable systems, funding partnerships must be both catalytic and impactful, and focusing on incremental change in outputs and activities is short-sighted. The funding collaborations between local and global philanthropy must pair knowledge, expertise, and existing networks to achieve tangible and sustainable change.

Given its rapid demographic changes and technological advances, Africa requires funders and investors who can adapt to a fluid environment that demands more strategic and systematic investment approaches.

The AU must play a continental leadership role in mitigating these risks and implementing solutions to address these challenges to secure the flow of philanthropic support across the continent and prevent the rich and powerful from grabbing the resources meant for the poor. Political will is a must, but there is room for government and philanthropic co-operational collaboration, including investing in human capital, financial systems, and the sustainable policies required to deal with this issue.

THE PATH FORWARD

Forging partnerships is essential, but it also carries risks for all involved. Each partner has to accept the challenge, invest time and resources without guaranteeing that others will do the same, adapt to dynamic ways of working together and prevent opportunism. One of the destructive elements of philanthropic practice has been using money as a substitute for local knowledge and expertise. No one wants to be in partnership when they think they are being used for image and reputation. Identifying the right partner and building mutual benefits that multiply impact are key to relationship-building.

OPPORTUNITIES FOR CONTINUED COLLABORATION

Philanthropic partnerships aimed at the COVID-19 response have been chiefly led by AU and Africa CDC, closely coordinated with local governments, civil society, and the private sectors. The response has been fuelled by generous donations from Africans and global partners. This large-scale collaboration and international solidarity are noteworthy and encouraging, but tenuous. As the pandemic went into its third year, sustaining partnerships became increasingly challenging due to complacency, reduced investment and donor fatigue. But it doesn't have to be that way.

Collaborative philanthropy that combines African philanthropists' insights with Western donors' global experience is imperative to boost efforts to reduce the burdens of poverty, ill-health, and injustice.

LEADERSHIP MATTERS

The pandemic has amplified the need for government inclusion and leadership, along with the positive impact of African-led collective action. At the height of the pandemic, this shared purpose and aligned interests increased the coordination and reach of response activities. This unprecedented scale of giving and coalition-building can serve as a springboard to create systemic and sustainable change if understood and executed on a continental-wide institutional level.

One of the lessons learned from the supply hoarding and vaccine apartheid seen during the COVID-19 crisis is that Africans must be their own saviours. These inequities serve as a rallying cry for the unity of purpose that is not solely driven by responses to public health or humanitarian emergencies but is rooted in self-reliance and interdependence to improve the quality of life for the continent's citizens.

As much as it enrages our leaders and upends Africa's bilateral and multilateral political relationships, it also provides an opportunity for the AU and African governments to continuously assert their leadership and vision for creating an internal sustainable resource base for holistic development.

HUMILITY GOES A LONG WAY

'Decolonise wealth' or 'decolonise aid' are not just social media slogans. They are grassroots movements stemmed in social justice, demanding greater equity and systems change (Villanueva, 2019).

Creating the conditions for enduring and trusting partnerships requires an end to the status quo and an earnest shift in how global philanthropy and development funding has historically operated in Africa. It demands an end to the transfer of financial resources meant for Africa through Western intermediaries instead of going directly to African-led NGOs or implementing partners. Regardless of the intended impact of this practice, the nature of the pandemic means that no foreign entity can operate alone or in silos without partnering and engaging African stakeholders.

Sharing power and relinquishing control are challenges that can be overcome by focusing on the value potential partners bring to the table. Building relationships with the right stakeholders willing to engage in an ongoing, open, and honest dialogue requires humility.

EXPANDING CHARITABLE VISION FOR PARTNERSHIPS

To bring everyone to the table, philanthropy must be grounded in what African countries and beneficiaries want and need versus what Western individuals and nations think they want.

Magic happens when partnerships are formed and sustained to engage everyone in the decision-making process and not dismiss constructive criticisms that inevitably arise along the journey.

For global funders new to the continent or those interested in doing things differently, leveraging the influence of African foundations whose projects get broader support across Africa may be beneficial. These donors have a track history of local partnerships and regional relationships to build capacity and promote best practices with their peers. Trusted partners can serve as ambassadors to inspire others to remain engaged in partnership-building during and after public health crises. They can advocate for more collective action to complement and advance the continent's strategic public health and development goals.

Furthermore, most diaspora Africans and HNWIs tend to fund and support programmes and projects in their local countries because it is easier to manage how the funds reach beneficiaries and track their contributions (Ansah, 2018). Expanding their charitable vision transnationally and harmonising their giving to continental priorities will ensure their impact on the continent for generations.

Powell et al. (2018) argue that when executed well, funder collaboratives can achieve significant results by creating economies of scale, but, to be sustainable, they need to articulate how their collective action will create value for beneficiaries, grantees, and themselves. Among the most reported benefits were greater ability to drive systems-level impact, greater reputation boost, and more or better non-financial support. The researchers also noted the importance of the positive emotional effects such as trust-building and networking that these collaborations have on individual leaders and organisations who actively participate in them.

FORMALISE PEER LEARNING

There is so much that is still unknown about partnerships, especially those that have been formed in response to public health crises. Facilitation of multi-sector philanthropy forums and gatherings adapted to the African context can help disseminate good practice models, tools, and strategies that can be replicated. They can create opportunities for private philanthropists to engage with the state at several levels and promote peer-to-peer exchange.

Corporations and HNWIs could be engaged more if governments provided them with opportunities and platforms for thought-leadership and advisory roles. AU appointing Strive Masiyiwa and other HNWIs as Special Envoys for policies and causes they care about is a good start, but more must be done to give such envoys wider exposure and help bridge the transparency gap.

Philanthropy networks, including the African Philanthropy Forum and other regional forums, provide platforms for philanthropists to engage in emerging topics and issues. They could be more strategic in engaging governments, supporting and increasing the pool of HNWIs, and aligning their giving to the continental development agenda. Spaces for sharing knowledge and experience with peers need to be more tailored to the nature of giving by the wealthy in the African context.

STUDY AND DISSEMINATE BEST PRACTICE

Engaging academia and supporting thematic research on existing partnerships in Africa, their impact, and lessons learned may provide more in-depth understanding of what works and what does not. Research can help all stakeholders have a clearer vision about how to solve problems and help them embrace evidence-based tools to measure impact. Funding and programmatic partnerships often conflate programme activities and outcomes with effectiveness. Investing in independent research and evaluations and other processes helps partnerships communicate more effectively to broader audiences and become vehicles for learning and growth for the sector, and holds partners accountable for their own contributions.

THE WHOLE IS GREATER THAN THE SUM

Collaboration is key to creating lasting solutions to society's biggest problems. Drawing on the lessons learned from the Dalberg report on African philanthropy, locally led giving has become focused, innovative, and fast-paced in response to crises. Yet, it can't transform the lives of Africans without building broad-based partnerships with the government and other stakeholders on the continent and beyond (Mwangi, 2020).

An African proverb says, 'it takes a village to raise a child', and it aptly applies to public-philanthropic-private partnerships. We know that UN set the vision for poverty elimination, but it alone did not lift more than 1 billion people out of extreme poverty since 1990 (UN,

2015). That level of achievement was only possible through long-term commitment and multilateral and multi-sectoral partnerships.

As Africa tries to fully vaccinate its population against COVID-19, prepare for future emergencies, and recover economies, mobilising its own resources will prove transformational. However, it will also need to bring on board its global donors, along with bilateral and multilateral partners to address gaps in scientific research, marginalisation, inequity, and the zero-sum premise of international power competition experienced on the continent.

Kituyi (2020) argues that global collaboration is crucial now more than ever: 'There is strength in numbers. We learn more, and faster, together – and the pandemic is underscoring the critical role of international collaboration on the frontiers of science and technology.' Yet the focus on partnerships and cooperation must remain on placing Africans at the forefront of philanthropic giving. The paradigm of Africans as helpless, barefoot, and hungry, and Western donors as saviours, has shifted permanently. Gone are the days when international donors and development partners parachuted projects and shoved their ideas onto Africans as needy beneficiaries who lack vision, creativity, and agency.

Africans have demonstrated unprecedented leadership and generosity in recent years. They are well positioned to ensure that charitable resources are deployed, with a deep understanding of the nature of the challenges they are intended to solve. As Africa recovers from the pandemic, it will need a new form of philanthropy that is collaborative, grounded in Africans' reality, and represents their vision and aspirations for the future.

REFERENCES

ADF Magazine. 2021. Somalia Opens First Oxygen Plant during Pandemic.

Africa CDC (Centres for Disease Control). 2016. *Africa Centres for Disease Control*. https://africacdc.org/about-us/.

Africa CDC (Centres for Disease Control). 2020. *Africa Joint Continental Strategy for COVID-19 Outbreak*. Africa CDC.

Africa CDC and AU (Africa Centres for Disease Control and Africa Union). 2020. *Partnership to Accelerate COVID-19 Testing (PACT) in Africa – Resources*, June.

Ansah, T. K. 2018. African Philanthropy for Africa is the Future. *Alliance Magazine*.

APHF (Africa Public Health Foundation). 2021. *Mobilizing Funds and Partnerships*. Africa Public Health Foundation.

Ayodele, J. 2020. US$100 Million Africa Pathogen Genomics Initiative to Boost Disease Surveillance and Emergency Response Capacity in Africa. *Africa CDC*. https://africacdc.org/news-item/us100-million-africa-pathogen-genomics-initiative-to-boost-disease-surveillance-and-emergency-response-capacity-in-africa/.

BBC. 2014. Ebola Outbreak: Africa Sets Up $28.5M Crisis Fund.

BMGF (Bill & Melinda Gates Foundation). 2020. Gates Foundation Honors Director of Africa CDC with 2020 Global Goalkeeper Award. *The Optimist*. www.gatesfoundation.org/ideas/media-center/press-releases/2020/09/gates-foundation-honors-director-of-africa-cdc-with-2020-global-goalkeeper-award.

Buffett, P. 2013. The Charitable-Industrial Complex. *The New York Times*, July, 26.

Crone, D. 2020. *Insights from Africa's COVID-19 Response: The Africa CDC*. Tony Blair Institute for Global Change.

David, L. 2021. *What Does Philanthropy Mean for Africa?* Philanthropy Circuit.

Donnenfeld, Z. 2021. *Africa Medical Supplies Platform: A Model for the World*. Institute for Security Studies.

Gachenge, B., Althoff, E., Lucking, K., and Ligi, A. 2020. *New Collaboration between Novartis and Africa Medical Supplies Platform to Facilitate Supply of COVID-19 Related Medicines*. Novartis.

Kapata, N., Ihekweazu, C., Ntoumi, F., Raji, T., Chanda-Kapata, P., Mwaba, P., and Mukonka, V. 2020. Is Africa Prepared for Tackling the COVID-19 (SARS-CoV-2) Epidemic? Lessons from Past Outbreaks, Ongoing Pan-African Public Health Efforts, and Implications for the Future. *International Journal of Infectious Diseases*, 90, 233–236.

Kelleher, F. 2021. *The African Continental Free Trade Area (AfCFTA) and Women: A Pan African Feminist Analysis*. FEMNET.

Kituyi, M. 2020. *Covid 19: Collaboration Is the Engine of Global Science – Especially for Developing Countries*. https://stli.iii.org.tw/en/article-detail .aspx?no=105&tp=2&i=171&d=8564.

Leland, O. 2017. A New Model of Collaborative Philanthropy. *Stanford Social Innovation Review*. https://ssir.org/articles/entry/a_new_model_of_collaborative_philanthropy.

Mastercard Foundation. 2021a. *Mastercard Foundation to Deploy $1.3 Billion Partnership with Africa CDC to Save Lives and Livelihoods*, 8 June. https://mastercardfdn.org/mastercard-foundation-to-deploy-1-3-billion-in-partnership-with-africa-cdc-to-save-lives-and-livelihoods/.

Mastercard Foundation. 2021b. *Saving Lives and Livelihoods*. Mastercard Foundation.

Medinilla, A., Byiers, B., and Apiko, P. 2020. *African Regional Responses to COVID 19*. European Centre for Development Policy Management (ECDPM) Discussion Paper No. 272.

Messick, R. 2020. Combating Money Laundering in Africa: John Hatchard's Latest Guide for African Corruption Fighters. *GAB | The Global Anticorruption Blog.* https://globalanticorruptionblog.com/2020/12/02/combating-money-laundering-in-africa-john-hatchards-latest-guide-for-african-corruption-fighters/.

Moyo, B., and Imafidon, K. 2020. *Barriers to African Civil Society: Building the Sectors' Capacity and Potential to Scale-Up*. Vodacom Foundation.

Musabayana, W. 2014. *The African Union Commission Pledges One Million to Ebola Response*. World Health Organization.

Musabayana, W. 2016. *The African Union's Intervention in the Ebola Crisis was a Game Changer*, 11 February. African Union.

Mwangi, J. 2020. *The Role of African Philanthropy in Responding to COVID-19*. Dalberg.

Mwathi, J. 2017. *Philanthropy in Contemporary Africa: A Review*. Brill.

Nkengasong, J., Djoudalbaye, B., and Maiyegun, O. 2017. A New Public Health Order for Africa's Health Security. *The Lancet Global Health*, 5(11), e1064–e1065.

Ntonjira, E. 2020. *Amref Health Africa Supporting Ministries of Health in Africa in Strengthening the Response to the Novel Coronavirus (COVID-19) Pandemic in the African Continent*, 13 March. https://newsroom.amref .org/press-releases/2020/03/amref-health-africa-supporting-ministries-of-health-in-africa-in-strengthening-response-to-the-novel-coronavirus-covid-19-pandemic-in-the-african-continent/.

Powell, A., Wolf Ditkoff, S., and Hassey, K. 2018. *Value of Collaboration Research Study: Literature Review on Funder Collaboration*. Taylor & Francis.

Ramaphosa, C. 2020. *Launch of Africa Medical Supplies Platform Media Briefing*, 18 June. www.gov.za/speeches/medical-supplies-platform-19-jun-2020-0000.

Schwier, J. 2020. *The Landscape of Large-Scale Giving by African Philanthropists*. The Bridgespan Group.

Schwier, J., and Holland, M. 2020. How African Philanthropy Responds in a Crisis. *Alliance Magazine*.

Sieff, M. 2018. Home Grown Help: The Rise of Africa's New Philanthropists. *Inside Philanthropy.*

Solidarity Fund. 2021. *Solidarity Fund Health Response Report.* Solidarity Fund.

Tendai, M. 2018. *African Philanthropy: Evolution, Practice and Change.* Research Gate.

UN (United Nations). 2015. *Goal 1: End Poverty in All its Forms Everywhere.* www.un.org/sustainabledevelopment/poverty/.

Villanueva, E. 2019. Money as Medicine: Leveraging Philanthropy to Decolonize Wealth. *Non Profit Quarterly*, 29 June.

Wigley, A. 2020. Philanthropy is Responding to HE's COVID-19 Challenges. *University World News*, 21 November.

6 Gender-Based Violence in South Africa and Multi-Stakeholder Partnerships

The Vodacom Foundation Experience

Takalani Netshitenzhe

INTRODUCTION

Gender-based violence (GBV) comprises one of the grossest human rights violations globally, and spiralled during the COVID-19 pandemic. It is referred to by United Nations Women as 'harmful acts directed at an individual or a group of individuals based on their gender. It is rooted in gender inequality, the abuse of power and harmful norms'.[1] South Africa, a constitutional democracy founded on the values of human rights and human dignity, has some of the world's highest levels of GBV, leading the country's president to declare GBV the second pandemic. Acknowledgement exists that GBV is systematic and addressing it effectively requires a comprehensive approach focused on prevention, response, and victim/survivor support through multi-stakeholder partnerships. Since 1994, the South African government – a signatory to UN frameworks on the protection of women – has put myriad of measures in place to address GBV but to little avail. With each government administration since 1994, GBV is of great concern, and in recent years, it is clear from media reports and the quarterly police statistics that the levels continue unabated. The causes of GBV are multifaceted and include cultural, legal, political, and economic factors,[2] and South Africa's violence

---

[1] UN Women, 'Frequently asked questions,' www.unwomen.org/en/what-we-do/ending-violence-against-women/faqs/types-of-violence#:~:text=Gender-based%20violence%20(GBV),of%20power%20and%20harmful%20norms.

[2] Council of Europe, 'Gender Matters: What Causes Gender-Based Violence?', www.coe.int/en/web/gender-matters/what-causes-gender-based-violence.

culture can also be traced to the apartheid era where violence was normalised as a response to resistance.

A rising phenomenon alongside GBV in South Africa is femicide, where women or perceived women are killed on the basis of gender identity.[3] In recent years, following a spate of horrific GBV reports and femicide, civil society organisations (CSOs) heightened their activism and started demanding decisive actions from government. This activism led to government in 2018 recommitting to a social compact with the business and civil-society sectors to step up the fight against GBV and femicide through the National Strategic Plan on Gender-Based Violence and Femicide (NSP). The NSP provides for 'accountability, coordination and leadership; prevention and rebuilding social cohesion; justice, safety and protection; response, care, support and healing; economic power; and research and information management'.[4] Where multi-stakeholder partnerships are forged, each partner must bring their own area of expertise to complement the others. The government, as the policymaker, should develop pragmatic policies and create a conducive environment in

---

[3] Department of Justice and Constitutional Development, 'What Is Femicide?', www .justice.gov.za/vg/femicide/docs.html.

[4] In 2019, an Interim Steering Committee (ISC) on GBV and femicide established by President Cyril Ramaphosa following a multi-party stakeholder summit, produced 'an Emergency Response Action Plan (ERAP)' providing for:

- 'Urgent response to victims and survivors of GBV.
- Broadening access to justice for survivors.
- Changing social norms and behaviour through high-level awareness raising and prevention campaigns.
- Strengthening existing architecture and promoting accountability.
- The creation of more economic opportunities for women who are vulnerable to abuse because of poverty.'

The ISC also developed the NSP with the following pillars:

- 'Accountability, Coordination and Leadership.
- Prevention and Rebuilding the Social Cohesion.
- Justice, Safety and Protection.
- Response, Care, Support and Healing.
- Economic Power, and
- Research and Information Management.'

which the other partners can operate; business and especially big business must bring agility and technical resources in the implementation of policies; and civil society must be the ears and eyes that hold both government and business accountable.[5] Vodacom

[5] Below is a summary of some laws on GBV, some of which were amended by the Parliament of the Republic of South Africa in 2021 and 2022 as part of President Ramaphosa's reform package:

- The Domestic Violence Act (Act 116 of 1998), which was amended in 2021, to inter alia, expand on definitions related to domestic violence, reporting of domestic or suspected domestic violence against vulnerable groups, authorisation for arrest without a warrant under certain circumstances, and simplification of the process of application for protection orders.
- The Sexual Offence and Related Matters Act (Act 32 of 2007), which was amended in 2021 as the Criminal Law (Sexual Offences and Related Matters) Amendment Act to inter alia amplify the national register for sex offenders; ensure children of a certain age are not held criminally liable for engaging in consensual sex; define sexual offences; and make it a duty to report sexual offences against vulnerable persons.
- The Protection from Harassment Act (Act 17 of 2011), whose main objective is the issuing of protection orders against general and sexual harassment, including the management of firearms involved in harassment.
- The Children's Act (Act 38 of 2005), which was amended in 2022 to further protect children from, amongst other issues, maltreatment, neglect, abuse, or degradation.
- Combating of Trafficking in Persons Act (Act 7 of 2013), which is aimed at combating human trafficking and effecting international agreements or instruments on human trafficking.
- The Criminal and Related Matters Amendment Bill, which was tabled in parliament in 2021 to amend the Magistrates Courts Act, 1944; the Criminal Procedure Act, 1977; the Criminal Law Amendment Act, 1997; and the Superior Courts Act, 2013, to inter alia impose stricter conditions for the granting of bail for criminal offences linked to GBV; allowing for virtual court proceedings; allowing victims of domestic violence to participate in parole proceedings; and regulating sentences for crimes committed against vulnerable people.
- The Prescription in Civil and Criminal Matters (Sexual Offences) Amendment Act (Act 15 of 2020), which amends the Prescription Act of 1969 to list sexual offences for which prescription does not run under certain circumstances and to amend the Criminal Procedure Act of 1977.
- Victim Support Services Bill of 2019 (not yet law), whose objective is to protect the rights of victims of violent crime against victimisation and ensure care, support, response, empowerment, and shelter for the said persons, with responsibilities assigned to relevant government departments and other stakeholders.
- Policy on the Prevention and Management of Learner Pregnancy in Schools General Notice 704 of 2021, issued by the Minister of Basic Education, whose objective is to minimise learner pregnancy through various interventions.

(Proprietary) Limited,[6] known as 'Vodacom South Africa', and its Foundation have been prominent partners in the fight against GBV since the early 2000s, working closely with government institutions and providing funding to CSOs that champion the rights of women and children. The Vodacom Foundation's partnership with both government and CSOs contributes to addressing policy implementation weaknesses including lack of access to reporting tools, toxic societal norms, rising teenage pregnancies, inaccurate reporting, and inadequate victim/survivor support and empowerment – including the government's inadequate support of CSOs at the forefront of the fight against GBV. The next sections examine how the Vodacom Foundation uses its resources to support the government and CSOs to address societal and policy challenges.

The Role of the Vodacom Foundation and Its Partners in the Fight against Gender-Based Violence

Founded in 1999, the Vodacom Foundation – the charitable arm of Vodacom South Africa – established itself as a pioneer of societal change by partnering with the government and CSOs to address challenges in education, health, and gender equality. Driven by the belief that companies are part of the society in which they operate, in 2017 the Vodacom Foundation streamlined its activities and adopted three of Vodacom South Africa's eight Sustainable Development Goals (SDGs) with an understanding that the goals are interrelated: education, gender equality, and partnerships, with technology as an anchor.[7] Under education, the Foundation has now created an education ecosystem that spans thirteen schools of excellence. The

---

[6] Vodacom South Africa is a subsidiary of Vodacom Group Limited, known as the Vodacom Group, and both are based in Midrand, South Africa. Vodacom Group is a subsidiary of Vodafone Group PLC, which is based in the United Kingdom. The Vodacom Foundation is the charitable arm of Vodacom South Africa, and the Vodafone Foundation is a UK registered charity (No. 1193984) under Vodafone Group and oversees twenty-seven foundations, which includes the Vodacom Foundation.

[7] The Foundation's revised strategy was approved in 2017 and subsequently in 2021.

ecosystem provides a comprehensive approach to education where the focus is not just on the learners, teachers, and infrastructure, but also on psychosocial support to address societal ills like GBV that hinder learner performance and educational outcomes. Under gender equality, the Foundation runs gender empowerment initiatives that support women and youth development, staff and public volunteering, and the fight against GBV. The latter serves as the flagship project in partnership with the Department of Social Development (DSD) and various CSOs. The GBV programme has now matured into an ecosystem that supports prevention, response, and victim/survivor empowerment, as outlined in what follows.

RESPONSE

One of the weaknesses in the fight against GBV is inadequate reporting and inaccurate statistics. In order to encourage victims of GBV to report abuse and ensure effective monitoring of the reporting, in 2013 the DSD approached the Vodacom Foundation to assist with setting up the GBV Command Centre. The Centre, which is currently managed by social workers from the DSD, is technology-driven through a short message system, voice, Unstructured Supplementary Service Data (USSD), video-conferencing, geo-location, and a data-capturing dashboard.[8]

The social workers, including a sign language specialist, take calls and provide confidential counselling to the callers. Depending on severity, they refer some cases to the police, community based-social workers, and shelters that house the victims of GBV. Although the Command Centre was created to respond to GBV, it also accepts calls on other societal challenges, some of which have a direct or indirect link to GBV, such as alcohol abuse, poverty, and joblessness.[9]

Inconsistencies in GBV reporting were glaring in 2020 at the onset of the COVID-19 pandemic national lockdown, when a number

[8] Republic of South Africa, Department of Social Development and Vodacom Foundation, https://gbv.org.za/about-us/ and https://vodacom.com/vodacom-foundation.php.
[9] See https://gbv.org.za/about-us/.

of general calls were conflated with GBV-related calls. A statement by the Minister of Police in the first month of the lockdown indicated that about 87,000 GBV calls were received through the National Joint Operations and Intelligence Structure (NATJOINTS) since the declaration of lockdown, and a few days later the Minister was reported to have said 2,300 cases of GBV were recorded in the first few days of the COVID-19 lockdown.[10] A Member of the Executive Council for Gauteng Social Development reportedly mentioned more than 120,000 such cases were recorded in the first three weeks of the national lockdown.[11] Further reports from non-governmental stakeholders noted tripled GBV cases received by the Command Centre in the first week of the lockdown.[12] Indeed, the number of GBV cases dramatically increased globally during the pandemic, and South Africa was not an exception, especially because GBV has always been a concern there. However, contradicting statistics from different sources published in the media were of great concern. As a partner that supplies communication technology to the GBV Command Centre, the Foundation deemed it necessary to pay special attention to the reported calls through the dashboard. By logging and monitoring all daily calls accepted by the social workers, it found the following trends:

- In 2019, the Command Centre recorded 96,620 calls, of which 1,846 were GBV-related.
- In April 2020, during the first month of the lockdown 23,041 calls were recorded, of which 690 were GBV-related.

[10] Bheki Cele, South Africa Minister of Police, 'Police Received About 87 000 Calls Related to Gender-Based Violence during Lockdown', 3 April 2020, https://youtu.be/uclZSledrZE; and 'Cele Welcomes Drop in Crime but Gender Based Violence Cases Still High', 5 April 2020, www.iol.co.za/news/south-africa/cele-welcomes-drop-in-crime-but-gender-based-violence-cases-still-high-46262416.

[11] See 'SA Records over 100 000 GBV Cases during Lockdown', 6 September 2021, www.sanews.gov.za/south-africa/Sa-records-over-100-000-GBV-cases-during-lockdown.

[12] See 'GBV Centre Calls Triple during Lockdown, 1st for Women Steps Up to Help', 2 April 2020, www.iol.co.za/news/south-africa/western-cape/gbv-centre-calls-triple-during-lockdown-1st-for-women-steps-up-to-help-45995727; and 'Shocking Stats on Gender-Based Violence during Lockdown Revealed', 1 September 2022, www.timeslive.co.za/amp/news/south-africa/2020-09-01-shocking-stats-on-gender-based-violence-during-lockdown-revealed/.

- In 2020, 180,909 calls were recorded, of which 6,726 were GBV-related.
- In 2021, 80,156 calls were recorded, of which 5,102 were GBV-related.

Social workers noted an escalation of calls during the hard lockdown levels 5 and 4 in 2020 when people's movement was most restricted; the highest number of calls was recorded in Gauteng Province, followed by Kwazulu-Natal and the Western Cape.[13] Close monitoring of the Command Centre dashboard helps ensure that accurate statistics are released from the Command Centre, so as not to mislead the public. This way, social workers are able to filter the calls to isolate GBV-related calls from general calls. However, the Command Centre is just one of the mechanisms provided by government to report on GBV cases. Some cases are reported directly to the police through the NATJOINTS and other emergency service numbers. However, these platforms are not integrated to give a single view of the cases, thereby contributing to contradictory reports.

Misaligned reporting on GBV is concerning and requires improvement, and this matter is now a priority for the Gender-Based Violence and Femicide Response Fund (GBVFRF) comprising private-sector business leaders and other professionals, which was established in 2019 to assist with fundraising to support programmes on GBV and femicide under the NSP. The GBVFRF has established a dashboard which attempts to provide comprehensive visibility and a monitoring tool of available data from some government platforms on GBV and femicide in South Africa, as the first step towards an integrated national reporting system.[14]

Although the Command Centre receives thousands of calls from desperate callers year on year, and is a vital platform to assist victims of GBV and perpetrators, after eight years there are areas that require attention to improve the quality of service:

---

[13] Foundation Board Quarterly Reports, 29 October 2020 (unpublished). The dashboard records daily calls from all technologies – voice, SMS, USSD. Video-conferencing calls are minimal and are reported manually.

[14] GBVF statistics dashboards, https://gbvfresponsefund1.org.

- The Command Centre has protocols on the turnaround time for answering calls, but the Foundation is aware of occasional service disruptions. Unfortunately, unlike with sales call centres where there is a customer service feedback mechanism, the Command Centre does not have a caller feedback mechanism to rate the service, and this feedback mechanism is required.
- Due to the confidentiality of the cases, Vodacom does not receive reports on referrals to other institutions, number of cases investigated, or those that have been successfully prosecuted. Whilst confidentiality is key, anonymous statistics would go a long way to enable monitoring and evaluation, in order to measure the impact of the Command Centre services, to instil confidence in the criminal justice system, and to encourage reporting.
- The technology requires upgrades to align with the emerging digital transformation developments. For instance, the video-conferencing facility may need upgrades to align with most commonly used platforms since the COVID-19 pandemic to ensure inter-operability for callers. Big data analytics which have now become an integral part of Vodacom South Africa's operations can be introduced to assist with caller experience, and with social workers' performance and decision-making, especially referrals.

VICTIM AND SURVIVOR EMPOWERMENT

Anyone can call the GBV Command Centre irrespective of social and economic class; perpetrators also call to seek counselling. However, most GBV victims are from lower social and economic classes who are economically and emotionally dependent on the abuser. This dependency is exacerbated by the high levels of poverty, unemployment, and inequality in South Africa; and women, children and youth are the most vulnerable. For these reasons, the NSP identified economic empowerment as one of its pillars in the fight against GBV and femicide. Although victim and survivor empowerment is pivotal in order to break the cycle of GBV, especially for underprivileged people who have no access to support services, the government's policy and support for victims through shelters is vague. Various reports found that the majority of the shelters in South Africa are owned by CSOs;[15] although shelters are a great resource for woman empowerment and protecting the rights of minor children, they are not adequately funded by government,[16] and the spend on victim care and support is less than the allocation for prevention and response.[17] Nevertheless, shelters provide short- to medium-term stays determined by the circumstances and nationality of the victim (some shelters exclude non-South-Africans) and availability of space, and some offer psychosocial support and skills development.[18]

Conscious of the socio-economic causes of GBV and challenges facing these CSO-owned shelters, the Vodacom Foundation introduced an information and communication technology (ICT)-based victim and survivor empowerment programme in some shelters to provide digital literacy training aiming to break the cycle of abuse. The trainers are graduates from the Foundation's youth academy education programme, who were trained in partnership with Microsoft Corporation and Cisco Systems, Inc., and they preserve the confidentiality of the victims and shelters in this support programme.[19] Since inception in 2018, the Foundation has trained over 1,600 victims and survivors. To further preserve confidentiality, the Foundation has no access to the programme beneficiaries and therefore cannot make follow-up enquiries in order to determine how the programme empowers the beneficiaries after leaving the shelter. This has been flagged as an area of weakness which precludes programme impact measurement.

---

[15] Watson, J., and Lopes, C. 2017. *Shelter Services to Domestic Violence Victims: Policy Approaches to Strengthening State Responses*, Policy Brief No. 1, September, p. 3&11, www.saferspaces.org.za/uploads/files/policy_brief_final_02_web.pdf.

[16] Commission for Gender Equality, *Report on Consultative Hearings into the State of Shelters in South Africa 2020*, https://static.pmg.org.za/1/CGE_Report_on_Shelters_2019.20.pdf, p. 6

[17] Vetten, L., and Lopes, C. 2018. *Out of Harm's Way: Women's Shelters in the Eastern and Northern Cape*. Cape Town: Heinrich Böll Stiftung, p. 1, https://za.boell.org/en/2019/05/30/out-harms-way-womens-shelters-eastern-and-northern-cape.

[18] Watson and Lopes, *Shelter Services*, p. 5. See note 15.

[19] Vodacom Foundation, 'Gender-Based Violence Program', www.vodacom.com/vodacom-foundation.php.

PREVENTION

Response and victim/survivor empowerment are pivotal to the fight against GBV. However, prevention is key, before pain and deep emotional scars are inflicted. Until the social norms that perpetuate GBV – such as the socialisation of boys and girls as unequal parties – are eradicated, it will be difficult to address GBV. To foster a culture of awareness and gender equality, in 2019 the Vodacom Foundation introduced the prevention pillar to pay attention to the root causes of GBV, in partnership with societal influencers who include gender activists, celebrities, CSOs, and men.[20] The involvement of men culminated in a men-led campaign called 'Be the Light', calling upon men to 'say no' to GBV, featuring Vodacom men and sportsmen from the football and rugby teams sponsored by Vodacom South Africa (the Kaizer Chiefs Football Club, Orlando Pirates Football Club, and the Blue Bulls (the Bulls in Vodacom Super Rugby)).[21]

The notable issue that partners amplify during dialogues is the intersectionality of gender, race, and social class. To this end, the Foundation also appointed an ambassador, Masingita Masunga – a media personality with cerebral palsy from an underprivileged upbringing – to inspire young people through her personal experiences on the intersection of gender, disability, race, and social class.[22] The partnerships with these 'influencers' are key in the fight against GBV and femicide because personal storytelling effectively delivers strong and impactful messaging, and, due to their media presence and societal standing, influencers reach a diverse pool of South Africans and create societal awareness. In essence, influencers play a delivery partner role for the Vodacom Foundation on GBV and femicide. In addition to delivering awareness messaging through influencers, the

[20] Vodacom Foundation, 'Vodacom's FaceBook Live Women's Month Event Puts Emphasis on Finding Lasting Solutions to the Scourge of Gender Violence', 26 August 2020, www.vodacom.com/news-article.php?articleID=7541.

[21] Vodacom Foundation, 'Be the Light against Gender-Based Violence', 3 July 2020, https://m.youtube.com/watch?v=cc2OXjvVx58.

[22] See note 20.

Vodacom Foundation and Vodacom executives participate in panel discussions with various partners to share learnings and experiences on how to leverage the GBV ecosystem to change the narrative on the societal stereotypes that fuel GBV and femicide.

INTEGRATION OF THE GENDER-BASED VIOLENCE ECOSYSTEM THROUGH PROSECUTION, DIGITAL TECHNOLOGY, AND PSYCHOSOCIAL SUPPORT

The ecosystem described cannot be successful if there is fragmented implementation on GBV, as this would make it difficult for victims to receive immediate and compassionate support. To provide an integrated strategy for prevention, response, and support for rape victims, in 2000 the National Prosecution Authority's Sexual Offences Community Affairs (SOCA), along with government partners and donors, rolled out 'one-stop' victim-friendly facilities called Thuthuzela (Comfort) Care Centres. Located in a public-sector medical health facility, these centres provide comfort to the victims of rape through immediate medical care, counselling, investigation, and prosecution, aimed at reducing secondary victimisation, improving conviction rates, and shortening the turnaround time for the finalisation of cases.[23] The Vodacom Foundation was one of the Thuthuzela Care Centres donors in the early 2000s at the inception of this integrated care model.[24] In spite of the disturbingly high rates of GBV and rape statistics in the country,[25] only sixty-three Thuthuzela

---

[23] National Prosecution Authority, 'Thuthuzela Care Centres Turning Victims into Survivors', www.npa.gov.za/sites/default/files/resources/public_awareness/TCC_brochure_august_2009.pdf.

[24] *Vodacom Annual Report 2003*, pp. 46–47, www.vodacom.com/pdf/investor/integrated-report/2003/integrated-annual-report.pdf.

[25] South African Government, 'Minister Bheki Cele: Quarter Two Crime Statistics 2021/2022', 19 November 2021, www.gov.za/speeches/speaking-notes-delivered-police-minister-general%C2%A0bheki-cele-mp-occasion-release-%C2%A0quarter; 'Minister Bheki Cele Releases Crime Statistics for the Third Quarter of 2021–2022', 18 February 2022, https://youtu.be/G23kQrXJJiI; and South African Police Services, 'Speaking Notes Delivered By Police Minister General Bheki Cele (MP) at the Occasion of the Release of the Quarter Four Crime Statistics 2021/2022 Hosted in Pretoria', 3 June 2022, www.saps.gov.za/newsroom/msspeechdetail.php?nid=40209.

Care Centres exist in South Africa,[26] and they are underutilised due to lack of awareness and stigma attached to rape.[27] The government's target to increase the number of centres was hampered by the COVID-19 pandemic.[28] Since 2022, the Foundation has been working with SOCA and the GBVFRF to revive its support to the Thuthuzela Care model to facilitate the construction of additional centres, starting with two in 2023. Going forward, the Foundation will also equip some centres with ICTs to provide digital literacy to the victims of rape whilst they receive Thuthuzela support. The Foundation's revived support to the Thuthuzela Care Centres is deliberately integrated into its GBV and education ecosystems, and demonstrates Vodacom Foundation's commitment to an integrated approach to GBV.

To deepen integration, in December 2020, the Vodacom Foundation launched the Bright Sky South Africa application (app) in three South African languages, integrating all three pillars of the Foundation's GBV ecosystem. The zero-rated app was first launched in some Vodafone European markets; it has been adapted to define and describe South African societal practices, norms, and stereotypes that fuel GBV for awareness purposes. The app interfaces with the criminal justice system institutions, shelters, and the GBV Command Centre. As a digital tool, it also provides awareness on cybersecurity threats and is available on Apple iOS- and Google Android-based devices.[29] The South African version of the app was

---

[26] Unpublished communications between the Vodacom Foundation and the GBVFRF in September 2023 on the establishment of the new centres.

[27] *Process Evaluation of NGO Services at Thuthuzela Care Centres*, 2018, p. 11, www .nacosa.org.za/wp-content/uploads/2018/09/GBV-Evaluation-Report-Web.pdf.

[28] *Department of Justice and Constitutional Development: Annual Report 2020–2021*, p. 97, https://nationalgovernment.co.za/department_annual/375/2021-department-of-justice-and-constitutional-development-(doj&cd)-annual-report.pdf.

[29] Vodacom, Sustainability Report for the Year Ended 31 March 2021, p. 46, https:// vodacom-reports.co.za/integrated-reports/ir-2021/documents/sustainability-report-2021.pdf; and Vodacom Foundation, 'Vodacom Zero-Rates Bright Sky SA Gender-Based Violence Awareness App', 21 January 2021, www.vodacom.com/news-article .php?articleID=7594.

written with the assistance of a Foundation CSO partner, Women & Men Against Child Abuse, to ensure the script is aligned to societal realities. In April 2021, the Foundation introduced USSD version of the app to cater for users with no smart devices.[30] Some psychosocial support experts who are partners of the Vodacom Foundation have started using this app in schools.

The psychosocial support programme was launched in 2021 by the Vodacom Foundation, working with a professor from the University of Stellenbosch in partnership with the Department of Basic Education (DBE) in the schools of excellence to complement the education ecosystem. Under the slogan 'change the world' the programme provides counselling support to teachers, parents, and learners. Rising cases of social ills such as bullying, teenage pregnancy, on-site general violence, and GBV motivated this programme. The presence of psychosocial experts in the schools creates space for the teachers to focus on pedagogical development while psychosocial experts provide counselling services on societal ills that disrupt learning. These experts engage with the school governing bodies, parents, the DSD, and the police, thereby building a community of support around the school.

So far, 22 psychosocial support experts are working in 17 schools in 6 provinces and the support currently covers approximately 17,000 community members, including teachers, learners, parents, and caregivers.[31] More than 50 per cent of cases attended to by the psychosocial experts in schools are GBV related. With rising teenage pregnancies during the COVID-19 pandemic, this psychosocial support programme is augmented by the Policy on the Prevention and Management of Learner Pregnancy in Schools.

---

[30] Vodacom Group Social and Ethics Committee Report, 3 November 2021 (unpublished).

[31] Vodacom Foundation, 'Vodacom Joins Forces with Government to Launch a New Ecosystem Using Public Schools to Fight Gender-Based Violence in Society', first reported on 12 August 2021 at inception of the programme, and from unpublished records the programme has now grown to wider reach, www.vodacom.com/news-article.php?articleID=7670.

Issued by the Minister of Basic Education in 2021, the objective is to minimise learner pregnancy through various interventions and make it mandatory for educators to report pregnancy of girls under 16 where the male partner is above 16.[32]

The integration of the GBV and education ecosystems creates a seamless approach to philanthropy and demonstrates the intersectionality between societal challenges and educational outcomes. Learners drop out of school not only because they lack the intellectual or coping abilities to excel, but also because of emotional, social, and economic challenges. Although the objective of psychosocial support is to address societal ills, from engagements with the psychosocial experts and a school principal, the programme is also contributing to self-esteem rebuilding through job creation for young graduates in social work and psychology who could not find jobs in the mainstream economy. Further, integrating more schools in one village helps to spread the message to the community at large about the impact of the programme, thereby positioning the Vodacom Foundation as a pioneer of sustainable development.

The integration approach outlined on prosecution, technology, and education with psychosocial support demonstrates the power of a multifaceted approach and multi-stakeholder partnerships in tackling GBV. With lessons learnt from this integrated approach, a concerted effort to scale up these services across the country can lead to the reduction of GBV cases in South Africa.

GENDER-BASED VIOLENCE SUPPORT FOR VODACOM EMPLOYEES

Inspired by the saying 'charity begins at home', to demonstrate focus on employee well-being in 2019, Vodacom Group Limited (known as Vodacom Group) launched a domestic violence and abuse policy

---

[32] See www.gov.za/documents/national-policy-act-policy-prevention-and-management-learner-pregnancy-schools-3-dec-2021, p. 28 (Government Gazette, No. 45580, 3 December 2021).

for its employees following a global launch, the first of its kind by Vodafone Group PLC. The policy which provides ten day's leave was introduced after extensive research commissioned by the Vodafone Foundation to understand the scale and impact of GBV on employees and workplace performance. To be effective, the policy is supported by training human resources (HR) personnel, and is linked to the company's total wellness programmes.[33] In 2020, during the COVID-19 pandemic, the Vodafone Foundation commissioned further research to determine the implementation progress across the twenty-seven foundation markets. The research found that impressive progress was made in the implementation of the policy since its introduction, with 95 per cent of the markets commending the policy for its significant contribution to support affected employees. Eighty per cent had completed or were on the path to completing training of supervisors and HR. Markets also attest to invoking various interventions such as referral to the internal and external total wellness programmes and providing flexibility to the work conditions of affected employees. Employees found that the policy creates uniformity in addressing domestic violence across the markets, fosters employer–employee trust, promotes intersectionality conversations, creates safe spaces for difficult conversation on domestic violence, and affords a gendered approach to GBV.[34] The first version of the policy focused just on the victim-employee, but in 2022 the policy was updated to address employee-perpetrators of GBV. This policy creates alignment on Vodacom South Africa's focus on communities, customers, and colleagues by giving employees on-site tools to address GBV whilst at the same time allowing them access to the tools of the Vodacom Foundation.

---

[33] Vodafone Foundation, *Vodafone's Domestic Violence and Abuse Policy Guide: A Briefing for Business*, July 2019, pp. 4–6, www.vodafone.com/content/dam/vodcom/files/Vodafone_Domestic_Violence_and_Abuse_Policy_Guide.pdf.

[34] Pillinger, J. 2020. *Executive Summary: Learnings from Vodafone's Global Policy on Domestic Violence and Abuse*, Vodafone Foundation, November, pp. 4–8, www.vodafone.com/sites/default/files/2020-11/learnings-from-vodafones-global-policy-on-domestic-violence-and-abuse.pdf.

The Transformation of CSOs to Strengthen Multi-Stakeholder Partnerships: A Vodafone and Vodacom Case Study

CSOs are an integral part of the fight against GBV because they operate within communities and are accessible. As such, the Vodacom Foundation has been working with CSOs since the early 2000s. However, the effectiveness of CSOs is hampered by lack of human and financial resources. A majority of CSOs, especially the small ones, depend mainly on donor funding and big corporations such as Vodacom South Africa. Corporates collaborate with CSOs as delivery partners because they bring community-based expertise due to their direct involvement with victims, survivors, and perpetrators. However, funding is drying out as more companies scale up their own programmes to embed integrated environmental, social, and governance (ESG) strategies within their businesses. In 2020, the Vodafone Foundation, Vodacom Foundation, and Safaricom PLC commissioned research to investigate the challenges faced by local African CSOs in accessing global donor aid.[35] The findings and recommendations from this report will enhance the Vodacom Foundation's multi-stakeholder partnerships to fight GBV.

The report highlights multiple barriers preventing African CSOs from operating at the same scale and capacity as international CSOs based locally, including funding and donor languages, trust and perceptions, governance and leadership challenges, the regulatory and policy environment, adaptability and agility of CSOs to fluid contexts (such as COVID-19), power relations especially related to the localisation, and domestication of international organisations in Africa.[36]

---

[35] Vodacom Group Limited owns approximately a 35 per cent stake and Vodafone Group PLC approximately a 5 per cent stake in Safaricom PLC.

[36] Vodafone Foundation, *Achieving Greater Equality in Global Philanthropy*, September 2020, www.raceandphilanthropy.com; and Vodacom Foundation, 'New Report Urges International Investment in African Philanthropy for Sustainable Social Impact', 13 September 2021, www.vodacom.com/news-article.php?articleID=7692, p. 6.

Findings and recommendations approved by the Vodafone Foundation include acknowledging that the relationship between Western donors and African CSOs is still premised on colonial mindsets and this power dynamic overwhelms local CSOs. Vodafone Foundation further agreed that the digitising and capacity-building of CSOs is pivotal, the private sector and government need to play a much more meaningful role to support CSOs, CSOs must invest in succession planning, and they must build relationships with local funders instead of just relying on international donor funding. Lastly, the Vodafone Foundation agreed that Western donors must acknowledge that local CSOs are best placed to address local societal challenges.

These findings and recommendations resonate with the work already started by the Vodacom Foundation to transform the relationships with its partner CSOs through capacity-building. The Vodacom Foundation currently funds ten CSOs, the majority of which depend solely on corporate donor funding to champion the rights of vulnerable women and abused, abandoned, and orphaned children. Only three of these CSOs also receive government funding.

However, the Foundation's support to these CSOs was tested when in 2016, the South African government introduced revised Codes of Good Practice on Broad-Based Black Economic Empowerment (B-BBEE), in order to address the imbalances created by apartheid, requiring companies in the ICT sector to inter alia, use ICTs to support philanthropy in order to receive maximum points in the B-BBEE score card.[37]

---

[37] The codes published in Government Gazette 40407, of 7 November 2016, aim to further deepen the implementation of the Broad-Based Black Economic Empowerment (B-BBEE) Act 53 of 2003, as amended by inter alia stimulating growth and promoting transformation of the ICT sector and access to ICTs. To contribute to these objectives, measured entities in the ICT sector must contribute 1.5 per cent of net profit after tax to support socio-economic development (SED), and the spend for such initiatives must be ICT-based in order for the entity to realise maximum points from the B-BBEE score card. This ICT requirement meant that Foundation and company SED activities which are not ICT-based would not be recognised for purposes of B-BBEE measurement. The B-BBEE Act was enacted in order to redress the imbalances resulting from the apartheid system, which excluded mainly black people, black women,

Unfortunately, none of the Foundation-supported CSOs had at the time deployed ICTs as a tool for development, instead the Foundation only provided them with an annual financial grant, which meant that under the new B-BBEE legislative arrangement, the Foundation would forfeit points to the score card as there was no ICT benefit to CSOs. A debate ensued in the company on the possibility of removing these CSOs from the Foundation beneficiary list. After several iterations, the Foundation decided to support these CSOs not for statutory compliance purposes, but as part of its commitment to connect for good and in support of the company's purpose to connect for a better future, by fostering digital literacy and gender equality.

Although the Vodacom Foundation continues funding these CSOs on an annual basis to deliver on their programmes, it has limited funding to support projects from other charitable institutions because it runs massive and costly infrastructure-related projects in support of government programmes in education and GBV. Consequently, the Foundation had to devise creative ways of providing sustainable support to these CSOs beyond just funding. In order to empower these CSOs to attract more funding from the government and to adopt digital transformation to improve their offerings to the vulnerable, a journey ensued to digitise the operations of these CSOs with costs borne by the Foundation. Most CSOs were eager to adopt digital transformation to improve their administration processes and to support their beneficiaries. The Foundation deployed twenty-four ICT graduates from its youth academy to eight CSOs that were open to additional support, and computer laboratories to

and black people with disability from participating in the economy. The measured entities are assessed against a score card to achieve the law's objectives with weightings assigned to the pillars of the score card thus: ownership (25); management control (23); board representation (8); top management representation (5); employment equity (10); skills development (20); enterprise and supplier development as follows – (procurement (25); supplier development (10); enterprise development (15)); and lastly, SED (12). Vodacom South Africa needs a minimum of B-BBEE level 4 in order to qualify for spectrum and some big government contracts (according to Global System for Mobile Communications Association spectrum refers to 'radio frequencies allocated to the mobile industry and other sectors for communication over airwaves').

three of these CSOs to provide digital literacy to the staff and some of their beneficiaries. The survey conducted by the Foundation in 2021 found that this deployment of ICT coordinators and computer laboratories multi-dimensionally transformed the way the CSOs operated. Two of the CSOs expanded their geographical footprint to another province as a result of the financial support from the Foundation. The partnership also contributes to job creation because these CSOs collectively employ a total of 267 people. Digital transformation provides ease of daily administration, empowers beneficiaries and staff with self-confidence in using ICTs, and puts the CSOs in good stead to apply for government funding.[38] The Foundation and Vodacom staff survey found that the partnership with these CSOs teaches the Vodacom staff compassion, boosts staff morale through volunteering at these CSOs, creates a mutually beneficial partnership, inspires development of ICT solutions to solve societal challenges, and enhances company brand and reputation.[39]

The Foundation continues to ensure that these partner CSOs comply with Vodacom South Africa's internal policies derived from national laws on CSO registration, anti-corruption, terrorism, money-laundering, and ensuring that there is no duplication of funding with other Vodacom South Africa programmes. However, this annual vetting process can be cumbersome and overwhelming for CSOs and may serve as a deterrent to funding renewal. So, the ICT coordinators will also assist with interpretation and completion of the required application forms.

The review of the relationship with these CSOs changed power dynamics between the Vodacom Foundation and the CSOs to a symbiotic relationship based on mutual respect. Today, the Foundation refers to and treats its CSOs as delivery partners, acknowledging that they have a community reach and field understanding on GBV that the Foundation lacks. Going forward, the Foundation will report on

---

[38] *Vodacom Foundation Report* (unpublished), September 2021. The report was tabled in the Vodacom Foundation Board Meeting of 3 September 2021.
[39] Ibid.

the work of these CSOs in its annual activities because the grants and capacity-building provided benefit not just to the CSO but also vulnerable communities which are the main focus of the Vodacom Foundation's work. From engagements with CSO managers, there is immense gratitude towards the transformative partnership between Vodacom Foundation and the CSO in the daily management of administrative functions and the benefits to children who would otherwise only have access to ICT at university level due to high levels of inequality in the country.

Conclusions and Recommendations

There is growing realisation by government, civil society, and big business of the need to work together to tackle GBV. However, GBV is a complex national crisis, which requires a capable state to manage with clear polices, multi-stakeholder partnerships, and a robust criminal justice system. The South African government is showing a positive trajectory in its commitment to addressing GBV in some areas like prosecutions,[40] DNA management,[41] and providing police stations with trained GBV officers.[42] However, there is still a concern that many cases remain unreported due to societal stigma or lack of confidence in the criminal justice system, and some cases are not prosecuted due to botched investigations.

In December 2021, ahead of the 16 Days of Activism Against Gender-Based Violence, and shortly after the release of crime statistics, President Ramaphosa gave high-level progress remarks on the response to the GBV crisis since the launch of the NSP, including updates on legislative reform, capacity-building in police stations, and psychosocial services. He admitted that despite the government's best efforts, the shameful picture on GBV in South Africa

---

[40] *Department of Justice and Constitutional Development: Annual Report 2020–2021,* p. 97, see note 28.

[41] See 'Cabinet Pleased with Clearing of DNA Testing Backlog', 2 March 2023, www .sanews.gov.za/south-africa/cabinet-pleased-clearing-dna-testing-backlog.

[42] South African Police Services, 'Speaking Notes'; see note 25.

continues unabated, thereby diminishing efforts to create a GBV-free society.[43]

Much has been said about the current state of South African prisons, which are not conducive for the rehabilitation of offenders due to overcrowding, gang activity, and sexual assault. Prevention and economic empowerment are key. However, where offenders are put behind bars, correction and rehabilitation require much more attention – in the first instance by accelerating the pace of addressing of overcrowding, stopping repeat offenders, and smoothly reintegrating ex-offenders into society.[44]

In its 2019–2020 annual report, the Department of Justice and Constitutional Development reported a 75.2 per cent conviction rate for sexual offences brought for prosecution, representing 4,098 convictions.[45] In 2020–2021, the number of convictions increased to 75.8 per cent, with 2,539 convictions, and this number increased to 3,402 in the 2021/22 year but is recorded in the annual report as a 74.2 per cent rate.[46] Although the conviction rates seem to be improving and this is commendable, there is criticism as the trend's focus is on cases brought for prosecution rather than all reported cases.[47] Consequently, reports on prosecution must give a full picture of successfully prosecuted cases against all reported cases to draw attention to the number of withdrawn and unattended cases (cases that were never brought to trial).

[43] The President, Republic of South Africa, 'From the Desk of the President', 22 November 2022, https://mailchi.mp/presidency.gov.za/from-the-desk-of-the-president-monday-22-november-2021.

[44] Cameron, E. 2021, 'Harsh Prison Terms Won't Solve the Crisis of Gender-Based Violence,' *News 24*, 9 August, www.news24.com/news24/analysis/edwin-cameron-harsh-prison-terms-wont-solve-the-crisis-of-gender-based-violence-20210809.

[45] *Department of Justice and Constitutional Development Annual Report 2019/2020*, pp. 107–108, www.justice.gov.za/reportfiles/anr2019-20.pdf.

[46] *Department of Justice and Constitutional Development: Annual Report 2020/2021*, see note 28; *Department of Justice and Constitutional Development: Annual Report 2021/2022*, p. 97, www.gov.za/sites/default/files/gcis_document/202210/justice-constitutional-development-annualreport.pdf.

[47] South African Broadcasting Corporation featuring Advocate Bronwyn Pithey, 'NPA's 75% Conviction Rate for Sexual Offences Questioned' 10 September 2020, https://youtube.com/watch?v=oWR5d2QFYIg&feature=share.

To improve accuracy in reporting of GBV cases, the role of all relevant organs of the state and other stakeholders needs to be augmented by technology, including big data analytics and a dedicated unit to collate and analyse the data before disseminating. CSOs in the GBV space should be digitalised, with costs for indigent CSOs largely carried by their private-sector partners and the remainder by government.

With the dire need for support, it is unclear why the Victims Support Services Bill, which was tabled in parliament in 2020, was not processed and passed together with the package of laws that were tabled in 2021, as part of the legislative reform package. This bill and the policy on shelters must be given priority to address the role of government in victim support, especially in shelters.

Government still has difficulties driving a coordinated and consistent approach to GBV. A disconnect exists between the work of line-function departments and private-sector initiatives, with some stakeholders questioning whether private initiatives such as the newly established GBVFRF are meant to replace the existing state or private-sector initiatives. Poor reporting on GBV and poor programme planning contribute to inadequate funding, thereby giving rise to requests for the private sector to fund some of the GBV programmes or initiatives, which is unsustainable. There needs to be clearly defined roles on what each partner brings to the partnership to avoid ambiguity, duplication, and competition.

Measurable targets underpinned by a performance-based remuneration model should be set for public servants dealing with GBV, with organisational performance assessed strictly against these targets. A monitoring and evaluation framework is also required to measure the impact of multi-stakeholder partnership programmes.

The Vodacom Foundation's contributions, while not insignificant, are broadly a drop in the ocean. Technology is not a *panacea* for societal ills, but efforts can be scaled up if there is clear delineation of roles between government, the private sector, and civil society.

More companies should actively join the fight against GBV beyond simply providing grants; they must offer sustainable solutions that contribute to the GBV ecosystem and the NSP. However, existing multi-stakeholder partnerships are hampered by a nagging suspicion from some government partners that the private sector is just revenue-driven and not genuine in its support to the developmental agenda. On the other hand, a view exists in some private-sector circles that government spends most time formulating policies and making statements on GBV but fails on implementation, as is evident from the crime statistics every quarter.

Lastly, this GBV crisis can only be resolved through multi-stakeholder partnership, guided by mutual trust, tight policies, clear role definition, and the willingness of all parties to effect change. However, partnerships should not usurp or replace government's constitutional and international obligations to promote gender equality, prevent GBV, and protect victims.

7 Philanthropy in Emerging Economies

A Call to Invest in Resilience

Maysa Jalbout and Katy Bullard

INTRODUCTION

The COVID-19 pandemic has sent deep shockwaves through our global and local economies, our health-care and education systems, and into our personal homes and lives. While the shock was universal, the impact and its long-term implications have been felt and will linger much longer for the most vulnerable countries, communities, and individuals. In emerging economies around the world, the pandemic has set back hard-fought progress in economic development and social equity. As we begin to understand the real cost of the pandemic for everything from children's learning to women's economic opportunity, every sector and actor must reflect on their role and re-evaluate their position in building a more resilient system for all, in emerging economies and beyond.

In this chapter, resilience is understood as sufficient stability within a system to protect communities, particularly the most vulnerable, and services from deep shocks. This system encompasses not only government, but also civil society, including philanthropy. To examine the role of philanthropy in supporting resilience in emerging economies, we consider three dimensions: what philanthropists invest in, how they invest, and with whom they invest.

THE CASE FOR PHILANTHROPY TO SUPPORT RESILIENCE

What Is Resilience in Philanthropy?

Within this understanding of resilience, there are several dimensions to consider. Lynn et al. (2021, p. 52) write of *strategic resilience*: '[a] philanthropic strategy is resilient when it supports the ability of grantees to collectively achieve long-term aims amid significant disruptions in context'. This resilience is drawn from the ability of networks of organisations to drive change. They argue that strategic resilience requires that funders: support networks, rather than strategies; focus on systems; do not aim to define the change process in place of the organisations they fund; support networks' capacity for transformative action in response to crisis; and use philanthropic power to supplement – not replace or overshadow – the power of community leaders and organisations. As such, strategic resilience has major implications for who, what, and how philanthropic organisations fund. This concept of strategic resilience underpins the way that resilience in emerging economy philanthropy is understood in this chapter.

It should be noted that resilience in philanthropy can also imply contributing to the stability of the organisations funded by philanthropists in the face of shocks. Given the massive funding gaps faced by many organisations – for instance, a recent Bridgespan report found that many African non-governmental organisations (NGOs) face funding gaps – this element should be held in mind. The COVID pandemic has been a challenge for many NGOs who rely on philanthropic funding (Layode et al., 2021). Organisations surveyed in 2021 by CAF America (Charities Aid Foundation America) in Argentina, Brazil, India, Russia, and South Africa have struggled with fundraising in the wake of the pandemic.[1] Most of those surveyed noted that building financial reserves and strategic planning were areas of support that would help them improve. Among respondents, 45 per cent and 43 per cent noted that support in contingency planning and developing risk management frameworks, respectively, would help them improve their preparedness to respond to crises. Foundations' willingness to recognise and respond to the needs of grantees is another dimension of resilience in philanthropy (Table 7.1).

---

[1] www.cafamerica.org/wp-content/uploads/CAFAmerica_CV19_Volume_FINAL.pdf.

Table 7.1 *Dimensions of resilience in philanthropy*

Who	What	How
Foundations	Strategic resilience: effective support for grantees' long-term impact even during crisis or disruption (see Lynn et al., 2021).	Supporting networks, focusing on systems, allowing grantees to design the change process, supporting grantees' capacity to respond to crisis, and augmenting grantees' and community leaders' power (Lynn et al., 2021). Unrestricted funding, giving grantees agency, utilising multiple financial instruments (OECD, 2021).
Grantees	Ongoing ability to provide services and/or support social and civic engagement amidst crisis.	Building financial reserves, institutional agility in adapting strategy and services as needed, put in place contingency plans or risk frameworks.
Philanthropic nexus of foundations, governments, and NGOs	System-level change.	Collaborative action to assess, build, and reform governments and other systems through data generation and usage, advocacy (OECD, 2021), and transformative system-wide programming.

COVID Poses Major Threats to Development

COVID has threatened decades of progress on economic and human development in many emerging economies. For example, Ram and Yadiv (2021) estimate that the economic consequences of COVID may double India's poverty rate, undoing consistent progress in recent years. Around the world, including in emerging economies like South Africa and countries in the Middle East and North Africa, the pandemic has exacerbated poverty, unemployment, and other inequalities (Futshane,

2021; Lopez-Acevedo and Hoogeveen, 2021). In Brazil, an emergency aid programme from the government reduced poverty substantially but is expected to be only a short-term improvement, as poverty rates have begun to bounce back as short-term pandemic aid slowed down, highlighting the need for more medium- and long-term investments in poverty reduction (The Brazilian Report, 2020; McGeever, 2021).

The pandemic has also raised severe challenges for several sectors. Notably in education, school closures have elevated major concerns about learning loss and growing inequities in learning outcomes. For low- and middle-income countries, the World Bank's calculations for a 'pessimistic scenario' about school closures projected that as many as 70 per cent of 10-year-olds may not be able to read a simple text (what the World Bank deems the 'learning poverty' rate); this would be a substantial increase from the already alarmingly high learning poverty rate of 53 per cent pre-pandemic (World Bank, UNESCO, and UNICEF, 2021).

Brazilian schools faced some of the longest school closures in Latin America and the Caribbean, and remote learning highlighted and deepened inequities in the Brazilian education system, with over 90 per cent of children in wealthy parts of the country able to access remote learning, compared to less than half in the poorest parts of the country (World Bank). In South Africa, according to the United Nations Children's Fund (UNICEF), by July 2021, students were between three-quarters of a year and a full school year behind where they should have been, and up to half a million students had dropped out of school in the preceding sixteen months.

Philanthropy and Resilience during COVID

Globally, while there is widespread acknowledgement of the need for investments in resilience – including attention to the systems and policies that contribute to vulnerability and inequity – these types of investments do not appear to comprise a large portion of overall philanthropic giving. Research (Candid and CDP, 2021b) on giving during COVID noted that while most foundation leaders interviewed see supporting advocacy for systems and policy reform as important, few of their foundations began supporting grantee advocacy during COVID. Candid and the Center for Disaster Philanthropy's (CDP's) analysis of the state of disaster philanthropy notes that disaster funding tends to focus heavily on relief and recovery, not the mitigation and preparedness efforts that can help reduce the likeliness or severity of crises (Candid and CDP, 2021a).

COVID has intensified existing challenges in the philanthropic sector in many emerging economy contexts, including the difficulties that small organisations face in trying to raise funds. Smaller organisations in Argentina, Brazil, India, Russia, and South Africa surveyed by CAF America have struggled to raise funds in the wake of the pandemic, in part due to their own limited staff resources.[2] Such a challenge is a reminder that the capacity and strategies of all actors within the philanthropic ecosystem – not only foundations themselves – must be considered when thinking about resilience. CAF America also found mismatches between donors and the communities they intend to serve during the pandemic. That said, the majority of organisations surveyed noted that their preparedness to respond to crises had improved in the second year of the pandemic. Most also note that building financial reserves and strategic planning were areas of support that would help them improve; 45 per cent and 43 per cent noted that support in contingency planning and developing risk management frameworks, respectively, would be useful. These issues point to non-programmatic work that foundations may play a crucial role in supporting for promoting resilience.

PHILANTHROPY IN EMERGING ECONOMIES

Significant Philanthropic Investment

The Organisation for Economic Co-operation and Development (OECD) estimates that 205 private philanthropic organisations gave $42.5 billion in philanthropy for development between 2016 and

---

[2] www.cafamerica.org/wp-content/uploads/CAFAmerica_CV19_Volume_FINAL.pdf.

2019. The sample included a large number (116) of organisations from emerging economies. In this period, middle-income countries received the most philanthropic funding (42 per cent) of the total, followed by lower middle-income countries (38 per cent), highlighting that emerging economies are major areas for philanthropic investment. Organisations based in emerging economies accounted for 19 per cent of total philanthropic giving for development, and many of these organisations give heavily domestically, with education as the largest sector for domestic philanthropy for development. Foundations in Colombia contribute about $100 million annually towards social programming, particularly education and small business, and large South African donors give about $76 million annually, much of it targeting education. With this large and growing role, the OECD sees domestic philanthropy in emerging economies as 'the next frontier' (OECD, 2021).

Pre-COVID, philanthropy appeared to be a growing sector in emerging economies, and existing philanthropic organisations in emerging economies tended to have tight geographic or thematic focus, often focused on vulnerable populations, and often implemented their own programming, some partnering with or funding local NGOs. Given these roles and, in some cases, their closeness to beneficiaries, philanthropic entities in emerging economies are well positioned to understand and collaboratively respond to challenges in their context; the philanthropic sector more broadly can learn from their knowledge and experience. In some of these contexts, funders are collaboratively working to make more data publicly available about the sector or governments are taking steps to mandate more reporting (OECD, 2021).

Traditional Approaches and Challenges

Many emerging economies have strong traditions of philanthropy in some form, but the modality and focus of giving has evolved over time, moving gradually towards strategic resilience in certain respects. Community aid and support for local social networks through individual giving have been long-standing practices, sometimes linked in part to religious traditions. Alongside these traditions, larger givers are innovating, becoming more collaborative, and placing growing focus on scale. In short, while lingering challenges from long-standing approaches can limit the focus on resilience in philanthropic giving, recent trends and opportunities also show signs of progress towards strategic resilience.

Ongoing Preference by Many Donors to Individual Giving
Community aid and support for local social networks through individual giving have been long-standing practices, sometimes linked in part to religious traditions. In India, for example, giving often takes the form of direct individual donations, rather than institutional philanthropic funding. For instance, crowdfunding – both before COVID and in the response to the devastating spike in infections that India faced – and other forms of online donations highlight how this direct style of giving allows for needs to be directly targeted by individual funders (sometimes to individual recipients). In line with this trend, more than two-thirds of respondents in a 2012 CAF report (cited in Hartnell, 2017) said they would prefer to give to beneficiaries, while less than one third reported giving to charities. Similarly, in the Arab region, Muslims often give their mandatory annual contributions such as *zakat* (annual percentage of their wealth) directly to individuals who they have identified as needing financial support or through religious institutions. As such, this funding rarely targets systems-level challenges.

Hesitancy to Fund Issues Viewed as Challenging Social Norms or Politically Charged
Though there have been some promising shifts towards resilience in philanthropy, in many contexts there is reticence to fund politically contentious issues or causes that may challenge the status quo. For example, in the Arab region, since the Arab Spring, philanthropy appears to be shifting away from controversial issues, which may mean that key systems challenges remain unaddressed by the sector (Hartnell, 2018). In Brazil, many donors, especially in the large

corporate-giving sector, tend to focus on non-contentious issues such as public education, rather than other more controversial rights- or democracy-oriented causes. Even as social justice philanthropy has grown in recent years in Brazil, including with the formation of the Philanthropy Network for Social Justice in 2009, the current political climate has become strained and has limited social justice giving (Hartnell and Milner, 2018).

Low Confidence by Philanthropic Entities in Investing in System Change, Due to Political Climate and Fragility

The political climate and fragility in many emerging economies have limited the interest of the philanthropic sector to invest in system-level change and therefore contribute to greater resilience. In the Middle East, where eight of the twenty-two Arab States are classified by the World Bank as fragile or conflict-affected, philanthropic entities do not view the government as a viable partner and are therefore often limited to working with NGOs to address the failure of governments to address issues systemically. Meanwhile, in Brazil, NGOs are not well trusted, which challenges the philanthropic sector and contributes in part to the prevalence of donors, the majority of which are corporate foundations, operating their own programmes rather than investing in strengthening civil society (Hartnell and Milner, 2018).

Legal Frameworks Inhibit the Philanthropic Ecosystem from Becoming More Robust

Legislation and policy around philanthropic giving are not particularly favourable in many emerging economies. For instance, in Brazil, donations are taxed, which may discourage some philanthropic giving (Hartnell and Milner, 2018). In the Middle East, too, legal restrictions limit the operations or innovation of philanthropic funders. Registering pooled funds is a challenging process, and more broadly, legal challenges with registration and operation mean that in some cases Arab philanthropists may operate their foundations from the United States or United Kingdom where laws are more supportive.

These legal barriers point to the need for changing legal frameworks for philanthropic entities (Jalbout, 2020).

Little Investment in Exploring New Innovative
Solutions – the Sector Remains Largely Risk-averse
Broadly, many philanthropic givers remain more inclined to give to 'safe' causes than to invest in innovative new opportunities. Unlike governments, who need to be more cautious about investing public funds, philanthropists are well positioned to explore and support innovation, even if some degree of risk is involved. Such investments, though, have historically been limited. In the Middle East in particular, funders often lean towards supporting low-risk opportunities such as scholarships, university infrastructure, or humanitarian relief (Jalbout, 2020).

New Trends and Opportunities

While these traditional approaches and ongoing challenges persist among many philanthropic actors, new trends and opportunities hold promise in helping philanthropy shift towards strategic resilience.

A Greater Use of Technology to Increase
Funding and Deliver It More Efficiently
Technology has played a critical role in facilitating crowdfunding as part of India's individual giving, as discussed in the section 'Traditional Approaches and Challenges'. The COVID pandemic brought this sharply into focus. The Indian online crowdfunding platform Ketto raised over $55 million from 220,000 donors supporting over 4,000 fundraisers as part of its COVID relief, according to the fund website. Fundraisers were started by both individuals and NGOs. Around the world, crowdfunding platforms and other forms of online or phone-based giving strategies have enabled more and more direct giving to beneficiaries chosen by donors, whether they are individuals or larger organisations. This scope and scale of giving would not be possible without technology.

A Stronger Understanding of the Magnitude of the
Challenges Facing Emerging Economies Coupled
with a Search for More Scalable Solutions

Across emerging economy philanthropy, there is growing interest in scalability. This has been facilitated, too, by engagement in pooled funding and partnerships with governments, as will be discussed in the following sub-section. Among larger donors in India, including venture philanthropists and impact investors, interest is growing in scaling, measuring impact, and exploring new strategies for supporting social enterprise. There is also increased openness to pooled funding and accountability for investments. While large-scale programmes are still focused on service delivery rather than system change, this attention to scale and openness to new approaches may point to a gradual shift towards resilience, at least in the strategies foundations employ, if not in the types of projects they support (Hartnell, 2017).

An Increase in Openness among Philanthropists to
Adopt Collaborative Approaches and Pool Funds

Philanthropic collaboratives are also a promising, if nascent, trend in Indian philanthropy. As of 2020, they accounted for only 1 per cent of giving in India, and most have emerged from the early 2000s, but hold exciting potential for the philanthropic landscape in India. These collaboratives bring together multiple actors – potentially including funders, implementers, governments, and others – under a collective strategy and vision for impact and with shared funds, allowing them to work for large-scale impact, often with interest in scale, building up encouraging innovations, sharing knowledge and research, and influencing policy. While such collaboratives can face challenges in formation and execution, they mark a potentially meaningful shift – albeit at a small scale within the Indian philanthropic landscape – towards strategic resilience (Venkatachalam and Shah, 2020). See the EdelGive Foundation case study (in the section 'Investing in Sustainable Education Change: EdelGive Foundation in India') for more discussion of the Collaborators for Transforming Education philanthropic collaborative, which brings together multiple funders, NGOs, and the Government of Maharashtra.

An Increase in Collaboration with Government

The Arab World also has strong philanthropic and charitable traditions, often with direct giving to support short-term challenges through local organisations or individuals, sometimes through religious institutions. Again, this community response helps individuals and responds to direct needs in the immediate term. Alongside this, social enterprise and impact investing are on the rise. With high rates of poverty or vulnerability to poverty – nearly two-thirds of the population of ten Arab countries are classified as poor or vulnerable (Khouri, 2019) – coupled with high youth unemployment and persistent refugee crises, there is growing recognition that governments may not be able to fulfil all community needs. In response, philanthropic institutions – including companies and high net-worth individuals (HNWIs) – play a bigger role. While high net-worth philanthropists in the region typically haven't used high-impact strategies, there have been some promising trends pointing towards more large-scale activity. Partnerships between the state and the private sector or civil society appear to be on the rise (Hartnell, 2018; Jalbout, 2020). This trend suggests emerging elements of strategic resilience in the sector. As will be discussed in the section 'Investing in Evidence to Inform Effective Education Systems: Community Jameel', Community Jameel has supported large-scale, systems-oriented activities that require collaboration with government and civil society, highlighting optimistic trends within the region's philanthropy landscape.

A Desire among a New Generation of Philanthropists to Make More Sustainable Investments

Social enterprises address unmet socio-economic needs through sustainable market-based solutions. Their approach can be attractive to philanthropic entities concerned with the long-term sustainability of their funding. It is not surprising, therefore, that there has been an increase in social enterprises in emerging economies. In the Arab region, social enterprises help tackle critical issues of youth unemployment among other social challenges, and some large funders have a growing interest in supporting social enterprises in scaling and sustaining their impact (Coutts, 2016).

While impact investing in the region remains nascent and venture philanthropy is relatively modest, both have large potential. For example, Alfanar, established in 2004, remains the only venture philanthropy organisation investing in social enterprises in the Arab region while Wamda is among the few entities publicly championing and investing in social enterprises. Both venture philanthropy and impact investing are expected to grow as more social enterprises are established and demonstrate the ability to scale. In Brazil, impact investing had $343 million in assets under management in 2018, according to a study by the Aspen Network of Development Entrepreneurs in partnership with the Association for Private Capital Investment in Latin America. Financial inclusion is the top area of investment with education, health care, and environment figuring prominently (Hartnell and Milner, 2018). Impact investing and venture philanthropy are also growing in India, where these strategies tend to target social enterprises in sectors such as agriculture and renewable energy (Hartnell, 2017).

THREE EXAMPLES OF PHILANTHROPIC ORGANISATIONS FROM BRAZIL, INDIA, AND SAUDI ARABIA INVESTING IN RESILIENCE

Education System Resilience: The Lemann Foundation in Brazil

The Lemann Foundation's work in Brazil builds education system resilience by focusing not only on the student level but also on the quality and stability of the education system more broadly. Like many other foundations, the Lemann Foundation works at the individual level, aiming to improve student access in the immediate term. Beyond this work, the Foundation focuses on long-term policy reform and development, helping to build the resilience of the Brazilian education system. This work involves engaging with political and educational leaders to ensure that education system strengthening efforts are effective and relevant. It also includes generating commitment to education quality from key stakeholders and political leaders to ensure that reforms are effective and enduring.

The Lemann Foundation works closely with partners to build Brazil's education 'ecosystem'. In any philanthropic work, such partnerships are essential, and they are particularly important for the enduring systems-level change needed to build education system resilience. Such partnerships include those with organisations such as Nova Escola, which supports school managers and teachers, and the Reúna Institute, which supports implementation of the national standards.

Part of the Foundation's work involves bridging disconnects between education policy and what happens in schools. As part of this, close collaboration with leaders at all levels has also been central to the Foundation's efforts to build educational resilience, which links to the Foundation's broader interest in building the next generation of Brazilian leaders across sectors. Two of the longest-running programmes funded by the Foundation – Formar and Educar pra Valer – show that schools involved in the programmes improve more quickly than similar schools and have outcomes that are above the national learning average. Both programmes help to implement education policies that improve learning or maintain strong learning results, with heavy reliance on partnership with regional leaders.

For instance, through the Formar programme, which has reached more than 840,000 students in 20 school districts, the Foundation, in partnership with education organisations, supports alignment between departments of education and schools. In particular, this work strengthens management, professional development, and communication. Similarly, the Partnership for Literacy via Collaboration

(Parceria pela Alfabetização em Regime de Colaboração, PARC) programme, which builds on learning from the strategies that helped
reform education in Ceará, provides a range of technical support to
help states develop policies on education topics such as teachers,
assessment, instructional resources, and incentives. The programme
relies on collaboration with city governments. These programmes
point to the ways in which building bridges between schools and
policymakers can help foster education system resilience by promoting policies that support equitable and high-quality learning
opportunities.

Critically, the Foundation has been active in supporting development of the country's National Learning Standards (Base Nacional
Comum Curricular, BNCC). These standards set out the curriculum – including lessons and competencies – that public school students should be receiving and developing throughout their schooling,
bridging education policy and classroom practice. The standards
were adopted by the federal government in 2017 and by the end of
2020, 74 per cent of Brazilian municipalities had approved the BNCC
(2020 annual report).

The Lemann Foundation has worked on a range of digital efforts
to strengthen the education system, including expanding internet
access for millions of students, a critical avenue for learning continuity in the COVID era. According to the Foundation's 2020 annual
report, over 12 million students were impacted by distance learning
initiatives and 27 institutions committed to supporting remote education. These efforts as a more immediate pandemic response have
been coupled by digital education efforts that hold potential to build
the education system's resilience in the longer term. Surveys conducted by the Foundation revealed that almost three quarters of educators plan to incorporate more technology into their teaching after
the pandemic than they did before COVID, though almost half do not
believe their internet connection is sufficient and almost a third do
not have internet in their schools, pointing to the need for support to
connectivity and tech-supported education to facilitate education for

all – including the most vulnerable – in the Brazilian system. In this way, the Foundation's support to expanded internet access may also be valuable for building education resilience in the face of future shocks.

According to the Foundation, their support for expanded internet access and digital learning infrastructure has facilitated systems-level initiatives, including projects aligned with the BNCC. In collaboration with the Omidyar Network, for example, the Foundation conducted a survey to find digital-based opportunities to support BNCC implementation, and the two partnered to create an alliance, launched in April 2020, for entrepreneurs developing tech-enabled opportunities to support the implementation of the BNCC. The foundation also worked with Google.org to develop six thousand digital lesson plans for teachers to facilitate learning aligned with the BNCC.[3] The alignment across investments to ensure implementation of policy measures for effective teaching and learning demonstrates a commitment to system-level reform.

INVESTING IN SUSTAINABLE EDUCATION CHANGE: EDELGIVE FOUNDATION IN INDIA

EdelGive Foundation supports grassroots NGOs that work with vulnerable communities in India. The Foundation's theory of change, as shared in their 2020 annual report, sees 'educated children, empowered women, and resilient communities' as the foundation of inclusive society. As such, '[their] development, in-turn develops stronger, more sustainable, and inclusive nations'. The Foundation works for systemic change, with a model built around cross-sectoral partnerships and empowerment of grassroots leadership. These three goals – systemic change, strong partnerships, and development of grassroots leaders – align and lay crucial groundwork for the resilience that is built into the Foundation's theory of change (EdelGive, 2021).

EdelGive began in 2008 disbursing small grants to implementing organisations across multiple states in India. The Foundation initially

---

[3] www.google.org.

focused on education, livelihoods, and women's empowerment, but, as their CEO explained, they increasingly saw that developing sources requires attention to the full ecosystem of social and human behaviour. With this recognition, the Foundation transitioned from a small funding organisation to a philanthropic asset-management foundation assisting institutional and individual givers in finding causes to fund. EdelGive currently supports about 200 NGOs across 20 states in India. Over the years, the Foundation has helped to facilitate about $70 million in commitments to their NGO partners. The Foundation holds a legacy of 150 capacity-building projects. EdelGive has also been awarded the National Corporate Social Responsibility (CSR) Award by the Ministry of Corporate Affairs, Government of India, for its work towards supporting education, women's empowerment, and the livelihoods of vulnerable communities.

The Foundation recognises the need for sustained investment over a long period of time and invests in NGOs with innovative models that could grow exponentially. It takes an equity-driven approach to stakeholder engagement, recognising that not all stakeholder groups have equal power, but approaching them all as equally important. EdelGive also recognises that through their work, EdelGive's investments (and the risks they take on in making those investments) benefit Indian society much more widely. And to ensure that change is sustainable, the Foundation and its partners provide NGOs with comprehensive support, not only through financial support but also through capacity-building and connections to other funding sources. This philosophy and approach point to a deep commitment to long-term resilience, recognising the need for a long-term lens on change, building up voices that often lack power in development and philanthropic conversations, and working for transformative change for society's benefit.

EdelGive's support to education reflects this interest in systems transformation. Working closely with the government, the Foundation has several strategies and initiatives to improve the education system. For instance, Collaborators for Transforming Education is an initiative that works to improve learning outcomes in Special Focus Districts in Maharashtra by implementing Pragat Shaikshanik Maharashtra (PSM), a state government initiative to strengthen education. The Collaborators is a public-private partnership with the Department of School Education and Sports, currently working in seven districts of Maharashtra with three non-profit organisations (NPOs), reaching over 1 million school children. Alongside improving education outcomes, Collaborators for Transforming Education builds system capacity and strengthens community engagement, with the intention of ensuring sustainability. The stakeholders involved in the project together identify and share practices to strengthen learning that can be incorporated into government systems. The project aims to cover all 36 districts of Maharashtra by 2026 to reach approximately 20 million students in 110,000 schools with about 760,000 teachers and over 10,000 civil servants. The Collaborators for Transforming Education was the first of the six collaboratives that EdelGive will be steering and or participating in in the coming years. Others focus on women, entrepreneurship, climate migration, and paying the true costs while supporting NGOs.

EdelGive's education interventions have had wide reach: according to the 2021 annual report, the Foundation has supported more than 67,000 teachers and government officials in delivering quality education and has reached over 19 million children.

EdelGive's newest initiative – the Grassroots, Resilience, Ownership and Wellness (GROW) Fund – is an initiative to build 100 grassroots organisations' capacity and resilience. The Fund is a highly collaborative effort that has received funding from several other foundations, including the Bill & Melinda Gates Foundation (BMGF), MacArthur Foundation, ATE Chandra Foundation, and Rohini Nilekani Philanthropies. According to Naghma Mulla, EdelGive's CEO, GROW Fund aims to build 'empathetic structures of funding', and its structure and approach highlight the growing need for blended approaches – in financing and in systems – to mitigate risks, especially in the wake of COVID (Lidji and Mulla, 2021).

While the GROW Fund is not specifically focused on education NGOs, this coalition-oriented approach to financing and systems strengthening demonstrates an understanding of resilience that is grounded in capacity-building and distributed risk to benefit the most marginalised. Almost 2,300 registrations were received from organisations across India through an open application process. After a four-month due diligence and selection process, the final cohort of 100 GROW organisations was announced in January 2022. The cohort is comprised of grassroots organisations from across the North, South, East, and West zones of India that work in nine social impact thematic areas.

This approach to building grassroots' capacity without trying to dictate the organisations' approaches points to EdelGive's strategic resilience. The Foundation's work and approach empowering grassroots NGOs is in contrast to the weak confidence in NGOs that often limits or undermines philanthropic efforts in India (Hartnell, 2017). That said, the Foundation's interest in collaborative philanthropy reflects another trend in India reported by Philanthropy for Social Justice and Peace (PSJP): a growing interest in pooled funding for high-impact models that can be implemented at a large scale.

INVESTING IN EVIDENCE TO INFORM EFFECTIVE
EDUCATION SYSTEMS: COMMUNITY JAMEEL

Following in the philanthropic tradition set by the late Abdul Latif Jameel more than seventy-five years ago, Community Jameel works to tackle education, health, and climate challenges through innovative and evidence-based approaches. Data and technology feature in much of the organisation's work. Community Jameel is interested both in individual support and in systems strengthening. In education, these can take a range of forms, from scholarships at the individual level and pedagogical and technological innovations to strengthen education for the most vulnerable.

One of Community Jameel's best-known support areas is the Abdul Latif Jameel Poverty Action Lab (J-PAL), a research centre at the Massachusetts Institute for Technology (MIT) that aims to 'reduce poverty by ensuring that policy is informed by scientific evidence'. The lab conducts randomised evaluations and works to promote evidence-based policy-making. The lab was founded in 2003 by MIT Professors Abhijit Banerjee, Esther Duflo, and Sendhil Mullainathan and named for the late Abdul Latif Jameel in 2005. It continues to receive support from Community Jameel. Since its inception, J-PAL has been a major force in poverty-reduction efforts. Its rigorous research has reshaped how governments and the development sector understand poverty and work to combat it.

J-PAL's work in education has transformed the way governments and development providers approach education. The lab's research on teacher training, pedagogy, school governance, incentives, and other key factors in education access and quality help policymakers incorporate rigorous research into decision-making.

J-PAL's research has played a critical role in demonstrating the impact of the Teaching at the Right Level (TaRL) approach, which aims to build foundational skills in primary students. The approach was developed by the Indian NGO Pratham and has since been used in a range of settings in India and Africa, in some cases as part of government interventions. J-PAL's multiple evaluations of the approach over almost two decades have demonstrated its consistent ability to raise learning outcomes when effectively implemented, and through ongoing collaboration with Pratham, it has informed adaptations to the model to make it more effective. TaRL is regarded globally as one of the most promising approaches to raising foundational learning, and particularly in the COVID era, when governments and other providers have been attuned to the foundational learning gaps that emerged during school closures, has been seen by governments and nongovernmental actors as a potentially transformative approach. J-PAL's rigorous evaluations of TaRL have been instrumental not only in strengthening the model but in making the case for its adoption in a wide range of contexts. J-PAL's work on TaRL is one of many examples of the ways in which the lab's rigorous education research has had profound impacts on education policy and practice in developing country contexts.

J-PAL's work offers a powerful example of how Community Jameel invests in resilience in emerging economies. Evidence-based policy-making is essential for systems effectiveness and resilience, including (perhaps especially) in education. Rigorous evidence on what works in education can guide policymakers towards decisions that build education system capacity, quality, and equity in the short and long term. Community Jameel's support for rigorous research – and, critically, for building bridges between researchers and policymakers – demonstrates interest in promoting system sustainability and effectiveness through effective policy-making. Investing in evidence gives community leaders, policymakers, and grassroots organisations tools for understanding what works without prescribing specific strategies to address them. This commitment and strategy puts Community Jameel at the forefront of a shift in current Middle East philanthropy: in a region that has historically been characterised by short-term, individually focused, giving, funders are gradually shifting towards more strategic long-term activities (Coutts, 2016; Hartnell, 2018).

CONCLUSION

Philanthropy in emerging economies, like most philanthropic giving globally, is not contributing to building resilience with the depth and at the pace that is needed. The COVID pandemic has underscored the fragility of current systems as it threatens to reverse hard-won socio-economic progress over the past two decades by pulling millions of people back into poverty, locking children out of school, and holding women back from achieving equality. The case for investing in greater stability to protect communities, particularly the most vulnerable, is clear.

Philanthropic entities in emerging economies must actively move away from focusing on funding individuals to supporting networks of organisations by strengthening their capacity to respond to crises through more flexible funding and building their long-term financial sustainability. Utilising technology more effectively, investing in social enterprises, and adopting more innovative financial instruments, including impact investing and venture philanthropy, are proving to be credible opportunities.

The challenges facing philanthropic entities in emerging economies are not insignificant. Fear of political reprisals, government weaknesses, fragile states, and limiting legal frameworks are hurdles to investing in systems but they are not insurmountable. As demonstrated by three large foundations from India, Brazil, and Saudi Arabia, philanthropic leaders can take decisive action towards strengthening the resilience of emerging economies by not shying away from longer-term investments such as education, by investing in scalable solutions, by pooling resources with other philanthropic entities, and by critically working with governments.

REFERENCES

The Brazilian Report. 2020. Coronavirus Aid Sees Brazil's Poverty Rates Drop to Lowest Level since 2004. *Wilson Center Blog*, 14 August. www.wilsoncenter.org/blog-post/coronavirus-aid-sees-brazils-poverty-rates-drop-lowest-level-2004.

Candid and CDP (Center for Disaster Philanthropy). 2021a. *Measuring the State of Disaster Philanthropy: Data to Drive Decisions*. https://doi.org/10/gm29bv.

Candid and CDP (Center for Disaster Philanthropy). 2021b. *Philanthropy and COVID-19: Measuring One Year of Giving*. https://doi.org/10/gh5dzk.

Coutts. 2016. *Middle East Report*. www.alliancemagazine.org/blog/coutts-million-dollar-donors-report-sees-growth-major-giving/.

EdelGive. 2021. *Annual Report 2020–21*. https://cdn1.edelweissfin.com/wp-content/uploads/sites/3/2021/09/IMAGINE_EdelGive-Foundation-AR-2020-2021.pdf.

Futshane, V. 2021. *Recovering from COVID-19 and Inequality: The Experience of South Africa*. Paper prepared for the United Nations Virtual Inter-Agency Expert Group Meeting on Implementation of the Third United Nations Decade for the Eradication of Poverty (2018–2027). www.un.org/development/desa/dspd/wp-content/uploads/sites/22/2021/05/Futshane_paper.pdf.

Hartnell, C. 2017. *Philanthropy in India: A Working Paper*. Philanthropy for Social Justice and Peace. www.psjp.org/wp-content/uploads/2017/10/Philanthropy-in-India-October-2017-1.pdf.

Hartnell, C. 2018. *Philanthropy in the Arab World: A Working Paper*. Philanthropy for Social Justice and Peace. www.psjp.org/wp-content/uploads/2018/03/Philanthropy-in-the-Arab-region-March-2018.pdf.

Hartnell, C., and Milner, A. 2018 *Philanthropy in Brazil: A Working Paper*. Philanthropy for Social Justice and Peace. www.psjp.org/wp-content/uploads/2018/05/PHILANTHROPY-IN-BRAZIL-MAY-2018.pdf.

Jalbout, M. 2020. Governments Simply Cannot Do It Alone: How Philanthropy Can Drive Development in the Arab World. *Dubai Policy Review*, 2. https://dubaipolicyreview.ae/governments-simply-cannot-do-it-alone-how-philanthropy-can-drive-development-in-the-arab-world/.

Khouri, R. G. 2019. How Poverty and Inequality Are Devastating the Middle East. *Carnegie Corporation of New York*. www.carnegie.org/topics/topic-articles/arab-region-transitions/why-mass-poverty-so-dangerous-middle-east/.

Layode, M., Schwier, J., Hayi-Charters, S., Holland, M., and Andrian, S. 2021. *Disparities in Funding for African NGOs: Unlocking Philanthropy for African NGOs as a Pathway to Greater Impact*. African Philanthropy Forum and the Bridgespan Group. www.bridgespan.org/bridgespan/Images/articles/disparities-in-funding-for-African-NGOs/disparities-in-funding-for-african-ngos-report.pdf.

Lopez-Acevedo, G., and Hoogeveen, J. 2021. COVID-19 Sets MENA Back on Poverty. *World Bank Group Blog*, 20 December. https://blogs.worldbank.org/arabvoices/covid-19-sets-mena-back-poverty.

Lidji, A., and Mulla, N. 2021. Naghma Mulla, CEO of the EdelGive Foundation, Talks about Philanthropy in India and Their New GROW Fund – Supporting 100 NGOs in India and Backed by the Likes of the Bill & Melinda Gates Foundation. *The Do One Better! Podcast – Philanthropy, Sustainability and Social Entrepreneurship*, 13 December. https://albertolidji.podbean.com/e/naghma-mulla/.

Lynn, J., Nolan, C., and Waring, P. 2021. Strategy Resilience: Getting Wise about Philanthropic Strategy in a Post-Pandemic World. *The Foundation Review*, 13(2), 52–63. https://doi.org/10.9707/1944-5660.1564.

McGeever, J. 2021. Millions in Brazil Thrown Back into Poverty as Pandemic Aid Dries Up. *Reuters*, 26 March. www.reuters.com/article/us-brazil-economy-poverty/millions-in-brazil-thrown-back-into-poverty-as-pandemic-aid-dries-up-idUSKBN2BI2OE.

OECD (Organisation for Economic Co-operation and Development). 2021. *Private Philanthropy for Development – Second Edition: Data for Action*. OECD. www.oecd-ilibrary.org/sites/cdf37f1e-en/1/3/1/index.html?itemId=/content/publication/cdf37f1e-en&_csp_=64f1aacd1c85e6f34404d7f4cde810a9&itemIGO=oecd&itemContentType=book.

Ram, K., and Yadav, S. 2021. The Impact of COVID-19 on Poverty Estimates in India: A Study across Caste, Class and Religion. *Contemporary Voice of Dalit.* https://doi.org/10.1177/2455328X211051432.

UNESCO, UNICEF, and World Bank. 2021. *The State of the Global Education Crisis: The Path to Recovery.* Washington, DC, Paris, New York: The World Bank, UNESCO, and UNICEF. https://documents1.worldbank.org/curated/en/416991638768297704/pdf/The-State-of-the-Global-Education-Crisis-A-Path-to-Recovery.pdf.

Venkatachalam, P., and Shah, K. 2020. Philanthropic Collaboratives in India: The Power of Many. *Bridgespan,* 18 February. www.bridgespan.org/insights/library/philanthropy/philanthropic-collaboratives-in-india.

How Strategic Philanthropy Can Shake Up the Ecosystem and Build Resilience

A Case Study on Increasing Access to Palliative Care in India

Rumana Hamied and Prakash Fernandes

CONTEXT

Traditionally, health-care philanthropy has focused on giving to individual patients, hospitals, and volunteering opportunities. This chapter aims to demonstrate how strategic philanthropy in health care can play an important role in purposefully driving giving to improve health outcomes.

The Constitution of India obliges the government to ensure the 'right to health' for all and requires each state to provide free universal access to health-care services. Unfortunately, the health sector in India has been highly fragmented, not just in terms of financing and provision of health care, but also in terms of the continuum of care and quality standards. While government hospitals offer free health services, these facilities tend to be inadequately equipped, understaffed, and based predominantly in urban areas. Many medical services are, therefore, provided by private institutions and 65 per cent of medical expenditures in India are paid out of pocket by patients.[1]

This chapter outlines how Cipla's (India's third-largest pharmaceutical company) philanthropy and corporate social responsibility (CSR) arms have, since the late 1990s, in tandem, been supporting

---

[1] Ambade, M., Sarwal, R., Mor, N., Kim, R., and Subramanian, S. V. 2022. Components of Out-of-Pocket Expenditure and Their Relative Contribution to Economic Burden of Diseases in India. *JAMA Network Open*, 5(5), e2210040. https://10.1001/jamanetworkopen.2022.10040.

the development of palliative care in India. In a fragmented health system, palliative care can potentially serve as the glue anchoring the patient at the centre of care by recognising that the challenges faced by a person with a serious illness are not just confined to the disease alone. Palliative care acknowledges that illness may cause pain and other symptoms related to the physical, social, and spiritual needs of both the patients and their families and that these should be holistically addressed. The palliative care team thus coordinates the care plan for each patient, seeking to connect a multidisciplinary team to provide all-round care to patients. Unfortunately, palliative care – though essential for quality patient care – is not a revenue source for the health-care industry and hence has been systematically neglected.

In 1997, Cipla's promoter family decided to invest their philanthropic efforts in setting up a palliative centre in Pune, despite being aware that they were not experts on this type of treatment. However, they believed that palliative care is essential to improving the quality of life of patients, and stepped forward to bridge this gap in the Indian health-care space. The single-minded clarity and focus of the family's vision – making palliative care accessible to all – has guided them develop a strategic model and has driven their philanthropic journey thus far.

Cipla's unique approach initially focused on providing direct patient support through palliative care in one Indian city, which then grew into a wider philanthropic strategy when the company mandated Cipla Foundation, its CSR arm to expand palliative care programmes across the country. Thus, the strategy for creating a palliative care ecosystem was informed by the practice and challenges of delivering care at the Cipla Palliative Care and Training Centre (CPC) in Pune. Simultaneously, through the expansion process came learnings from partners across the country, which informed the services at the palliative care centres and ensured they were strengthened over time. Wearing multiple hats as a funder, funder and implementer, has broadened Cipla's philanthropic scope and perspective of palliative care.

This chapter highlights how palliative care emerged as part of the philanthropy agenda, and how philanthropy was directed to set up a 'proof of concept' and lay the foundation to before being used strategically create access to care across the country. In doing so, the chapter also outlines the lessons the team learned and how it responded to challenges along the journey.

It is important to share this story as the Cipla team believes that philanthropy, when used strategically, can play an important role in creating a ripple effect, especially for issues such as palliative care that are neglected by market forces.

CIPLA'S PHILANTHROPY AND PALLIATIVE CARE: THE ROOTS

Palliative care is a niche area in India – one that has found little support on the list of health causes popular with philanthropic funders despite being a gaping unmet need. Only 4 per cent of patients in India with a serious illness receive access to pain relief – the majority live and eventually die in discomfort with their caregivers suffering alongside them.[2] As people live longer with serious and complex illnesses owing to general advancements in medical care, the gap in access to palliative care is only widening in India's fractured and under-resourced health-care system.

In 1997, it was commonly perceived that palliative care equalled hospice care; hence, palliative care was likened to end-of-life care. Therefore, the few available services in the late 1990s only offered this care to patients when curative treatment had ended.

Given that palliative was not clearly understood, from the start Cipla's CPC focused on the importance of using the term palliative care to emphasise addressing 'total patient pain' – whether physical, social, emotional, or spiritual. The vision also held that in order for palliative care to make a real difference to patients and families, it

---

[2] Knaul, F. M. et al. 2017. Alleviating the Access Abyss in Palliative Care and Pain Relief: An Imperative of Universal Health Coverage: The *Lancet* Commission Report. *The Lancet*, 391(10128). www.thelancet.com/commissions/palliative-care.

needed to be introduced close to the time of diagnosis. This would allow for the Cipla team to integrate with the physician to provide a holistic care plan supporting both patients and their caregivers.

The impetus to provide palliative care services in India first came to Cipla in the early 1990s when Dr Lucito D'Souza, a leading cancer surgeon and the founder of Mumbai's first hospice Shanti Avedna Sadan, spoke to Cipla's promoter family about manufacturing morphine sulphate tablets for terminal patients admitted to his facility. Cipla not only supplied the morphine tablets, but the family also visited the hospice in Mumbai to understand pain management for patients with serious illnesses. Upon further study, the family found an abysmal lack of professional palliative care services in India and felt that in such a scenario, simply manufacturing medicines to alleviate the suffering of patients would not be enough.

The second turning point came when the family attended a programme organised by Macmillan Cancer Support, a London-based charity. Macmillan had launched a project to train Indian doctors and nurses in specialist palliative care. The family realised the need for bringing such care to patients in India and the seed for Cipla's Palliative Care Centre was sown. In 1993, when palliative care was still relatively unknown in India, the family acquired a five-acre plot in a quiet suburb of Pune. To translate the vision into action in 1997, the Macmillan nurses in Britain were invited to Pune to demonstrate what a world-class palliative centre should look like and how it should function. This vision has continued to guide the work of Cipla palliative care since the late 1990s, allowing its services to reach over 22,500 patients and caregivers.

USING PHILANTHROPY TO ESTABLISH
A PROOF OF CONCEPT

From the outset, it was clear that the Cipla Centre (CPC) would not be a hospital, neither would it be a hospice for end-of-life patients. It was envisaged that Cipla's CPC would care for a person with cancer at any stage of the illness. A dedicated team of doctors, nursing staff, social workers, specialists, and volunteers would work together to provide the highest level of care to patients and their loved ones, completely free of cost.

After four years of planning and designing the service, on 1 May 1997, CPC welcomed its first patient, and over 20,000 patients and their families have been served ever since. Since 1997, several additions have been made to CPC's services driven by the goal of making quality palliative care accessible to patients and families.

The fifty-bed centre is designed to provide personalised care and exudes an atmosphere of peace and serenity. It is built around the concept of an *aangan*, an open courtyard, to foster a sense of community. The wards are named after flowers and patients are known by their names, not their bed numbers. Furthermore, the thoughtful architectural design of CPC allows even those patients who are confined to their beds who cannot even sit in wheel chairs, to be wheeled outside, on their beds, to enjoy the beautiful surroundings.

The service deeply embeds itself in the Indian ethos of family and community, where patients and caregivers are equally cared for at the Centre, at their home, or in an outpatient department. This model aims to equip family members by giving them the confidence and skills needed to care for their loved ones. Family members also receive ongoing emotional and psychological support, including much-needed grief and bereavement counselling. Box 1 illustrates an example of the difference palliative care can make to both the patient and their family.

Over the course of this process, the Centre's team has learned that to make philanthropy more strategic, they must listen and respond to the voices of all stakeholders to work towards providing quality care.

From patients and caregivers the team learned that they required services suited to their unique needs and phase of illness. From 2004, CPC therefore started home care teams to visit patients and provide services of equal quality in their homes. In 2007, the Centre began outpatient clinics so that palliative care support could be closer to patients when they met their treating physicians and continued to expand home care and outpatient clinics over the subsequent years. In 2020, as COVID-19 struck, CPC responded to patients by strengthening its telephonic and video consultations so that patients could continue to receive care. It also began a patient support programme to provide financial assistance to those seeking treatment.

In services like palliative care, Cipla has learned that the teams delivering the care are agents of change and their insights from practice become instrumental in developing a particular service. Through documenting CPC's interventions on a hospital management system, Cipla has used data and reflections from the team to make changes including: *improving patient care* through sharper assessment tools, *embedding feedback mechanisms* to better understand expectations from patients and caregivers, and *strengthening our services* by understanding the referral sources of patients and strategies to expand referrals from health-care professionals to palliative care.

Doctors helped Cipla understand the gap in communication between physicians and palliative care professionals, along with missed opportunities for information-sharing about pain-relief protocols. CPC responded by finding avenues for enhanced collaboration between these groups through exchange visits, workshops, and training sessions.

Case Study: Early Integration

FIRST MEETING WITH PUSHPA

The team first met Pushpa and her daughter-in-law when they were referred to the CPC by a relative in February 2013. They had been told that CPC doctors are 'different from other hospitals' and 'you don't have be afraid to talk to them'. Pushpa had had a biopsy done three days earlier at a government hospital but was too afraid to collect her reports; she wanted to know if the CPC team could ease her pain. The social worker and the palliative care physician talked with Pushpa to find out more about her journey so far, her fears and expectations. Pushpa and her daughter-in-law also had the opportunity to tour the Centre. At the end of the visit, she agreed to collect the biopsy report but was still unsure of the benefits from any medical interventions. She agreed to have the palliative care team visit her at home to discuss further. After her visit to CPC, she collected the reports that confirmed her cancer diagnosis. Pushpa felt shame, anger, and guilt as a result of this diagnosis and resolved not to undergo any curative treatment.

SUPPORTING PUSHPA IN SEEKING CURATIVE TREATMENT

Two days after her first visit to the Centre, the CPC home care team paid Pushpa a visit, went through her reports that she had just collected, and talked to her about the symptoms she was experiencing. They gave her information about the biopsy procedure, what the results indicated, and how they could be addressed. The CPC team also provided her with a prescription for present symptoms, including hypertension and breathlessness. At the time, Pushpa was not ready for further curative treatment. The home care team told her they would come back in two days to check on her symptoms. When the team visited again, the patient reported that she had some symptomatic relief and again spoke about her fear of cancer and the stigma around being a cancer patient. The home care social workers spoke to her about these fears, discussed her strengths and her methods for coping in the past, and the support that could be available through the CPC. After two more counselling sessions, Pushpa said she was ready to go ahead with curative treatment. The team explained the surgery and what to expect in the aftermath, and identified a local general practitioner whom the team could also contact if necessary.

MANAGING THE EFFECTS OF SURGERY

Pushpa underwent surgery in April 2013 and after discharge she agreed to be admitted at CPC for post-surgery and wound management. Looking back on her two-week stay at CPC, Pushpa describes this experience as one of the most life-changing and peaceful times in her life, where she learnt about caring for herself. The clinical team of doctors, nurses, physiotherapists, and social workers helped prepare and implement a care plan for Pushpa till after her wounds had healed well, she was no longer in pain and felt ready to go back home. She said she was more confident now to face her life ahead and more positive about facing any problems. The home care team assured her that she could call at any time and also briefed the local GP on Pushpa's condition.

ESTABLISHING A HOME CARE ROUTINE

The CPC home care team visited Pushpa two days after she left the Centre and advised her to see her oncologist as well for a check-up. They also went through her medications, diet, and exercise routine. At this visit, she explained her worries about the ill health of her youngest son, who was seeking treatment but did not seem to be getting better. Before the next visit scheduled for the following week, Pushpa called the home care team with news that her son had passed away – she was feeling guilty that due to her illness, she had neglected her son's health. The home care team spent time with Pushpa to listen to her worries and reminded her of all the support she had provided as a mother. The team continued to support Pushpa in addressing her guilt, and after a month she said she had now accepted the situation. The home care team began visiting once a month from that point forward.

CONTINUING CARE FOR PUSHPA

The home care journey continued for Pushpa over the next several years. In September 2015, Pushpa mentioned on a call that she felt some pain in her left hand. The team asked her to come to the Centre and realised that she was developing mild lymphedema; she visited CPC regularly for physiotherapy and in two weeks was completely cured. The routine home visits and telephone calls continued – the home care team continues to be part of Pushpa's life and joins in during family wedding and birthday celebrations, as well as difficult times for the family.

Pushpa's case exemplifies a successful story of early support where the CPC team built trust and rapport with a patient, allowing for the establishment of a longer-term palliative care arrangement. There are many more patients like Pushpa who require support and CPC hopes to reach as many of them as possible in the years ahead.

WHY PALLIATIVE CARE CONTINUES TO BE NURTURED AND STRENGTHENED

In 2016, when Cipla Foundation – the CSR arm of Cipla – began to engage strategically in palliative care, there was a strong conviction that palliative care had the power to transform the health-care system. This conviction stemmed from the positive health outcomes the Pune Centre achieved despite facing challenges. In striving to overcome difficulties at CPC, the below critical concerns emerged:

- **Need for greater awareness, understanding and acceptance about the benefits of palliative care**: Many misconceptions remain among health-care providers and patients about the concept of palliative care as being 'end-of-life' care rather than 'complementary' care that should run alongside curative treatment protocols. Doctors and patient family members, who may be focused on curing an illness until the very end, misunderstand palliative care as a failure to adequately treat and help patients.[3] In addition, the use of opioids for pain relief, which are used in palliative care, are shrouded in misapprehensions as addictive drugs that can result in legal risks and misuse. This results in a double-edged challenge for health-care providers, who may not refer patients to palliative care facilities, and for patients, who may not demand palliative care in time.
- **Increasing access to holistic healing and total pain management**: The CPC team observed that health-care providers focus primarily on physical pain relief. As a result, the vast majority of patients live a poor quality of life, especially just before death. Additionally, there is a lack of awareness about the use of opioids in pain relief.[4]
- **Improving communication between health-care providers, patients, and families**: In an overburdened health-care system patients with serious illnesses and their families often feel rushed, with inadequate support and information about their disease prognosis and care plans. This is further exacerbated by the lack of communication within the family due

---

[3] Salins, N., Ghoshal, A., Hughes, S., and Preston, N. 2020. How Views of Oncologists and Haematologists Impacts Palliative Care Referral: A Systematic Review. *BMC Palliative Care*, 19, 175, https://doi.org/10.1186/s12904-020-00671-5.

[4] Kar, S. S., Subitha, L., and Iswarya, S. 2015. Palliative Care in India: Situation Assessment and Future Scope. *Indian Journal of Cancer*, 52, 99–101. www.indianjcancer.com/text .asp?2015/52/1/99/175578.

to the stigma of certain health conditions as well as fear of discussing the impact of the condition on the patient.

- **Enhancing palliative care skills amongst health-care providers**: The Centre's team realised that there is an acute shortage of trained palliative care professionals, including physicians, nurses, and social workers. They also learned about the lack of evidence-based palliative care training opportunities available for health-care providers to deepen their skills. The team's on-ground experience of the difficulty in getting trained palliative care professionals for the Centre fuelled Cipla's belief that training was an essential component of the strategy to scale up palliative care work in India.
- **Focusing on the needs of caregivers**: Family members who visited the Centre in Pune told the team how their own physical, financial, emotional, and spiritual needs had been neglected, and described the support they required to cope with the relentless demands of caregiving. A key guiding principle in Cipla's work therefore became ensuring that the patient's family also receives ongoing emotional and psychosocial support, including much-needed bereavement counselling. Throughout the patient's journey, the palliative care team assesses the needs of both the patient and the caregivers and has a care plan for both. This aspect of palliative care ensures that the focus remains on holistically observing how the illness impacts both the patient and caregiver.
- **Ensuring a continuum of care**: The CPC team members learned that successful palliative care ensures that no patient with a serious illness suffers because of pain, whether in hospital or at home. In addition to inpatient care, they realised the immense scope and value of providing patients with the choice of providing quality services at outpatient clinics or at their homes. Patients and families told the Centre's team that they often spend longer periods of time than needed at hospitals for fear of losing access to quality care back home. Cipla's goal was therefore to achieve the same standard through home care services.

These key insights not only guided the philanthropic strategy in running the Palliative Care Centre in Pune, but further informed Cipla's vision to strengthen palliative care access across the country. The aim of this type of strategic philanthropy centres on building an ecosystem where all health-care providers embody the essence of palliative care and adopt its responsive approach to meet patient needs, delivering care based on patient preferences.

USING PHILANTHROPY STRATEGICALLY TO CREATE ACCESS TO CARE

To take forward Cipla's palliative care vision, Cipla Foundation's (CF) strategy is to invest in direct services that will create greater health-care access for Indians. The Foundation supports this aim by partnering with organisations interested in developing palliative care services in their locations or with those seeking to consolidate and expand their existing palliative care work.

By October 2023, CF was supporting thirty partner organisations across twenty-four Indian cities, as illustrated in Figure 8.1. The Foundation's budgets over the past five years have also grown to reflect the commitment to palliative care, from 12 crore rupees (£1,255,000) in 2019–1920 to 16 crore rupees (£1,675,000) in 2021–2022.[5] From April 2021 to March 2022 alone, Cipla CPC and its partners offered palliative care services to over 10,000 patients.[6]

The strategy of CF, whilst creating access, has been to partner with like-minded organisations already working in this space and find champions willing to take on palliative care in their geographies. Further focus on training and building a cadre of health-care professionals with a palliative care approach has supported strong collaborations at a national level to take forward changes in policy and resource allocation to palliative care.

IDENTIFYING AND SUPPORTING CHAMPIONS

A key process for the Foundation has been identifying champions for palliative care and supporting them in strengthening services. In doing so, CF has focused on a variety of service models in palliative care, examined how palliative care can move beyond oncology, and demonstrated that partnerships with the government are important to scaling up the work and making it accessible.

---

[5] *Cipla Annual Report 2021.*
[6] Cipla Foundation financial reports.

FIGURE 8.1 Palliative care services supported by the Cipla Foundation

- **Strengthening existing palliative care providers**: Initially, the Foundation began partnerships with partners that enabled cross-sharing of work between teams. CF recognised innovative work being implemented by other organisations and supported these partners to strengthen their service delivery. For example, many partners have existing inpatient facilities but lacked home care services. The Foundation's support enabled them to provide a continuum of care to patients ensuring that health facilities are accessible to the most vulnerable.
- **Setting up palliative care in new geographies**: The Foundation also identified champions in locations that had no palliative care services available

and supported their development of integrated outpatient clinics offering palliative care services, with the aim of having a more equitable distribution across the country.

- **Developing palliative care services beyond oncology**: The Foundation supported the establishment of a novel inclusive inpatient palliative care facility in Mumbai. It has also partnered with India's premier institute for neurology to set up an outpatient clinic for patients with neurological conditions in Bengaluru.
- **Demonstrating that palliative care is for children and adults of all ages**: CF has partnered with champions in charitable and state hospitals to set up paediatric palliative care units, supporting six of these centres across the country to date.
- **Piloting community projects along with the state governments**: To work towards integrating palliative care within the public health-care system, the Foundation has been supporting a project with the state government. Through this community-based project, it trains government health workers to use a checklist of symptoms to identify patients requiring palliative care and refer them accordingly. Additionally, CF trains doctors, nurses, and multipurpose workers to provide palliative care at primary health-care centres, subcentres, and rural hospitals. The project has now been scaled up to an entire district with the hope that this pilot will encourage an uptake at the state level.

CASCADING PALLIATIVE CARE THROUGH TRAINED PROFESSIONALS

The need for training has been a consistent theme that emerged from Cipla's experience at the Centre and through its partnerships. At the Foundation, the strategy uses an evidence-based curriculum, focuses on partnering with premier training institutes in the country, identifies key audiences for training, ensures the follow up of training activities, and allows for practical hands-on training.

The Foundation has forged partnerships with End-of-Life Nursing Education Curriculum (ELNEC) USA and Education in Palliative and End-of-Life Care (EPEC) USA to design training modules along with palliative care professionals in India to adapt this to local needs. CF's support has enabled this face-to-face collaboration, ensuring that jointly the organisations developed and piloted modules to deepen knowledge and skills on palliative care. By supporting the ELNEC and EPEC programmes, Cipla trained 2,600+ nurses including 35 trainers, and over 120 physicians. Such training also includes a training-of-trainers component with a professional development workshop to create a cadre of lead trainers who cascade the training across the country.

CF has, further, trained professionals across the country by partnering with institutions that have a national presence in the Indian public health-care system, including the All India Institute of Medical Sciences (AIIMS), New Delhi, and the Tata Memorial Hospital. A key aspect of all these training programmes centres on providing a mentorship programme for participants that extends beyond the core training.

Based on the existing services supported by the Foundation, oncologists and paediatricians were identified as key professionals to train in palliative care. It has therefore partnered with the SAARC Federation of Oncologists (SFO) as well as the Indian Academy of Paediatricians (IAP) to train their members. To date the Foundation has trained 450 oncologists and over 100 paediatricians in palliative care.

As palliative care becomes integrated into the health-care curriculum of doctors and nurses, the need to design a training programme for faculty in teaching hospitals has emerged. The Foundation will continue to intensify its efforts to support such programmes.

NATIONAL COLLABORATIONS FOR POLICY CHANGE

Whilst the Foundation's team does not directly lobby state and national governments, it supports and collaborates with its partners to advocate for better access to pain relief, training of doctors and nurses, and greater allocation of government resources for palliative care. CF supports training programmes and best-practice exchange, in addition to bringing members together on national, regional, and theme-based platforms to promote palliative care. It also supports partners in pressing the government for better allocation of resources to palliative care and adding this important service area to the agenda for the broader national health-care system.

The Foundation has thus been striving to work alongside its partners to create access to palliative care by generating a ripple effect through its support in direct services, training, and collaborations, so that access becomes a basic right for patients and caregivers.

USING PHILANTHROPY AS A CATALYST FOR SUSTAINABLE CHANGE

When analysing the role of Cipla's philanthropy and CSR in supporting sustainable change in palliative care, key themes that emerge are:

- **Integrated models of care in the public health system**: Cipla Foundation's work has focused on strengthening services in outpatient clinics in key government and charitable hospitals. Its support enables the overstretched public health-care system to recruit for an embedded palliative care team. This multidisciplinary team then works in close collaboration with the treating physician to coordinate care for the patient, and to answer questions from the patient and caregiver about their concerns, treatment options, and how the treatment is impacting them, thus reducing time required by the treating physician. This integrated clinic model further enables palliative care to be offered earlier on to patients and caregivers, given its availability within the hospital itself. Through these programmes, the CF demonstrates the value of housing a specialised team within a larger institution to deliver care, train other professionals, facilitate interdisciplinary working, and achieve better health outcomes. Once the value proposition of these interventions is felt within the hospital, it becomes easier to discuss further funding or co-funding partnerships with the hospital leadership team.
- **Bringing partners together to increase reach and impact:** The Foundation upholds the belief that changing the health-care ecosystem requires a truly collaborative movement to embed and integrate palliative care. CF has taken every opportunity to join forces with committed, passionate individuals and organisations working in the palliative care space,

strengthening its resolve to bring partners together, share knowledge and skills, and leverage best practices. The Foundation even attempted this during COVID-19 through the establishment of a national palliative care helpline – Saath Saath.

During the height of COVID-19, several palliative care services, and especially home care services, were interrupted. The extremely vulnerable subset of palliative care patients experienced difficulty accessing medical care in the event of increased symptom burden, obstacles in reaching hospitals during emergencies or at end of life, limited access to medication, and isolation due to social distancing regulations, all of which led to psychosocial impacts and a lack of bereavement support. The Foundation consulted with partners and experts internationally to draw up standard operating procedures that guided the care at Cipla's Centre as well as at its partner organizations. This enabled palliative care to safely continue for both staff and patients. CF also facilitated regular discussions amongst partners to share experiences and learn how best to support patients especially through telemedicine services.

The value of reaching out to patients and caregivers through technology became apparent during COVID-19 and initiated the development of a national palliative care helpline.

The Foundation played a leading role in bringing together its partners to develop the helpline Saath Saath, a toll-free number for patients, caregivers, and professionals that launched in October 2021. This is the first national palliative care helpline in India, linking callers to their nearest palliative care service. Calls in the first 2 years (over 4,500 calls) demonstrate the value of having a single point of contact for patients, and further highlight the gaps in service provision which need to be addressed.

- **Aligning with government priorities:** State governments have been developing their non-communicable disease (NCD) programmes in recent years, offering crucial opportunities to integrate palliative care. Cipla Foundation learned about this opportunity through supporting a community-based project with the National Health Mission. The community-based project supported by CF strategically aligned with the NCD so that prevention, promotion, palliation, treatment, and rehabilitation are all integrated into the care programme. This enabled the training of health-care workers and identifying patients with serious illnesses early in their disease trajectory. As a Foundation, Cipla will continuously review the latest government priorities and find relevant partners in order to dovetail palliative care within such programmes.

- **Attracting more philanthropists to the palliative care space:** To broaden funding to palliative care services, Cipla has been engaging with funding agencies and philanthropists to deepen their support towards palliative care services. Of the twenty-three projects Cipla Foundation supported between 2021–2022, nearly one third of them were able to raise additional funds from donors for these projects.[7] Cipla recognizes that whilst government funding to palliative care may increase over time, there is an urgent need for more philanthropists and corporations to include palliative care projects within their scope of health-care work.

CHALLENGES IN ADVANCING PALLIATIVE CARE

Notable challenges faced during implementation of the services work have included:

- **Changing the perception of palliative care:** Misunderstandings around palliative care are a substantial barrier inhibiting all stakeholders, including patients, health-care professionals, and donors, from deeper involvement in this area. Shifting mindsets is extremely important for palliative care to truly become embedded in the health-care system. Cipla attempts to change this perception by avoiding certain terms such as 'life limiting', 'threatening', and 'beyond cure' whilst explaining palliative care. However, this requires a larger behavioural-change campaign to enable stakeholders to see the supportive nature of palliative care as well as the medical science of care in palliation.
- **Measuring impact:** India lacks clear evidence of impact in palliative care. There have been some studies outside of India that demonstrated how early integration of palliative care leads to better health-related quality of life, improved communication, fewer emergency hospitalisations, less distress, and better satisfaction with care. However, there is a lack of India-specific research and data. Additionally, outcome tools in palliative care have been developed and standardised outside of India and need to be standardised based on the country's national norms. Cipla, through its Foundation is now embarking on a research programme aiming to develop guidelines and standard operating principles for palliative care service provision.

[7] Cipla Foundation annual report 2021.

- **Financing health care**: Given that palliative care is not seen as part of the health-care continuum, funding is very limited in an already underfinanced broader system. This challenge forces the Cipla team to prioritise and strategise on how to achieve maximum reach. To ensure lack of funding does not limit newer initiatives, more philanthropists and donors need to co-fund palliative care projects, especially for home care services that reach patients most in need.
- **Supply of trained palliative care professionals**: Related to the issues of awareness and funding, there is a dearth of health professionals opting to specialise in palliative medicine. This challenge requires deeper awareness in all medical, nursing, and social work colleges about palliative care as well as the development of specialised courses for professionals to further enhance their skills.

Whilst the Cipla team has attempted to mitigate some of these challenges in a limited way, it feels confident that now is the time for a concerted effort from all stakeholders to further advance the palliative care agenda. Cipla Foundation is committed to furthering this movement.

CONCLUSION

Through its philanthropy and CSR efforts, Cipla has worn multiple hats as a programme funder and implementer, broadening its scope and perspective on how to strategically shape the palliative care ecosystem. After twenty-five years working in this space, Cipla Foundation is now poised to move forward with its legacy. Whilst the Foundation hopes to continually be flexible in responding to emerging needs, the principles that guide its strategic focus will be based on a commitment to increasing access to palliative care, strengthening collaborations and partnerships, and collecting evidence to improve practice and policy.

Cipla Foundation believes that the pathway to achieving its goal requires collaborations at all levels. As it strengthens and forges new partnerships, it will continue to identify champions, work with the public health-care system, and ensure integrated models of care so that the needs of patients remain at the core of the service.

CF is further committed to facilitating platforms to increase dialogue and communication between stakeholders. It hopes this will lead to greater awareness about the key issues, attract more talent into the space, increase funding to palliative care, and develop more training opportunities and dissemination of information on palliative care.

Cipla's work in service delivery through its Centre at Pune, has strengthened its conviction that palliative care, when understood as responsive care for patients with a serious illness, has the potential to transform the Indian health-care system to one that is more person-centred and can improve health-related outcomes. Cipla strives to make a difference with a strategy guided by keeping people, especially the most disadvantaged, at the heart of the health-care system. It hopes that this strategy of philanthropic commitment to palliative care that engages all stakeholders will create a ripple effect in the entire health-care ecosystem.

9 Building Resilience for the Malaysian Education Ecosystem during the Pandemic and Beyond

Kathleen Wai Lin Chew

INTRODUCTION

Malaysia is a young nation, one that seeks to establish itself as an example of a dynamic melting pot of Asian cultures that has grown out of its colonial past and embraced the global economy. As the wealth of the country has increased, there has been a growing awareness since the early 2010s that investment in a vibrant social sector is necessary to address the inequalities that often accompany rapid economic growth. In other words, Malaysia not only needs more social purpose organisations, but also a strong and resilient ecosystem that supports those working in the social sector.

The COVID-19 pandemic taught Malaysians the importance of having a strong education ecosystem. Schools closed for a total of thirty-seven weeks in 2020 and 2021, and the usual way of working through schools to deliver the programmes we at YTL Foundation offered was no longer possible. We therefore turned to partners like Teach For Malaysia, who have played a key role in building the education ecosystem since the early 2010s, and other content partners, then sought the skills of an education technology ('edtech') solutions provider. Finally, we brought in a telecommunications company, and together we provided the devices, connectivity, and online learning resources to keep children learning during lockdown.

In those first dark days of the pandemic, as we worked around the clock to deliver our solution, it was stories of the families that we managed to reach that kept the team engaged and motivated.

LOCKDOWN

Chinese New Year, one of the major celebrations in Malaysia, was just over, and the country was reeling from the second political upheaval in two years. For the first time in Malaysian history, the Opposition had won the general election in 2018. In a strange twist of events, the 94-year-old prime minister resigned after less than two years into office, making room for a realignment of loyalties and the installation of a new coalition government. Just days later, the country went under a total lockdown to protect its citizens from the new coronavirus that was spreading at an unprecedented speed across the world.

The usual panic buying of food and essential items started, and businesses braced themselves for a new regime of working from home while closing their shops and factories. Most believed that this situation would only last for a few months at most.

Schools across the country closed and parents started worrying about their children's lessons while considering how they would cope with having to tutor them from home. Most schools were not prepared for delivering online classes even though the Ministry of Education had for many years tried to implement edtech solutions, including providing virtual learning environments, and then Google Classrooms for all schools. And even if schools were capable of pivoting to online classes, did families have the devices and data necessary for students to attend these classes? What if the pandemic could not be controlled for a prolonged period and children continued to be locked down at home?

These were questions that absorbed us at YTL Foundation in the first weeks of the pandemic. As an education foundation that has worked with Malaysian public schools for many years, we understood the challenges that the entire community would face during lockdown. We worried about learning loss, especially for the most vulnerable and disadvantaged children.

There was an urgency to do something to address this gap whilst the government worked on its own solution, but we knew we could not do it alone. The immediate need was to make available devices, data, and learning resources, and we had to find partners to help us provide these. Racing against time, we mobilised YTL Communications, edtech solution provider FrogAsia, and volunteer teachers from Teach For Malaysia. Two weeks after lockdown began, we launched the Learn From Home initiative in late March 2020.

Over the course of 2020, we gave out over 100,000 smartphones to low-income families, 18 million gigabytes of free data, 450,000 data SIM cards, and created over 1,200 digital lessons mapped to the Malaysian school curriculum in the subjects of English, Mathematics, Science, and Malay, and launched a gamified quiz app with over 13,500 quizzes. In 2021, through subsidies provided by the government, we gave out another 750,000 smartphones, onboarded new partners, and continued to work on expanding the lessons to other core subjects.

We started this journey to address a need we saw during the early months of COVID-19, but we have learnt that the need extends far beyond the pandemic. We must ensure that the Malaysian education ecosystem is both flexible and resilient enough to face new challenges by investing in technology, and supporting learners, parents, and educators to make the best use of the solutions available to them.

In this chapter, we will discuss the challenges faced in rolling out the Learn From Home initiative nationwide during lockdown, the partners we brought in that enabled us to do this, and how engaging the government and continuing to forge new community partnerships is vitally important to scale up and build a resilient education ecosystem for the long term.

THE MALAYSIAN CONTEXT

While the pandemic was the spur for action, it was the context in which the Learn From Home initiative operates that informed the need for urgency in our response. Malaysia's education system is in crisis and despite many attempts at addressing the issues, progress has been slow.

In the 2012 Programme for International Student Assessment (PISA),[1] Malaysia came out in the bottom third out of the sixty-five participating countries, and among the Asian countries that participated, it only outperformed Indonesia and lagged behind even lower-income countries such as Vietnam.

A year later, Malaysia launched the Malaysian Education Blueprint 2013–2025 (known as the Blueprint),[2] a comprehensive plan for a rapid and sustainable transformation of the education system through to 2025. There was a general recognition in the Blueprint that whilst access to education had improved significantly, the quality of the student outcomes had deteriorated. Poor teacher quality and weak school leadership resulting from the rapid expansion of schools in the country, the use of rote learning techniques against teaching higher-order thinking skills, poor language skills, and the lack of autonomy of schools are some of the factors that contributed to the decline.

In 2018, Malaysia showed a slight improvement in the PISA scores but was still below the Organisation for Economic Co-operation and Development (OECD) average.[3] Whilst PISA scores alone may not reveal the true state of the quality of a country's education system, they provide some indicators and track whether improvements have been made over time.

There is also a trust deficit felt by parents towards the national education system in Malaysia, as reflected in the significant increase in student enrolment in private education at primary, secondary, and tertiary levels since the early 2010s. For example, in the five years from 2013 to 2017, enrolments in private schools grew from 172,684 to 209,966, an increase of approximately 21.5 per cent.[4] This flight to private education has meant that it is the bottom 40 per cent of the population, particularly in rural areas, who suffer most from the gaps

[1] OECD Programme for International Student Assessment (PISA) Results from PISA 2012.
[2] Malaysia Education Blueprint 2013–2025 (Preschool to Post-Secondary Education).
[3] OECD Programme for International Student Assessment (PISA) Results from PISA 2018.
[4] Malaysian Ministry of Education: Quick Facts 2013 and 2017, Malaysian Education Statistics.

in the public education system and there is less urgency to address these gaps because the economically better-off populations do not experience them.

Malaysia also has a large number of refugees who have fled to the country as a transit point for resettlement to other countries like the United States or Australia – this includes both refugees from regional neighbours like Myanmar as well as a significant number of refugees from other countries. As of October 2021, there were some 179,830 refugees and asylum-seekers registered with UNHCR (United Nations Higher Commission for Refugees) in Malaysia.[5] This includes 45,870 children below the age of 18. However, refugee children in Malaysia are denied access to the formal education system and must resort to obtaining their education via an informal parallel system of community-based schools run by their own communities, non-governmental organisations (NGOs), and faith-based organisations. While these organisations provide much-needed services, the quality of education offered is understood to lag behind the education offered in mainstream schools.

The country has a relatively good internet infrastructure, with the World Bank reporting internet penetration at 90 per cent in 2020.[6] YTL Foundation's programmes have therefore been aimed at helping schools improve teaching and learning using the many innovative tools and solutions that technology provides in education. It has also supported NGOs that work with refugee children, and the two learning centres it operates provide additional support for these children as well as those from low-income families, classified as B40.

Such was the state of the education system when the pandemic brought everything to a standstill.

Soon after the country went into lockdown, many stories were carried in the media of teachers doing their best to continue

---

[5] UNHCR Malaysia, 'Figures at a Glance in Malaysia', www.unhcr.org/en-my/figures-at-a-glance-in-malaysia.html.

[6] World Bank, 'Individuals Using the Internet (% of Population) – Malaysia', https://data.worldbank.org/indicator/IT.NET.USER.ZS?locations=MY.

teaching online but finding that many of their students could not participate due to the lack of devices or data. A survey conducted by the Ministry of Education in April 2020 revealed that nearly 37 per cent or up to 900,000 students affected by school closures due to the COVID-19 outbreak had no access to an electronic device for e-learning purposes.[7] Even if a household had a device, family members would have to share it among themselves for work and/or study. Unsurprisingly, those with the lowest access were students from B40 families, including refugee children.

Teachers were also struggling to cope with having to use unfamiliar online tools whilst caring for their families at home. Some used WhatsApp or Telegram groups to keep in touch with their students and to give out homework but many were at a loss as to how to deal with online classes.

Cheryl Fernando, Country Director for Pemimpin Global School Leaders, who worked with over 200 school leaders across 90 schools to help them cope with the situation during the first months of the pandemic said, 'Many teachers and school leaders are not adequately trained on using tech tools to teach. Many also wait for the directives from the government on what tools to use in their online teaching.'

A paper published by Khazanah Research Institute on 28 April 2020 titled 'COVID-19 and Unequal Learning' concluded, 'In addition to strengthening broadband penetration, more needs to be done to ensure all children have access to the needed devices, including making devices more affordable/accessible. It is especially urgent to develop high quality digital content, perhaps even translating appropriate foreign materials, and to equip teachers with the skills to more effectively use e-learning technologies.'[8]

A few of the large Malaysian telecommunications companies offered an additional one gigabyte of data daily to their customers,

---

[7] *The Edge Malaysia*, 'Edu Nation: Let's Get Digital Learning Right', www .theedgemarkets.com/article/edu-nation-lets-get-digital-learning-right.

[8] Hamid, H. A., and Khalidi, J. R. 2020. *COVID-19 and Unequal Learning*. Kuala Lumpur: Khazanah Research Institute, p. 43.

but that was not enough: it generally did not help those without any devices or any internet plans.

In this context, there was an urgent need to provide devices, data, and high-quality digital content to students in the country, especially to those from B40 families.

THE LEARN FROM HOME INITIATIVE

The YTL Foundation, and YTL Group entities FrogAsia and YTL Communications, came together early in the pandemic and rapidly developed a coordinated emergency response to support learning in Malaysia, particularly for children in low-income families.

Their aim was to address key barriers to educational continuity and advancement during the COVID-19 period through providing devices and data to support access to compelling, curriculum-aligned learning materials.

Under the Learn From Home initiative, they put together a package of free 4G SIM cards, mobile phones with data plans, and digital lessons in English, Malay, Mathematics, and Science (later expanded to include all core subjects by the end of 2022). An app with more than 13,500 revision quizzes was also released for free download in the App Store and Google Play Store.

Each aspect of the Learn From Home response is detailed as follows.

Free SIM Cards with 40 Gigabytes of Data

YTL Communications provided free 4G SIM cards, each pre-loaded with 40 gigabytes of data.

Whilst YTL Communications is a relatively new telecommunications company, it has the widest mobile footprint across Malaysia when it comes to the provision of 4G services, especially in the rural areas. The company has built its network to cover about 80 per cent of schools in the country, some quite remote. With the exception of those living in the interiors of East Malaysia and along the mountainous regions of Peninsular Malaysia, populations with school-going children tend to live close to schools and therefore within network coverage.

A major challenge at the time was verifying the identity of the parents receiving the free SIM cards as the country was completely under lockdown. YTL Communications had to find technical solutions to comply with regulatory requirements surrounding the registration and verification of parent identities, which had hitherto only been done through in-person interactions at physical stores. Working around the clock, the engineers managed to develop and deploy online registration systems and optical character-recognition technologies within two weeks of lockdown.

As hundreds of thousands of applications streamed in, teams from other parts of the company had to be redeployed to assist in the processing of the applications. Once the applications were approved, more resources had to be brought in to handle the dispatch and delivery of the SIM cards across the country. Over 750,000 applications were received and processed in 2020 when the country was in total lockdown.

Free Mobile Phones with 12 Month Data Plan

Whilst the free data SIM cards were made available to all students, the more pressing need was to put devices into the hands of students from B40 families. The challenge here was to find a solution that would:

- ensure that the mobile phones would be given to B40 students only and not those from higher-income families; and
- assist B40 families in applying for the mobile phones, as many have low literacy and technical skills.

Standard communication channels like the press and news channels would only reach a limited number of families and probably leave out those most in need. We at the Foundation therefore decided to launch an extensive social media campaign to seek nominations for these families from the public.

The nominator could be a teacher, community leader, religious organisation, an NGO, or even a kind neighbour. The nominator would attest to the income status of the nominee and provide the basic information required for the nominee to qualify. Once qualified, nominators were asked to assist the nominees to complete the online application process.

The strategy paid off. The free mobile phone campaign went viral and nominations flooded in, with the website briefly crashing from the high initial traffic. At the start of the initiative, YTL Communications had an existing stock of 20,000 mobile phones. It soon became clear that this would not be sufficient to help the many who needed the phones.

We at the Foundation increased our budget, set a target to give out 100,000 mobile phones, and mandated YTL Communications to procure the balance of the phones. With factories closed in most countries and global supply chains disrupted, this proved to be another significant challenge, but we finally managed to secure supplies and by the end of 2020 had reached our target of delivering 100,000 mobile phones to those who needed them most.

Digital Learning Resources

Digital Lessons in English, Malay, Mathematics, and Science
The Learn From Home initiative's edtech partner, FrogAsia, had worked with Malaysian schools since 2012 to deliver a virtual platform for teaching and learning. FrogAsia therefore had a deep understanding of curriculum delivery in schools as well as the challenges of digital adoption by teachers.

FrogAsia was able to rapidly deploy its team to work on creating new, engaging, and interactive lessons on its platform. An early question from the team was who would be teaching using the lessons, parents or teachers? It was agreed that as children were now learning from home and not in school, the lessons would be framed to address parents. In this new environment, parents would have to play the role of teachers and facilitators for their children's lessons.

We in the partnership also decided to dispense with the requirement for parents and students to register or login to access the digital lessons. The lessons would be available on the website with just a simple click. Whilst this would mean the loss of some of the features of the platform and some data tracking functionality, it would lower barriers to access and address the immediate need during the crisis.

While the FrogAsia team was able to build the digital lessons on its learning platform, we at the Foundation still faced the problem of sourcing for teachers familiar with the national curriculum to create the necessary lesson plans and content. The teachers we needed required the skills to work online, innovativeness in their approach, and willingness to sacrifice their time for this mission.

Our first thought was to reach out to Teach For Malaysia, as they have been a grantee of YTL Foundation since the start of their Fellowship Programme in 2012; their pool of fellows and teaching alumni would tick all the necessary boxes. Their trustees and CEO immediately embraced the vision and from April through to September 2020, about fifty of their fellows and teaching alumni worked on the digital lessons with FrogAsia.

Later, other partners like MYReaders, a social enterprise working on English literacy, along with final-year and master's students from the linguistics department of Universiti Kebangsaan Malaysia were brought in to work on completing the entire suite of English lessons and start work on the Malay lessons.

By the end of 2021 we had more than 1,200 lessons available on our website covering the entire curriculum for English, Malay, Mathematics, and Science from Year 1 to Year 11. Currently, we are working on adding lessons in all other core subjects with funding provided by CIMB Foundation.

Kindity, a preschool, also joined us in creating lessons for preschool children.

Launchpad Learning App

To support the Learn From Home Initiative, FrogAsia developed Launchpad (formerly known as 'FrogPlay'), a gamified revision quiz app and fast tracked it through the App Store and Google Play Store.

Pelangi Publishing, a major education publisher in Malaysia, agreed to release its bank of quizzes for public use through the app. Over the course of 2020, FrogAsia continued to create and release additional quizzes, making up over 13,500 quizzes in all core subjects, including Mandarin and Tamil, on Launchpad.

Today all our digital lessons are also available on the app so students can both learn and use the revision quizzes on their mobile phones.

As of the end of 2021, the lessons and quizzes have been accessed more than 1 million times.

UNIQUELY ENGAGING PARENTS

Providing data, devices, and digital lessons would allow learning to continue online but if teachers were unable to connect with their students, parents would have to step into the role of teacher.

For this reason, we at YTL Foundation specifically aimed to engage parents. Many parents felt overwhelmed by the sudden, urgent need to play the role of teacher while maintaining a full working schedule during the pandemic. Our lessons were therefore developed with parents in mind and helped parents support their children while learning from home.

The United Nations Children's Fund's (UNICEF's) Research Brief 'Parental Engagement in Children's Learning' of September 2020 concludes:

> It is crucial, in these difficult times of school closures, to provide reading material and support for parental engagement and to ensure that the most vulnerable are not left behind. All policy decisions on continuing education remotely should also be cognisant of parents' capability to help their child learn in order to prevent further exacerbating the global learning crisis and amplifying the learning gaps across socio-demographic groups.[9]

[9] UNICEF, 'Parental Engagement in Children's Learning: Insights for Remote Learning Response during COVID-19', September 2020, https://docs.edtechhub.org/lib/AIRLRUKJ.

Other solutions that we have seen during the pandemic, and certainly most edtech solutions overall, are primarily aimed at helping teachers. Whilst research clearly shows the need to support parental engagement, there are few initiatives targeted at parents. We at the Foundation tested our approach with education specialists and parents and received positive reviews, giving us the confidence to continue this strategy.

Professor Colin Diamond CBE, Professor of Educational Leadership, University of Birmingham, after reviewing the lessons, said:

> I have had a good look around and imagined that I was a dad at home brand new to teaching. And it worked! The approach at the beginning is well-structured and took me into thinking about 'what is a lesson?' and how to get things going. You have lots of online materials in the different subject and age level areas with the quizzes to back up learning. I was just looking at the 'Imagine you are the Prime Minister' English lesson where you write down all the things that your country will need during the pandemic – really 'on the money' contemporary curriculum.[10]

LEVERAGING PARTNERSHIPS

When YTL Foundation first conceived the plan for rolling out the initiative in the first weeks of the national lockdown, it drew on the strengths and capabilities of a range of partner entities within the broader YTL Group, one of Malaysia's leading multinational corporations. This allowed the Foundation to act quickly and mobilise existing resources despite the confusion and uncertainties that pervaded the country at the time.

As the plans developed and we at the Foundation could see beyond the first response to the crisis, we tapped into the strengths of Teach For Malaysia, as well as our network of local NGOs and

---

[10] University of Birmingham, 'Becoming the Teacher – Hopes and Fears Taking on the Job at Home', https://blog.bham.ac.uk/socialsciencesbirmingham/2020/03/25/becoming-the-teacher-hopes-and-fears-taking-on-the-job-at-home/.

universities. These partners helped to curate and develop the content for our lessons and learning resources.

We set out with the objective of developing lessons and resources for parents to help their children learn at home during lockdown. However, these resources can equally support anyone who needs material to teach to national curriculum standards. The Teach For Malaysia fellows who helped with the development of the lessons naturally use the lessons for their own classes in school.

We therefore sought out partners who would benefit from using the lessons and resources, and trained them in these online resources. Our partners included teachers' unions, community schools, NGOs, and faith-based volunteer groups that provide after-school tuition to underprivileged students, and corporations like Deloitte who have an internal volunteer programme for teaching English to students in low-cost housing communities.

National Union of the Teaching Profession

The National Union of the Teaching Profession (NUTP) is the largest teachers' union in the country with over 230,000 members. Engaging teachers is important as they are at the front line, tasked with delivering home-based learning during school closure and dealing with the learning loss experienced by students during the lockdown.

A recent World Bank analysis of early evidence from the pandemic reveals that while remote learning has not been equally effective everywhere, hybrid learning is here to stay.[11] The report concludes that for remote learning to deliver on its potential, a key element is having effective teachers with high subject-content knowledge, skills to use technology, and appropriate pedagogical tools and support.

Whilst we at the YTL Foundation had started out with the aim of supporting parents at home to teach their children, we believe that

---

[11] Muñoz-Najar, A., Gilberto, A., Hasan, A., Cobo, C., Azevedo, J. P., and Akmal, M. 2021. *Remote Learning during COVID-19: Lessons from Today, Principles for Tomorrow*. Washington, DC: World Bank Group.

supporting teachers will become more important as we settle into a hybrid approach to teaching and learning. Teachers can use our lessons as a baseline, since they follow the national curriculum standards and use a range of strategies to keep children engaged. They can also use their own skills to adapt the lessons to suit their students as they become more proficient with using technology.

Working with NUTP, we provided free data to their members as well as trained them in the use of the resources on our platform. It will be teachers who shoulder the task of helping Malaysian students get back on their feet again.

Community Schools

There are some 45,870 children below the age of 18 who are registered with the United Nations High Commission for Refugees (UNHCR) in Malaysia as of October 2021. These refugee children are denied access to the formal education system and obtain basic education via an informal parallel system of community-based learning centres run by their own communities, NGOs, and faith-based organisations. Many of these schools lack a structured curriculum as they depend on volunteers who teach for short periods of time.

These schools were perhaps among the hardest hit during the pandemic. During the first lockdown in March 2020, these schools closed and volunteer teachers were ill-equipped to continue teaching online. Limited access to devices and data, the same problem faced by the B40 students, was a barrier to keeping children learning.

Before the pandemic, YTL Foundation operated two learning centres in Kuala Lumpur for the underprivileged and underserved, including refugee children, providing after-school enrichment classes to them.

When the pandemic struck, we at the Foundation moved our classes online and started using the Learn From Home lesson resources to teach. We provided smartphones with data to some of the children from these community schools and brought them into our online classes. It soon became obvious that our online lesson resources could be used to provide a much-needed structured curriculum for community schools.

As these schools have started operating again, we are developing a programme to train volunteer teachers to use our resources and adapt them to their particular needs.

PARTNERSHIP WITH GOVERNMENT

The need for people to stay connected during lockdown and the affordability of data and devices for the most disadvantaged citizens were concerns that the Malaysian government was aware it needed to address. As a private-sector organisation, the YTL Foundation could act swiftly and started rolling out its Learn From Home Initiative a mere two weeks after lockdown. However, it took the government some time to develop its own programme to provide data and devices to those most affected by the pandemic.

In November 2020, the Minister of Finance, in his 2021 budget speech,[12] announced that a subsidy programme funded by the Malaysian government would allow B40 individuals to claim a RM15 ($3.71) credit per month for internet data or RM180 ($44.55) for the purchase of a phone plan from approved telecommunications companies. The Ministry of Finance subsequently increased the phone plan subsidy for families to RM300 ($74.25) to make it more affordable for them to purchase a device for home-based learning.

We at the YTL Foundation immediately saw this as an opportunity to work with the government to extend the impact of our Learn From Home Initiative. On our own, we were able to set a budget for giving out 100,000 phones and data, but working with the government and utilising the subsidy, we could stretch our dollars much further. We approached the Ministry of Education with an offer to work with them to identify the students who needed a device for home-based learning and to co-fund a phone plan for them using the government subsidy.

---

[12] Ministry of Finance Budget 2021: Budget Speech by Minister of Finance, 6 November 2020.

Whilst we received support from the highest level in government to do this, the Ministry of Education was preoccupied with having to deal with the closure and reopening of the 10,000 schools in the country, setting standard operating procedures for the safety of the students, supporting their teachers, rescheduling public examinations, and more.

As the Ministry of Finance had its own database of B40 families with school-going children, they encouraged us to work through YTL Communications to provide the subsidised phone plans to these families. YTL Foundation absorbed the balance of the cost of the phone plans not covered by the government subsidy so that these families would each receive the phone plan completely free.

The subsidised government programme ran for five months, from May 2021 through to September 2021, and during that period the Foundation gave out smartphones with data plans to over 750,000 families.

IMPACTING THE COMMUNITY

Sifting through the thousands of applications in the first weeks of the launch was just short of chaotic. Applications had to be reviewed for authenticity and postal addresses checked to ensure that the Foundation's delivery partners could in fact locate the applicants, especially as many were from rural areas where their addresses were merely PO boxes in remote villages. Addresses such as 'behind the Mosque' or 'above the Fire Station' confounded the team, but through Google Maps we managed to verify even addresses as strange as these. It gave us an insight into those we were reaching: real people in difficult circumstances who needed help.

As always, there were pranksters who submitted pictures of their pets or cartoons instead of their ID cards, and it was exhausting for the team to scan through the thousands of submissions to eliminate these. Then one morning we awoke to see a blurred picture of a family of three in a fishing village, the children holding up their father's death certificate. The father had recently passed away and the mother had lost her job as a waitress during the pandemic. The picture saddened us deeply and strengthened our resolve to press on as we knew we were making a difference to the lives of children like these.

We were also encouraged by so many in the community who went the extra mile to help the B40 families apply for the free smartphones and data. Neighbours were helping neighbours, teachers helping their students, and families helping each other. We had a teacher who painstakingly filled in the applications for 126 of her students.

At the time of lockdown, it was only through stories like these that we were able to gauge our impact on the ground.

While the Learn From Home initiative is a COVID-19-era response meant to meet the extraordinary challenge of the moment, we at the Foundation plan to further expand its features, particularly the learning resources. An independent evaluation to inform development of Phase 2 of the initiative is currently underway.

THE NEED FOR BUILDING RESILIENCE INTO THE EDUCATION ECOSYSTEM

We have seen enough in our lifetimes to accept that change is inevitable and yet we often think that we can control the rate at which change happens. Perhaps it is in our DNA that we need to feel in control in order to cope with the uncertainties of life.

If nothing else, the pandemic has taught us that the unexpected can come suddenly and swiftly and affect not just one community or country but the entire world. In an age where cheap global travel had become an accepted norm, borders closed overnight, airlines went out of business, and for almost two years we were locked within our own borders, not by political force but for fear of a virulent microbe.

In Malaysia, we have had floods that prevented children from attending school for several days per year. In recent times, the poor air quality resulting from forest fires has kept children indoors and out of school for several weeks. We have managed to cope with these incidents, but the total lockdown experienced in the two years of

COVID-19 has tested our education system to the limit. Thirty-seven weeks of school closure and inconsistent home-based learning will undoubtedly leave a lasting impact on our children, especially the most disadvantaged in our society. We are not only dealing with the learning gap that has arisen because learning could not continue during this time, but we are also grappling with the issue of potential loss of knowledge or reversals in academic progress.

As we start to build back after the pandemic, we need to think much broader and work on building resilience into our education ecosystem.

When we at the Foundation launched the Learn From Home initiative, our objective was to support continuity of learning during the months of lockdown. This affected the programme design, including the choice to simultaneously remove barriers to digital access at the same time as we increased availability of suitable learning resources. It also affected the approach we took to engaging parents as key stewards of learning for children.

As we have continued to work on these areas, we understand that these same elements of digital access and suitable learning resources are necessary if we are to build resilience into the Malaysian education ecosystem. However, advocating change and transformation in a system with entrenched bureaucracy can be risky; there is an in-built inertia to change. Previous attempts to introduce the use of technology into public schools have met with limited success and it has been too easy to blame the technology rather than the implementation. Moreover, the dependency between digital infrastructure and the digital skills of teachers creates high risk of failure.

A common mistake in many developing economies is the tendency to invest in infrastructure without at the same time investing in the upskilling of teachers and school leadership. We need to do both if we are to give ourselves the best chance of success.

Whilst the private sector can mobilise philanthropic capital at speed to address a crisis, as we have done with our Learn From Home initiative, we need to engage government to set clear policies and to put in place the long-term investments that create resilience. The pandemic brought to light the gaps in our system and created an environment where stakeholders from both public and private sectors are more open to change and innovation.

To move forward, we must continue to foster strong partnerships between the government, the private sector, and NGOs. Partnerships should not be limited to those working in the education sector, and cross-sector collaboration has been proven to be extremely effective. In the case of the Learn From Home initiative, it was necessary for a telecommunications company as well as suppliers of smartphones to get involved in what was essentially an education-led initiative.

YTL Foundation will continue working on providing digital access and digital learning resources as students in the country start on the journey of recovering the learning loss experienced over during the pandemic. It will also deepen its partnerships with the government, NGOs, and other private-sector companies to build resilience and preparedness for the next disruption. We at the Foundation have learnt that to build a resilient education ecosystem, we need everyone to be involved.

10 Creating Resilience and Rebuilding India through Philanthropy

Deval Sanghvi

IMPACTS OF COVID-19 ON INDIA'S SOCIAL SECTOR

The world will not achieve the Sustainable Development Goals (SDGs) until 2094 – sixty-four years after the deadline set by the United Nations (UN). If that estimate isn't humbling enough, it was projected *before* the COVID-19 pandemic. While the last two decades have given us great reason to celebrate historic progress in fighting poverty and improving health around the globe, the tumultuous pandemic period has forced us to confront our current reality with absolute candour: this progress has now been reversed.

India, a nation with large vulnerable populations including women and girls, migrant workers, and tribal communities already disproportionately disadvantaged with regard to basic human needs, has been hit particularly hard by COVID-19, experiencing consequences graver than that of any other external disruption that the country's social sector has faced. With over 33 million Indians having contracted COVID by late 2021, public health-care facilities facing unimaginable stress and shortage of essential equipment, herds of migrant workers fleeing back to their hometowns with little or no financial, food, or health security, and over 230 million people pushed back into poverty, discrimination against already marginalised communities intensified and frontline non-governmental organisations (NGOs) reached a breaking point.

The devastating impacts of COVID-19 in India can be seen across certain key areas:

- **Health care**: With over 22,000 new cases of COVID-19 each day at the height and only 20 per cent of eligible Indians fully vaccinated, lack of access to quality health care, inadequate support for ongoing health needs, and poor awareness around COVID-19 prevention continued to threaten health and well-being. This was particularly true among the country's most marginalised populations. On the infrastructure side, shortage of critical health-care equipment, dearth of adequate capacity and training for community health workers, and weak systems for contact tracing and testing were remain serious challenges.

- **Education**: Beyond the staggering impact on human life, COVID-19 has greatly disrupted access to education in India, with 247 million primary and secondary students out of school. Given that only one in four children has access to digital devices and internet connectivity, many were not able to avail themselves of online learning opportunities, leading to the poorest children being disproportionately impacted by pandemic-related school closures.[1]
- **Economic livelihoods**: Millions of people in India have been laid off and businesses have had to close their doors. These closures hit small and medium-sized businesses hardest, along with many daily wage workers in India's informal economy. While unemployment is of concern, the lasting problem of the pandemic is a lower labour-participation rate (41 per cent), which has still not recovered from its pre-pandemic levels (42.7 per cent).[2]

Of even greater concern, the very organisations with the greatest proximity to vulnerable communities and expertise to address these challenges are on the brink of collapse. With funding to these non-profits under greater threat than ever before, these organisations have found themselves in a difficult scenario concerning financial and institutional health, compelling them to rethink their strategies for future sustainability and resilience. In May 2020, Dasra surveyed over fifty-five non-profit organisations (NPOs) in India using its ResiLens Stress Test, and uncovered worrying findings:

- Seventy-one per cent of non-profits had cash balance to cover barely nine months of operations;
- Only 40 per cent of non-profits could cover more than 80 per cent of personnel costs;

---

[1] www.unicef.org/india/press-releases/COVID-19-schools-more-168-million-children-globally-have-been-completely-closed.

[2] www.cmie.com/kommon/bin/sr.php?kall=warticle&dt=20210628142621&msec=546.

- Close to 60 per cent had a highly restricted funding base with little flexibility to repurpose funds; and
- Several organisations reported considering drastic measures, including suspension of core programmes and trimming staff if funding for indirect costs is not forthcoming.

Recognising that grassroots and community-based organisations have a critical role to play at the local level in supporting communities through last-mile efforts, there is an urgent need to invest in strengthening their financial and institutional health. Furthermore, their strategies and efforts for their longer-term sustainability and resilience must be supported. When such organisations become resilient, they can in turn effectively support and rebuild the vulnerable communities worst impacted by the pandemic.

CHALLENGING TRADITIONAL PHILANTHROPY AND REIMAGINING APPROACHES TO INDIAN GIVING

While critical, it is not enough to simply unlock greater philanthropic capital towards non-profits. In the midst of the ever-widening inequality gap as a result of COVID-19, the need for philanthropy to deliberately engage and approach giving in a way that enables dignity, equality, and social justice for the most marginalised communities across India has never been more significant. There is an urgent need to improve grant-making practices and change both the discourse and direction of mainstream philanthropy to one that puts social justice at its core.

This includes supporting local partners with innovative opportunities to exercise power, agency, and leadership, seeking regular feedback from communities, investing in strengthening the institutional backbone of organisations, participating deeply in opportunities for collaboration and learning, and reimagining systems-change process as one led by local organisations and inclusive of all Indians.

DASRA'S COVID-19 RESPONSE

Recognising the scale of devastation caused by COVID-19 in India and the urgent need to shift giving practices towards a more inclusive and

Dasra's Response Rested on 4 Critical Pillars...

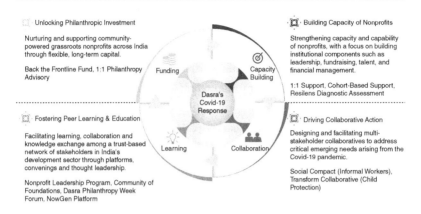

Unlocking Philanthropic Investment

Nurturing and supporting community-powered grassroots nonprofits across India through flexible, long-term capital.

Back the Frontline Fund, 1:1 Philanthropy Advisory

Building Capacity of Nonprofits

Strengthening capacity and capability of nonprofits, with a focus on building institutional components such as leadership, fundraising, talent, and financial management.

1:1 Support, Cohort-Based Support, Resilens Diagnostic Assessment

Fostering Peer Learning & Education

Facilitating learning, collaboration and knowledge exchange among a trust-based network of stakeholders in India's development sector through platforms, convenings and thought leadership.

Nonprofit Leadership Program, Community of Foundations, Dasra Philanthropy Week Forum, NowGen Platform

Driving Collaborative Action

Designing and facilitating multi-stakeholder collaboratives to address critical emerging needs arising from the Covid-19 pandemic.

Social Compact (Informal Workers), Transform Collaborative (Child Protection)

Funding *Capacity Building* *Dasra's Covid-19 Response* *Learning* *Collaboration*

FIGURE 10.1 Dasra's COVID-19 response

equity-focused approach, Dasra launched the Rebuild India initiative, a movement focused on supporting locally led scalable solutions that have measurable outcomes of justice, equity, diversity, and inclusion. This global initiative takes a holistic view, providing rapid response funding for local frontline organisations. It simultaneously unlocks greater and more thoughtful philanthropy that supports long-term resilience by strengthening the organisations' institutional backbone through capacity-building support and promoting knowledge exchange between key stakeholders to accelerate India's development (Figure 10.1).

We now lay out the specific initiatives that Dasra undertook to support non-profits and funders across each of its four pillars.

Unlocking Philanthropic Investment

Dasra introduced the # BacktheFrontline Rebuild India Fund to nurture and support locally led community-based non-profits in India. The Fund prioritised speedy deployment of relief funding, while ensuring reach to remote areas and demographics rarely covered in mainstream discussions. The Fund further highlighted the diversity of community-powered organisations and local decision-making on utilisation of funds. Given the emphasis on trust-based relations and

ground-up learning, it soon transformed into a model for connecting global and local philanthropy with community-trusted organisations in the Global South. Having already raised $20 million in
unrestricted funding to support over seventy-five grassroots non-
profits over five years, BacktheFrontline has become a $50 million
fund. Moreover, we at Dasra plan to raise an additional $30 million
of flexible, unrestricted, long-term funding from Indian and global
foundations and families to support 150 non-profits through this
platform.

Building Capacity of Non-Profits

Recognising that capacity-building is a critical element to ensuring non-profits' sustainability and effective functioning, over the
years Dasra has built the capacity of over 1,000 NPOs across diverse
sectors to scale their impact. It works to strengthen not only pro
grammatic aspects of these organisations but also institutional
components including leadership, fundraising, talent, and financial
management, while facilitating the knowledge, tools, and confidence
to better understand NPOs' indirect expenses and effectively raise
unrestricted funding. Several of these organisations, such as Educate
Girls, Naz Foundation, and Muktangan, have gone on to scale up
exponentially and grow into sector leaders as a result of the catalytic
funding and capacity-building support that it enabled.

With the onset of the COVID-19 pandemic, Dasra undertook a
focused effort to strengthen the institutional backbones of organisations serving the needs of the most vulnerable communities across
diverse sectors and regions in India, while maintaining a sharp focus
on institutional sustainability. Specifically, it focused on the following key approaches:

- **One-to-one support**: Dasra provided financial coaching and customised
  capacity-building support to non-profit leaders, helping them think through
  key programmatic and institutional pivots as a result of COVID-19, assess
  progress and make necessary course corrections, and learn and adapt to
  the communities' fast-evolving needs while keeping the organisations'
  financial sustainability at the forefront.

Industree Foundation: Capacity-Building Support for Regenearth Programme

Dasra helped Industree design and operationalise its pathway to scale, through the Regenearth Programme, which trains organisations/ incubators that work with social entrepreneurs setting up enterprises via a cohort programme. This programme kicked off in October 2020 and helped Industree disseminate its decades-long learnings to other enterprise-building organisations through an eleven-month, action-based learning programme. Dasra and Industree used a human-centred design approach to conceptualise the solution, test it with potential customers, and finally roll it out. Dasra also helped create a 'Regenearth Handbook' to institutionalise the model, programme design, approach, tools, frameworks, and learnings within Industree Foundation.

COVID-19 PIVOT

While Industree had always envisioned their scale-up via a one-to-many approach, the onset of COVID-19 really forced the team to push the limits of what was feasible, leading to an online action-oriented programme catering to organisations from India and other developing nations.

- **Cohort-based support**: Since 2006, Dasra's flagship programme, the Dasra Social Impact Leadership Programme, has helped NGOs achieve ambitious plans to deepen impact. In 2021, Dasra brought together non-profit leaders who previously participated in this programme to provide them with access to tools, knowledge, and resources towards navigating the COVID-19 crisis and building institutional sustainability.
- **ResiLens diagnostic assessment**: Dasra created the 'Institutional Resilience and Impact Optimization Toolkit' for Indian non-profits to conduct data-enabled stress tests and decision planning to best cope with the crisis, and reinvent their organisations to be more impactful post-crisis. Administered among 250 non-profits across India, the toolkit enabled organisations to analyse their risk levels on institutional and programmatic parameters and outline potential solutions the organisation should consider to build institutional resilience. Similarly, a toolkit was designed for funders to support their grantees by equipping them to undertake stress tests in order to weather the crisis.

> ## Resilens: The Institutional Resilience and Impact Optimization Toolkit
>
> The Dasra Resilens Toolkit consists of a self-assessment and recommended decision-making framework, which allows organisations to identify their stress areas and consider potential decisions, enabling non-profit leaders and their boards to understand current scenarios, make assumptions and identify relevant options, and proactively plan critical decisions for the sustainability of their organisation.
>
> 'Doing the COVID Stress Test Toolkit was a very useful exercise to assess SNEHA's sustainability. It forced us to re-look at our numbers, converse with donors, analyse our funding pipelines, which was extremely helpful. The results were a wakeup call on how we operate in order to still be impactful and relevant.'
>
> *Vanessa D'Souza, CEO, SNEHA*

Fostering Peer Learning and Education

With the pandemic having only exacerbated the depth and scale of the already complex development challenges in India, it is clearer than ever that no single individual or organisation is capable of addressing them alone at the scale and pace that the country requires. With this recognition, facilitating learning, collaboration, and knowledge exchange among key players in India's development sector has been a core part of Dasra's work, particularly at this defining time when coming together to support the country's most vulnerable has never been more important. Following are specific initiatives that Dasra undertook towards this:

- **Non-Profit Leadership Programme**: For many years, Dasra has been facilitating the Dasra Social Impact Accelerator and Leadership Programmes – structured, peer-learning based programmes in partnership with the Harvard Business School and Ashoka University, providing non-profit leaders with access to tools, knowledge, and resources designed to help them build stronger, scalable organisations and accelerate their impact. Through these programmes, we at Dasra have built a community of over 400 unique leaders, representing close to 600 organisations working across multiple sectors, including education, health, and livelihoods. With the onset of the COVID-19 crisis, Dasra launched the Dasra Social Impact Alumni Engagement Programme, curated specifically for alumni of the Accelerator and Leadership Programmes to help them build organisational resilience, adjust their operations, manage strategy execution, and lead their teams effectively through uncertainty with a long-term perspective.

'The overall experience in the programme was very good with valuable learning from the classroom as well as peer discussions. Based on the tools introduced in the modules, I have initiated some changes in my organisation and have started exploring some new ideas to bring organisational efficiencies. The networking opportunity this platform gave was very good.'

Amit Naphade, Co-Founder, Krushi Vikas
va Gramin Prashikshan Sanstha

- **Community of Foundations**: In February 2020, Dasra launched the Community of Foundations – comprising leaders of nineteen influential domestic and international foundations – to learn from each other's experiences, failures, and best practices, foster collaboration, and drive collective thought leadership towards strengthening India's philanthropy ecosystem. The group convenes quarterly, with discussions focusing on topics including understanding grant-making pivots due to COVID-19, navigating legal amendments and implications, and outlining 2021 trends in Indian philanthropy. In March 2021, the group collectively published the *India Philanthropy Trends 2021* thought-leadership piece, which garnered attention from over twenty national and regional media platforms across India.
- **Dasra Philanthropy Week Forum**: Dasra has also brought together a number of domestic and global philanthropists through the Dasra Philanthropy Forums, in cities including Bengaluru, London, New York, Houston, and San Francisco. Beyond these programmes, over the last four years alone, it has conducted over seventy-five multi-stakeholder

and cross-sectoral events globally, with attendees across non-profits, government, domestic and diaspora philanthropists, and academic institutions. In March 2021, Dasra hosted the twelfth edition of the Dasra Philanthropy Week Forum, which convened diverse stakeholders on a common virtual platform focused on strengthening dialogue on India's development. The event sparked powerful discussions led by 110+ thought leaders who highlighted the rising significance of justice, equity, diversity, and inclusion in philanthropy, and covered themes such as mental health, the plight of migrant workers in COVID-19, and data for good.

- **GivingPi**: To harness the full potential of family philanthropy in India, in July 2022, leading philanthropists and Dasra launched GivingPi—India's first and exclusive family philanthropy network, with the intent of enabling learning, sharing and collaboration between philanthropic families in India. This invite-only network has, in just over a year, brought together over 200 philanthropic families from over 23 cities across 6 countries. It has curated 15+ gatherings across 7 cities and initiated conversation on a range of topics such as Education, Climate Change, Disability, Arts etc with sector leaders, experts and philanthropists. With 59 percent next-gen representation in GivingPi, one sees the emergence of a promising new wave of philanthropy in India and Dasra hopes to engage with this community to foster dialogue and action on bolder aspirations for building a stronger India.

Driving Collaborative Action

Dasra seeded collaborative impact programmes in two new sectors – informal workers and child protection – given the emerging needs during COVID coupled with multi-stakeholder interest in investing across these issues. The former has taken the form of Social Compact, a collaboration with 150+ companies to create a more enabling environment for informal workers to thrive in Indian companies. It is a collective effort between philanthropists, foundations, non-profits, and industry federations led by Indian promoter families and anchored by Dasra. The latter is an effort to strengthen child protection at a systems level within the State of Maharashtra. Dasra is engaging with foundations and family philanthropists to shape their long-term vision, investment, and partnership strategies directly driving $10–15 million over the next

Social Compact

The Social Compact aspires to ensure greater dignity and equity for informal workers within industries in India and mainstream the aspiration that responsible business equates to successful business. It brings together diverse stakeholders to lend their skills, expertise, voices, and networks in driving change through better business practices across the value chains.

Based on the needs, vulnerabilities, and aspirations of these workers, the collective aims to work towards *six key outcomes* that will holistically transform the lives of the most vulnerable workers in company ecosystems: (1) secure living wages, (2) maximise safety against accidents, (3) ensure health and social security coverage, (4) foster gender equity, (5) facilitate access to entitlements, and (6) enable participation in future work.

The Social Compact is enabling action on the ground via two distinct impact pathways: individual action which companies adopt for their own workers and their value chains, and action through Worker Facilitation Centres. In the last two years, we at Dasra launched five Worker Facilitation Centres across Pune and Gujarat, leveraging a hub-and-spoke model to ensure scalable impact for informal workers across regions. The centres have already impacted 9,500 + workers and continue to work towards impacting one million informal workers and their families by linking them to government entitlements, building agency through on-ground awareness amongst the labouring communities, providing access to remedial support, facilitating financial inclusion, and utilizing the collected data to identify systemic issues and address them through policy advocacy.

decade or so, building a case for investment within the giving community, and enabling learning among various funders within the Dasra network on this issue.

LEARNINGS AND RECOMMENDATIONS

Derived from Dasra's many years of experience in India's development sector, including its support to funders and non-profits during the COVID-19 pandemic, we include below several key learnings and insights that Dasra has gained, along with recommendations for stakeholder groups towards strengthening the philanthropy ecosystem and building a more inclusive, equitable India.

Funders

• **Invest in institutional resilience**: With the combination of philanthropists largely redirecting funding to COVID-19 relief programmes, the accessible pool of corporate social responsibility (CSR) funds expected to diminish drastically, and core operational costs for many non-profits increasing significantly to address growing needs of vulnerable communities, the institutional and financial resilience of non-profits is under serious threat. The Centre for Social Impact and Philanthropy surveyed fifty NPOs in May 2020 to understand how many months they can cover their fixed costs with their existing funds. What they found was worrying: 54 per cent could cover fixed costs for a year, 16 per cent could cover costs for even longer, and an astounding 30 per cent could cover only six months or less. Several of these organisations reported considering drastic measures, including suspension of core programmes and trimming down team strength if funding was not secured.

Such a concerning situation highlights the urgent need for funders to support partner organisations with flexible capital to strengthen their institutional backbones. Offering non-financial assets in the form of capacity-building opportunities, resilience-building tools, and advisory support is also an important way that funders can help build grantees' organisational resilience over the coming years.

'Tarsadia Foundation and Dasra are working closely together to ensure our grant making efforts are thoughtful in meeting long term challenges and systematic vulnerabilities. As philanthropists, we leverage "trust based" principles; we are driven by the belief that our local non-profit partners understand the community needs better than we ever could, and it is our role as funders to follow their guidance, how we can work together to create lasting change.'

Maya Patel, President, Tarsadia Foundation

- **Adopt a strong gender-equity-diversity-inclusion (GEDI) lens**: The COVID-19 crisis has been a wake-up call that unveiled deep fault lines around the inequities seeping through India's development systems. Whether it is the millions of migrant workers who fled back to their hometowns with little financial or food security, the thousands of children who were left homeless, or the many women who experienced increasing incidences of domestic violence during lockdown, there has never been a more important time than now for India's philanthropy community to think about how they as a society are caring for their most vulnerable communities. We must further make an intentional shift to fund organisations that work with the most marginalised communities – especially at the intersection of caste, class, gender, and poverty – that have the greatest chance of falling through the cracks. This focus can be adopted through both funding decisions with grantee partners as well as increased incorporation of the GEDI lens within the culture and principles of grant-making institutions.
- **Support rural, localised, community-led efforts**: Having recognised that grassroots organisations with greatest proximity to vulnerable communities played a critical role at the local level in engaging and supporting these communities through the pandemic, there is a growing need for funders to expand their focus beyond large, well-established city-based non-profits to also support more grassroots organisations. Only these organisations can enable last-mile efforts where government services are unable to reach those in need.

Intermediaries

- **Build philanthropy infrastructure and create spaces for cross-learning**: The ecosystem of family philanthropy in India has grown and matured significantly since the early 2010s. However, when viewed alongside the country's need and true giving potential, the gap is stark and there remains much to be done. Efforts are largely taking place in siloes, data and research around strategic giving are fragmented, there is a dearth of concrete investment-ready vehicles, opportunities for peer learning and knowledge exchange are limited, and a cohesive and powerful narrative around philanthropy is lacking in India, with this topic largely invisible in mainstream conversations. Intermediaries have a critical role to play in enabling common goods and platforms that the sector can leverage, and in building India's philanthropy infrastructure through thought leadership, peer learning, and narrative-building, to ultimately accelerate equitable giving in India.

- **Strengthen capacity of grassroots non-profit leaders**: With Indian non-profits under greater threat and pressure than ever before, intermediaries must look to invest in building NPOs' capacity to effectively catalyse funding from philanthropists. NPOs must further build leadership capabilities, and strengthen other institutional aspects that will enable them to sustain their work and achieve impact at scale while leveraging capital most effectively. Given the rising significance of community-based organisations in addressing the many COVID-19 related challenges, there is a need to double down on giving a voice to and empowering the country's grassroots leaders who form a pivotal backbone of Indian society and play a catalytic role in transforming communities and the nation. While there are several initiatives focused on the economic empowerment of grassroots leaders, there are limited initiatives highlighting leadership training and development. Such leaders also often get overlooked due to language and technology barriers, accessibility issues, and lack of contextualised offerings that cater specifically to their needs.

- **Facilitate collaborative action**: There is a fast-growing realisation that no individual stakeholder is singularly capable of creating change at the scale and pace urgently required to move India forward, and that the magnitude, complexity, and seriousness of development challenges in this country necessitates collaborative action among multiple stakeholders at a greater scale than ever before. This presents a significant opportunity for intermediary organisations to invest in building and facilitating multi-stakeholder collaboratives to drive collective impact at scale. (As per Bridgespan's definition, collaboratives are defined as 'entities that are co-created by three or more independent actors – including at least one philanthropist or philanthropy – and that pursues a shared vision and strategy for achieving social impact, using common resources and

> 'To achieve resilience, family philanthropists, NGOs, foundations, corporates and governments will need to work together regularly exchange knowledge and learnings, align on shared vision, build a collective voice, and combine resources to invest in scalable, inclusive and sustainable solutions.'
>
> *Neera Nundy, Co-Founder, Dasra*

prearranged governance mechanisms.') While the important role of collaboratives in India was present even before 2020, the COVID-19 pandemic has brought with it an increased sense of urgency and action, underscoring the need for intermediaries to accelerate impact by serving as creators and backbones of such platforms.

Non-Profits

- **Empower communities to design and lead solutions**: Models where non-profits or other external stakeholders assess community needs, design and implement solutions, and account for results are common, and even effective for delivering immediate aid. However, such models have shown to be disempowering to communities and less sustainable over time.[3] On the other hand, approaching communities as partners or owners (rather than as mere recipients), and actively involving them in prioritising their needs, designing solutions, and supporting implementation, has shown to be a more effective model to build lasting community resilience – an approach that non-profits must incorporate as they seek to rebuild communities in a post-COVID India.

> 'Involving the community in every decision is time consuming, however, it helps in effective implementation of programmes with high adoptability from the communities.'
>
> *Dr Dhanya Narayanan, Director, ASHWINI Hospital*

- **Invest in strengthening institutional capabilities**: With long-term sustainability of non-profits threatened by the COVID-19 pandemic, organisations must invest significantly in strengthening their institutional resilience through undertaking focused efforts to fundraise for flexible capital, and participating in capacity-building opportunities such as webinars, workshops, mentorship, and 1:1 advisory support, while continuing to engage in various modes of peer learning.
- **Participate in collaborative action**: Joining forces with multiple stakeholders to drive collective impact through collaborative platforms offers non-profits the opportunity to drive deeper and faster impact by

[3] https://idronline.org/engaging-communities-is-critical-to-the-COVID-19-response/.

leveraging greater resources, a wider network, and more diverse skillsets. Given the rapidly growing inequities as a result of COVID-19, the need for non-profits to move away from siloed efforts and participate in such multi-stakeholder collaborative platforms has never been more important. Several Indian collaboratives have emerged during the pandemic, including COVID Action Collaborative and Rapid Community Response to COVID-19 (focused on immediate COVID relief efforts), as well as Saamuhika Shakti, Revive Collective, and Migrants Resilience Collaborative (focused on adjacent issues like supporting India's migrant workers).

CONCLUSION

Dasra's mission post-pandemic continues to focus on creating an inspiring, audacious narrative and movement for strategic philanthropy, to shift the focus of giving from 'how much' to 'how'. The pandemic disproportionately impacted already disadvantaged groups and NGOs faced acute funding crunches. It is critical for the philanthropic community to be guided by on-ground realities and provide patient and flexible funding to NGOs for them to deploy where it will be most effective for the communities. Philanthropists, families, and foundations are also increasingly coming to understand this. Intentional efforts are being made to narrow the power imbalances between NGOs and funders and to empower NGOs to make decisions in the best interest of the marginalised communities they support. There is a need to understand that a siloed approach isn't the best way forward, which is why efforts must be focused on building a community of empathetic philanthropists who are cognisant of the social sector's needs, and are willing to adopt newer giving practices and lead by example by engaging in an open dialogue to exchange learnings from each other's giving journeys.

The only way for India and other developing nations to rebuild with resilience and perseverance from the pandemic is by ensuring that the needs of the vulnerable communities are at the core of the interventions. We must give NGOs greater autonomy to make informed decisions and patient capital to meet the community's ever-changing needs, in order to make Dasra's vision of a billion people thriving, with dignity and equity, a reality.

Index

Printed in the United States
by Baker & Taylor Publisher Services